MW00559383

THE COLLEGE PRESS NIV COMMENTARY

MARK

THE COLLEGE PRESS NIV COMMENTARY

MARK

ALLEN BLACK, Ph.D.

New Testament Series Co-Editors:

Jack Cottrell, Ph.D.
Cincinnati Bible Seminary

Tony Ash, Ph.D.
Abilene Christian University

COLLEGE PRESS
PUBLISHING COMPANY
Joplin, Missouri

Second printing 2001

Printed and Bound in the
United States of America

Library of Congress Cataloging-in-Publication Data

Black, Allen, 1951-
Mark / Allen Black
p. cm. – (The College Press NIV commentary)
Includes bibliographical references.
ISBN 0-89900-629-9 (hard cover)
1. Bible. N.T. Mark–Commentaries. I. Bible. N.T. Mark. English. New International. 1995. II. Title. III. Series.
BS2585.3.B56 1995
266.3'07–dc20 95-46248
CIP

FOREWORD

No story is more important than the story of Jesus. I am confident that my comments do not do it justice. Even granting the limitations of a historical commentary (see the Introduction) there is so much more to be said. Nevertheless, the completion of a commentary on the Gospel of Mark accomplishes a goal I have wanted to reach for many years. I pray that my comments will help readers to develop a deeper understanding of Mark's story of Jesus as a basis for reflecting on Jesus' significance for their own lives.

I thank College Press for the opportunity to write in this series. I thank my colleague at Harding Graduate School Richard Oster (whose commentary on 1 Corinthians has appeared in the same series) for reading my manuscript and making many valuable suggestions. Another friend and colleague John Mark Hicks also provided helpful comments on several sections.

Most of all I thank Nancy, Amy, and Stacey, whose love and support are the dearest things on earth to me. The blessing they have been to me is second only to the blessing God has given to us all in the story about which I have been privileged to comment.

A WORD FROM THE PUBLISHER

Years ago a movement was begun with the dream of uniting all Christians on the basis of a common purpose (world evangelism) under a common authority (the Word of God). The College Press NIV Commentary Series is a serious effort to join the scholarship of two branches of this unity movement so as to speak with one voice concerning the Word of God. Our desire is to provide a resource for your study of the New Testament that will benefit you whether you are preparing a Bible School lesson, a sermon, a college course or your own personal devotions. Today as we survey the wreckage of a broken world, we must turn again to the Lord and his Word, unite under his banner and communicate the life-giving message to those who are in desperate need. This is our purpose.

ABBREVIATIONS

BAGD . . . A Greek English Lexicon of the New Testament, 2nd ed., eds. Bauer, Arndt, Gingrich, and Danker

DJG . . . Dictionary of Jesus and the Gospels

LXX . . . The Septuagint (An ancient Greek translation of the Old Testament)

NIV . . . The Holy Bible, New International Version

NRSV . . . The Holy Bible, New Revised Standard Version

SNTSMS . . . Studiorum Novi Testamenti Societas Monograph Series

UBS^4 . . . The Greek New Testament, United Bible Societies, 4th ed.

WUNT . . . Wissenschaftliche Untersuchungen zum NT

INTRODUCTION

ABOUT THIS COMMENTARY

The intended audience of this book is the general reader with a serious interest in Scripture. This is not a work for scholars seeking to explore and press forward the edges of contemporary scholarship on Mark. Rather, I seek to make some of the fruits of others' scholarly research available to the general reader. I have been especially influenced by the commentaries by William Lane and Robert Gundry, the incomplete commentary on 1:1-8:26 by Robert Guelich, and the magisterial work on the death of Jesus by Raymond Brown.[1] I often refer the reader to their scholarly works for further information, and even where I do not the reader would be well advised to consider them for a scholar's depth of treatment. Another fine source for further treatment with respect to many topics that arise in Mark is the *Dictionary of Jesus and the Gospels*, edited by Joel Green and Scot McKnight.[2]

The purpose of the commentary is to provide a historical interpretation of the Gospel of Mark; that is, an interpretation of what Mark meant to say to his ancient audience. I

---

[1]William L. Lane, *The Gospel according to Mark*, New International New Testament Commentary (Grand Rapids: Eerdmans, 1974); Robert H. Gundry, *Mark: A Commentary on His Apology for the Cross* (Grand Rapids: Eerdmans, 1993); Robert A. Guelich, *Mark 1:1-8:26*, Word Biblical Commentary, vol. 34A (Dallas: Word, 1989); Raymond E. Brown, *The Death of the Messiah*, Anchor Bible Reference Library, 2 vols. (New York: Doubleday, 1994).

[2]Joel B. Green and Scot McKnight, eds., *Dictionary of Jesus and the Gospels*, consulting ed. I. Howard Marshall (Downers Grove: InterVarsity, 1992).

write with the conviction that modern readers can only determine God's message to us after and on the basis of a determination of Mark's message to his ancient contemporaries. Because I believe God worked through Mark and inspired his work, I believe it has great relevance to every reader in every age. But we can only determine what it means to us if we have first determined what it meant when Mark wrote it. It is this latter task that it the focus of most commentaries, including this one. I will occasionally make comments about what a given passage means today, but not consistently. I will consistently comment on what Mark meant to say to his ancient readers. I hope and pray that my readers will recognize the contemporary relevance of Mark's work even though it will not be my purpose to point it out or illustrate it. My purpose is to provide a base to build on for contemporary application.

The commentary deals with historical meaning or intention on two levels. The first of those is the meaning intended by Mark for his contemporaries. John 21:25 says, "Jesus did many other things as well. If everyone of them were written down, I suppose that even the whole world would not have room for the books that would be written." John points out that every Gospel writer must be selective. That is true with respect to which stories or sayings are selected and with respect to the perspective from which they are told and the amount of detail which is provided. The commentary consistently asks why Mark might have made his particular choices (which I assume were made under divine guidance).

The second level of meaning is the level of the intent of the historical characters Mark wrote about, especially Jesus. What did Jesus intend to convey to his contemporaries by his words and actions? A major part of Mark's intended meaning is to convey his understanding of Jesus' intended meaning. Therefore, it is important to ask both "What did Mark want his contemporaries to understand from this action or saying?" and "What did Jesus want his contemporaries (two to three decades earlier) to understand from this action or saying?" Concerning the latter question, the commentary will focus primarily on what one could learn about Jesus' intentions from Mark's account alone. On a few occasions, another Gospel will be brought into the discussion – but primarily for the purpose of solving some ambiguity or otherwise illuminating Mark's account.

I have generally not commented on the scholarly disputes concerning the historicity of various events and sayings in Mark.[3] Most of them arise from the presupposition that Jesus did not work miracles. In this commentary I presuppose that he did and I assume the basic historicity of Mark's account. I comment only on a few well known problems of historicity which do not stem from antisupernaturalistic presuppositions.

In general, I have sought to provide deeper treatment of any recurring subject at the point where it is first mentioned in the text. For example, the titles "Christ" and "Son of God" are discussed primarily when they first arise in 1:1, and "Son of Man" is discussed in connection with 2:10. This means that the first chapter of the commentary is particularly important. It also means that readers will often want to look at the first text that mentions a particular theme. For example, it is important to supplement the comments on the centurion's confession of Jesus as the Son of God at 15:39 with the comments on the Son of God title at 1:1.

I have commented on the NIV text. In some places where it seems deficient, I have provided an alternative translation, often from the NRSV. The commentary makes note of the most significant textual variants and my opinions concerning them, but does not provide a list of manuscripts, versions, or church fathers. Interested readers should use the United Bible Societies *Greek New Testament*.[4]

---

[3]On issues of historicity see Craig Blomberg, *The Historical Reliability of the Gospels* (Downers Grove: InterVarsity, 1987).

[4]*The Greek New Testament*, 4th rev. ed., ed. Barbara Aland, Kurt Aland, et al.(United Bible Societies, 1993). See also the discussions in Bruce M. Metzger, *A Textual Commentary on the Greek New Testament*, 2nd ed. (United Bible Societies, 1994).

AUTHORSHIP

The author of the Gospel of Mark is not indicated within the text itself. However, the traditional understanding of the author is supported by the title and by early Christian writers.

The titles of the Gospels are first found in ancient manuscripts dating from the late second or early third centuries. Some scholars readily dismiss them as late second century creations.[5] It is true that they seem to be creations of early church tradition rather than of the authors themselves. This can be observed by noting their stereotypical form "The Gospel according to ________" and by the clearer evidence that other New Testament book titles were not original. For example, Paul would hardly have designated the letter we know as 1 Corinthians by that name. Not only did letters not need a name but in 1 Cor 5 he speaks about a former letter he had written them. The titles of Paul's letters and of the Gospels represent the perspectives of those who collected and circulated them.

But that does not mean they are not to be trusted. Martin Hengel has well argued that the titles of the Gospels go back to the earliest days of their collection and distribution.[6] Papias, a bishop in Asia Minor in the early second century, apparently knew of them.[7] So did his source, "the elder" – presumably a generation older than Papias. Hengel correctly argues that as soon as there was more than one Gospel to read at church, it would have become necessary to name them. The lack of competing titles suggests that these titles were uniformly applied from the earliest days.

The second most important piece of information concerning the authorship of Mark is a paragraph written by the above-named Papias, bishop of Hierapolis (near Colossae and

---

[5]E.g., Joseph A. Fitzmyer, *The Gospel according to Luke I-IX*, Anchor Bible Commentary 28A (Garden City, NY: Doubleday, 1981), pp. 35-36.

[6]Martin Hengel, *Studies in the Gospel of Mark*, trans. John Bowden (Philadelphia: Fortress, 1985), pp. 64-84.

[7]See the next paragraph.

Laodicea). The pertinent statements were preserved by Eusebius from Papias's work, *Expositions of the Sayings of the Lord*, which was probably written within the first three decades of the second century.[8] According to Eusebius[9] Papias wrote:

> And the presbyter used to say this: "Mark became Peter's interpreter and wrote accurately all that he remembered, not indeed, in order, of the things said or done by the Lord. For he had not heard the Lord, nor had he followed him, but later on, as I said, followed Peter, who used to give teaching as necessity demanded but not making, as it were, an arrangement of the Lord's oracles, so that Mark did nothing wrong in writing down single points as he remembered them. For to one thing he gave attention, to leave out nothing of what he had heard and to make no false statements in them."[10]

Papias believed a) that the author was a Mark closely associated with Peter and b) that what he wrote was essentially the preaching of Peter. These traditional understandings were repeated favorably by subsequent church fathers. Justin Martyr (writing c. A.D. 155-60) spoke of Mark's Gospel as "Peter's memoirs."[11] In the late second century Irenaeus and Clement of Alexandria described Mark as writing Peter's preaching.[12] In the early third century Origen and Tertullian affirm the same tradition.[13] The early date of Papias and the widespread support of his statements suggest that they might be correct.[14]

The connection between Peter and Mark is supported by

---

[8]Gundry, pp. 1027-1029.

[9]An early fourth century church father.

[10]Eusebius, *Ecclesiastical History* 3.39.15 as translated in the Loeb Classical Library edition of Eusebius, *Ecclesiastical History*, ed. and trans. Kirsopp Lake, 2 vols. (Cambridge, MA: Harvard University Press, 1926).

[11]Justin Martyr, *Dialogue with Trypho* 106.3.

[12]Irenaeus, *Against Heresies* 3.1.2; Clement of Alexandria, *Hypotyposes* according to Eusebius, *Ecclesiastical History* 6.14.5-7.

[13]Origen is cited in Eusebius, *Ecclesiastical History* 6.25.5; Tertullian, *Against Marcion* 4.5.

[14]Although he was also widely supported in antiquity in his statement that Matthew wrote his Gospel in Hebrew, an opinion disputed by most modern scholars. See D. A. Carson, Douglas J. Moo, and Leon Morris, *An Introduction to the New Testament* (Grand Rapids: Zondervan, 1992), pp. 67-70.

Peter going to John Mark's mother's house in Acts 12:12 and by Peter's reference to "my son Mark" in 1 Pet 5:13. The idea that Mark's Gospel was based on Peter's preaching is probably trustworthy.[15] It is probably also true that what Peter usually did was tell various individual stories about Jesus rather than a sustained account. Mark's Gospel, like the others, is not in strict chronological order,[16] although it does generally follow chronological lines.[17]

Acts 12:12 and 25 suggests that the Mark that Peter would later refer to as "my son" was the same as the John Mark who was a companion of Paul and Barnabas on the first missionary journey and a source of dispute between them over whether to take him on their return trip (Acts 15:36-40).[18] Col 4:10; Phlm 24; and 2 Tim 4:11 indicate that Paul was eventually reconciled with John Mark (and that John Mark was Barnabas' cousin). According to Acts 12:12 John Mark was from Jerusalem, but Papias and other ancient writers say that he did not follow Jesus before Jesus' death.[19]

---

[15]Mark's use of what he learned from Peter is no more inconsistent with divine inspiration than Matthew or John's use of their own experiences with Jesus. The doctrine of inspiration is not restricted to the revelation of the unknown, but includes supervision of the use of existing knowledge.

[16]Probably most scholars understand Papias's comment about "order" to mean that Mark did not put all the events in chronological order. Others suggest Papias was speaking of a lack of rhetorical order. Cf. Guelich, p. xxvii; Gundry, pp. 1036-1037.

[17]Cf. Blomberg, *Reliability*, p. 27: "From at least as long ago as the time of St. Augustine, it has been recognized that the gospels did not set out to supply a detailed itinerary of Jesus' ministry with every event in its proper chronological sequence, but frequently arrange passages in topical or thematic order instead."

[18]Some scholars identify the author as a companion of Peter named Mark, but not the John Mark of Acts and Paul's letters. So, e.g., Ernest Best, *Mark: The Gospel As Story* (Edinburgh: T. & T. Clark, 1983), pp. 25-26.

[19]The Muratorian Canon, a list of canonical books written near the end of the second century, is mutilated at the beginning, but its first words apparently refer to Mark. It begins, " . . . at these, however, he was present and so he set them down." The author of the Canon believed Mark was present at some events he records. On the Muratorian Canon see F.F. Bruce, *The Canon of Scripture* (Downers Grove: InterVarsity Press, 1988), pp. 158-169.

I will assume the author was John Mark of Jerusalem and that his Gospel was to some extent based upon the preaching of Peter.

AUDIENCE[20] AND PLACE OF COMPOSITION

In the late second century Clement of Alexandria commented on the circumstances of Mark's writing, including the audience he wrote for and the place where he wrote. According to Eusebius Clement believed that:

> When Peter had publicly preached the word at Rome, and by the Spirit had proclaimed the Gospel, those present, who were many, exhorted Mark, as one who had followed him for a long time and remembered what had been spoken, to make a record of what was said: and that he did this, and distributed the Gospel among those that asked him. And that when the matter came to Peter's knowledge he neither strongly forbade it nor urged it forward.[21]

However, Clement is not a very trustworthy source and his contemporary Irenaeus contradicted him by saying that Mark wrote his Gospel after the death of Peter.[22]

Clement could be correct about Rome as the location for

---

[20]Recent scholarship (e.g., Best, *Mark,* pp. 17-19) has correctly emphasized that most of Mark's "readers" were actually "hearers." Few would be able to own a hand-copied manuscript. Mark would have envisioned his work being read out loud to groups of listeners. I will use the term "reader" loosely. I will not enter significantly into the current discussion concerning how aiming at listeners might affect Mark's style, although it is certainly a question worth investigating.

[21]From Clement's *Hypotyposes* according to Eusebius, *Ecclesiastical History* 6.14.5-7.

[22]Irenaeus, *Against Heresies* 3.1.1. "After their death [the death of Peter and Paul] Mark, the disciple and interpreter of Peter, also handed down to us in writing the things preached by Peter." Gundry, pp. 1042-1043, advocates a minority position that the prevailing interpretation of Irenaeus which this translation represents is in error. He argues that Irenaeus did not say that Mark wrote after Peter's death, but that he wrote before it.

Mark's audience and his place of composition.[23] Two other factors provide mild support for Rome.[24] In 1 Pet 5:13, where Peter mentions Mark and calls him "my son," he indicates that he and Mark were in "Babylon." Most scholars believe Peter is referring to Rome, thus placing himself and Mark in Rome.[25] Furthermore, Gundry and others argue that the frequent Latinisms (Latin loan words or other Latin influence on Mark's Greek) point to Italy.[26] The Latinisms argument is, however, problematic. Some are not persuaded because many of the Latin terms used in Mark are military, judicial, or economic in nature and would be present throughout the empire.[27]

What can be affirmed with more confidence is that Mark's audience contained many Gentiles.[28] This is made clear in 7:3-4 when Mark must explain ritual cleanliness customs which he says are the practice of "all the Jews." Mark must envision non-Jews who would not know these practices. This does not mean he did not envision some Jews reading his work, but only that he included comments clearly aimed at Gentiles.

It is probable that the readers Mark had in mind were

---

[23]The so-called Anti-Marcionite Prologues say Mark wrote his Gospel in Italy. Although many scholars once believed these prologues were written in the late second century, the usual current assessment is that they were written no earlier than the fourth century. Their value is minimal. See Bruce, *Canon*, pp. 154-157.

[24]Scholars who believe Mark wrote in Rome and for Romans include Lane, pp. 24-25; Gundry, pp. 1043-1045; Best, *Mark*, pp. 35-36. Scholars who consider the Roman locale possible but weakly attested include Guelich, pp. xxix-xxxi; and Carson, Moo, and Morris, *Introduction*, pp. 95-96.

[25]J. Ramsey Michaels, *1 Peter*, Word Biblical Commentary, vol. 49 (Dallas: Word, 1988), pp. 310-311.

[26]Gundry, p. 1044.

[27]Joel Marcus, "The Jewish War and the Sitz im Leben of Mark," *Journal of Biblical Literature* 111 (1992): 443-446.

[28]There is widespread agreement that Mark addresses Gentiles. See Carson, Moo, and Morris, *Introduction*, p. 99, although they should not cite Mark's translation of Aramaic terms as evidence for a Gentile audience without careful qualification. Most Diaspora Jews would not know Aramaic.

already Christians.[29] Beginning with the citation of Scripture in 1:2-3 he occasionally cites or alludes to Scriptures in a way that seems to assume knowledge of and appreciation for the Old Testament. Coupled with the indications of a Gentile audience, the assumed knowledge of the Old Testament suggests either Gentiles who had been attracted to the synagogue or who had become Christians. Occasionally, more distinctly Christian knowledge seems to be assumed. For example, Mark never explains what John meant by Jesus baptizing with the Holy Spirit (1:8). Christian readers would know. A particularly interesting case is 15:21, which identifies Simon of Cyrene as the father of Alexander and Rufus. Apparently, the readers of Mark knew the two sons. But they were not well-known public figures. The most likely hypothesis to explain Mark's assumption is that they were known within the Christian community or at least that element of it which he had in mind.[30]

Mark may have written his Gospel in Rome and for Roman Christians. In any case, he probably envisioned a Christian audience with many Gentiles.

DATE

As noted above, the earliest comments reflecting the date of Mark are by the late second century writers Irenaeus and Clement of Alexandria, who disagree on whether Mark was written prior to or after Peter's death. Very little concrete data is available to supplement their conflicting reflections.[31]

---

[29]This is also a matter of widespread agreement, although there are a few dissenters. See Best, *Mark*, pp. 19-20, 93-95.

[30]Gundry, pp. 953-954; Brown, p. 913.

[31]Guelich, p. xxxi, observes that most scholars place the writing of Mark after Peter's death, which probably occurred between A.D. 64 and 68. For conservative scholarship (e.g., Lane, p. 17) this is primarily due to accepting the witness of Irenaeus (and in some cases the so-called Anti-Marcionite Prologues). For liberal scholarship it is primarily due to the opinion that

The most significant data in my opinion is the widespread hypothesis that Luke was dependent upon Mark[32] coupled with a relatively early date for Luke-Acts.[33] If Luke-Acts was complete by c. A.D. 62 and if Luke used Mark's Gospel, then Mark completed his work by the early sixties.[34]

MAJOR THEMES AND STRUCTURE

A number of scholars agree that two themes stand out in Mark and that they are developed in a two-part structure for the book.[35]

1. CHRISTOLOGY

One of the pervasive concerns of Mark is to portray Jesus as the authoritative Son of God and as the ultimate model of sacrificial service to God and humanity.

From the opening verse, "The beginning of the Gospel of Jesus Christ, the Son of God" (1:1), it is clear that Mark wants to paint a portrait of Jesus. Although it is an obvious oversimplification, it is useful to look at Mark's portrait by emphasizing a key word for the first half of the book, "authority," and a key word for the second half, "service." The pivotal center of Mark's Gospel is the confession by Peter in 8:27-30 and the

---

the predictions in Mark 13 go awry at some point shortly before or after the destruction of Jerusalem in A.D. 70, thus providing a date of perhaps 67 to the early 70s. See Guelich, pp. xxxi-xxxii.

[32]See Carson, Moo, and Morris, *Introduction*, pp. 32-34.

[33]Ibid., pp. 116, 190-194.

[34]Gundry, pp. 1042-1043, agrees with this conclusion and for the same basic reasons. He supports it with weak traditional materials and a minority interpretation of Irenaeus that denies that Irenaeus meant to say Mark wrote after Peter's death.

[35]Compare the discussions in Guelich, xxxvi-xl; Best, *Mark*, pp. 55-92, 129-130.

crucial discussion that follows in 8:31-9:1.[36] The turning point is the disciples' confession that Jesus is the Christ. The first half of the book leads to this confession; the second half builds on it and defines the role of the Son of Man as that of service unto death.

In 1:1-8:30, the focus is on the authority of Jesus as exhibited in his miracles and teaching and in the testimony of others. John the Baptist says, "After me will come one more powerful than I" (1:7). God declares, "You are my Son, whom I love" (1:11). Jesus summons fishermen, and they drop everything to follow him (1:16-20). When he teaches, the people "were amazed at his teaching, because he taught them as one who had authority" (1:22). When he casts out demons, they declare, "He even gives orders to evil spirits and they obey him" (1:27). The first eight chapters are permeated with features like these examples from the first chapter. Jesus' authority is repeatedly emphasized.

The question underlying most of these stories surfaces plainly in 4:41, "Who is this? Even the wind and the waves obey him!" Who, indeed, is this one with such authority that his teaching transcends that of the teachers of the law, that he forgives sins, that he controls sickness, disease, demons, nature, and even death?

The resounding answer is already given to the reader in 1:1, but is finally clear to the disciples in 8:29. At this point a new stage is opened up: "He then began to teach them that the Son of Man must suffer many things . . ." (8:31). The disciples do not readily grasp this new understanding either. Peter immediately objects (8:32). Throughout the remainder of the book, Jesus repeatedly works with the disciples to try to get them to see that the Son of Man "did not come to be

---

[36]Guelich, p. xxxvi, and others divide Mark at 8:26/8:27. This keeps the flow of the single storyline in 8:27-9:1 together. On the other hand, Lane, p. 292, and others divide Mark at 8:30/8:31. Peter's confession in 8:27-30 is the conclusion to the first part of the book. Then, as Lane suggests, "With verse 31 an entirely new orientation is given to the Gospel" (p. 292).

served, but to serve, and to give his life as a ransom for many" (10:45).

The fact that this authoritative figure who commanded nature, disease, demons, and death would submit to death in suffering service is a key theme permeating everything after 8:31. Even though the second half of the book continues to emphasize Jesus' authority, the focus turns more and more toward the cross. This focus is explicit in Jesus' own statements about his coming suffering (8:31; 9:12, 31; 10:32-34, 45; 14:18-21, 24-25, 27, 41). The shadow of his death lies over the second half of the book in other ways as well. One thinks, for example, of the fate of the son in the parable of the wicked tenants (12:6-8) or the anointing at Bethany (14:1-9) and of all the events from the Lord's Supper to the end of the crucifixion (14:12-15:47). In the second half of the book, Mark underscores the fact that the powerful, authoritative Son of God willingly submitted himself to the most shameful and inhumane of deaths because he had the heart of a servant.

2. DISCIPLESHIP

The theme of Christology carried out in the emphasis on Jesus' authority and then his suffering service is brought to bear on Mark's readers' lives through the emphasis on discipleship. To submit to Jesus' authority involves following in Jesus' footsteps in suffering service.

This point is first enunciated in 8:34-35 and then driven home by repetition, especially in 9:33-37 and 10:35-45. It is no accident that these sections of vital instruction on discipleship immediately follow the three repetitions of Jesus' predictions regarding his own death in Jerusalem. Disciples are to be like their master.

In each of these three instances, Jesus' prediction is followed by immediate indication that the disciples are out of step with their Lord. In 8:32, Peter even "rebukes" Jesus for what he said would happen. Having rebuked Peter, Jesus calls all the people together with his disciples and explains that what he plans to do bears not only on him but on what it means to be a follower: "If anyone would come after me, he must deny himself and take up his cross and follow me" (8:34).

In the second instance Mark writes that the disciples did not understand Jesus' prediction concerning himself (9:32), then immediately shows that they did not grasp its implications for themselves. They are interested in establishing which of them is the greatest (9:33-34), but Jesus tells them that followers of one who takes the role of a servant must be servants themselves (9:35).

The third instance is similar. Here, again immediately following a prediction concerning Jesus' death, James and John seek the chief places in the coming kingdom (10:35-37). Jesus' reply is explicit in the way it ties discipleship to Christology: "whoever wants to become great among you must be your servant, and whoever wants to be first must be slave of all. For even the Son of Man did not come to be served, but to serve, and to give his life as a ransom for many" (10:43-45). These verses, 10:43-45, provide a convenient summary of the main point with respect to discipleship. This emphasis permeates the second half of the book.

3. FURTHER OBSERVATIONS ON MARK'S STRUCTURE

In addition to the major division of Mark at 8:30/8:31, a few further divisions may be discerned with varying levels of confidence.

Most scholars identify either 1:1-8, 1:1-13, or 1:1-15 as an introduction. I have chosen 1:1-15 for reasons that are described at the beginning of the comments on chapter 1. These verses set the stage for all that follows.

It is questionable whether there is a clearly discernible substructure for the rest of the first half of the book (1:16-8:30). I have chosen the popular three-part structure proposed by

Leander Keck[37] largely as a matter of convenience for the memory. Keck's outline is easily learned because each section begins with a new stage in the disciples' development: the call of the four fishermen (1:16-20), the appointment of the twelve apostles (3:13-19), and the mission of the twelve (6:6b-13).

The second half of the book is easily divisible according to stages in Jesus' ministry. In 8:31-10:52 he journeys to Jerusalem. Beginning at 11:1 Mark focuses over one third of his book on Jesus' last week, from the triumphal entry to the resurrection.

In addition to the overall structure of the book, there are smaller structural features discernible in various sections. Some of these are identified in the outline, such as the collection of five controversy stories in 2:1-3:6 or the parable section in 4:1-34. Others are discussed as they arise in the commentary, such as the "sandwich" phenomenon discussed first at 3:20-35.

PURPOSE

Mark does not provide a statement of purpose for his work. It is difficult to construct a hypothetical statement of purpose that is well focused and yet broad enough to include all of Mark's material. Any statement of Mark's purpose should take into account his intended audience, particularly the probability that he wrote primarily for those who had already become Christians.

Mark's overall purpose might be stated as follows: to tell the story of Jesus from his baptism to his death and resurrection in order to strengthen the faith and deepen the understanding of his readers.[38] The weakness of this statement is

---

[37]Leander E. Keck, "The Introduction to Mark's Gospel," *New Testament Studies* 12 (1965-66): 352-370.

[38]Best, *Mark*, pp. 51-54.

that it is so broad as to include virtually anything Mark might have known about Jesus.

As stated above on pages 11-13, each Gospel writer had some particular emphases that guided his selection. In Mark's case there is one particular emphasis that dominates the overall structure of the book and presumably was the primary principle of selection for much of its contents: the emphasis on discipleship as self-sacrificing service.[39] Mark presents Jesus as the model of service: "the Son of Man did not come to be served, but to serve and to give his life as a ransom for many" (10:45). As is demonstrated in the above section on the structure of the book, Mark organizes his book around Jesus' effort to explain this to his disciples and to bring them to the understanding that "whoever wants to be great among you must be your servant, and whoever wants to be first must be slave of all" (10:43-44). This focus may account for many of Mark's choices.

Lane (and others) would be more specific.[40] In particular, he believes the purpose of Mark was to encourage Roman Christians to sacrificial service during the time of the Neronian persecution of A.D. 64. But I have argued above that Mark was probably written by A.D. 62 and that the tradition that his intended audience was in Rome is possibly true, but not a tradition to hold with confidence. It is questionable whether Mark wrote primarily for a persecution setting, Neronian or otherwise.[41] There are only a few explicit references to persecution (4:17; 8:34-38; 10:29-30, 39; and 13:9-13). Certainly Mark's Gospel could have been used for encouragement by persecuted Christians, but it is preferable to state his primary focus in broader terms of sacrificial service.

---

[39]E.g., ibid., pp. 83-92; Carson, Moo, and Morris, *Introduction*, p. 101.
[40]Lane, pp. 12-17.
[41]Best, *Mark*, pp. 52-53.

SUMMARY OF INTRODUCTORY CONCLUSIONS

The Gospel of Mark was written by John Mark of Jerusalem, an associate of Paul and of Peter. It probably reflects Peter's preaching about Jesus. Mark composed it by the early sixties. The audience he had in mind were predominantly Gentile Christians, possibly in Rome. He wrote the story of Jesus in order to strengthen their faith and deepen their understanding, particularly with respect to their need to follow Jesus in the path of sacrificial service to God and humanity.

Mark focused on christology and discipleship and their interrelationship. In the first part of the Gospel (1:1-8:30) he focused on Jesus' authority and the need for disciples to believe in him. Then, beginning in 8:31, he focused on how Jesus submitted himself to death in sacrificial service and on the need for disciples to follow his example.

OUTLINE

I. INTRODUCTION – 1:1-15

- **A. The Beginning of the Gospel** – 1:1-8
- **B. John Baptizes Jesus** – 1:9-11
- **C. Temptation in the Wilderness** – 1:12-13
- **D. The Gospel Jesus Preached** – 1:14-15

II. THE GALILEAN MINISTRY, SECTION ONE – 1:16-3:12

- **A. The Call of the First Disciples** – 1:16-20
- **B. Jesus Demonstrates His Authority in Capernaum** – 1:21-28
- **C. Healing Simon's Mother-in-Law** – 1:29-31
- **D. Other Healings at Capernaum** – 1:32-34
- **E. What Jesus Came to Do** – 1:35-39
- **F. Healing A Leper** – 1:40-45
- **G. Stories of Controversy between Jesus and the Religious Authorities** – 2:1-3:6
  1. Controversy over Forgiving Sins – 2:1-12
  2. Controversy over Eating with Tax Collectors and Sinners – 2:13-17
  3. Controversy over Fasting – 2:18-22
  4. Controversy over Picking Grain on the Sabbath – 2:23-28
  5. Controversy over Healing on the Sabbath – 3:1-6
- **H. Summary Statement about the Crowds and Healings** – 3:7-12

III. THE GALILEAN MINISTRY, SECTION TWO – 3:13-6:6a

- **A. The Appointment of the Twelve Apostles** – 3:13-19
- **B. Jesus Accused of Lunacy and Being Possessed** – 3:20-35

4. Warnings Against False Messiahs during the Birth Pains – 13:20-23
5. The Second Coming – 13:24-27
6. The Significance of the Birth Pains for the Second Coming – 13:28-31
7. No One Knows the Day or Hour of the Second Coming – 13:32-37

F. Jesus Honored and Betrayed – 14:1-11

G. The Passover Meal – 14:12-31

1. Preparation for the Passover – 14:12-16
2. Jesus Predicts His Betrayal – 14:17-21
3. The Institution of the Lord's Supper – 14:22-25

H. Jesus Predicts the Flight of the Disciples and Peter's Denial – 14:26-31

I. Prayer in Gethsemane – 14:32-42

J. Betrayal, Arrest, and Flight – 14:43-52

K. Jesus and Peter Put on Trial – 14:53-72

1. Jesus' Trial Before the Sanhedrin – 14:53-65
2. Peter's Denials – 14:66-72

L. Jesus' Trial Before Pilate – 15:1-15

M. Pilate's Soldiers Mock Jesus – 15:16-20

N. The Crucifixion – 15:21-41

O. The Burial of Jesus – 15:42-47

P. The Resurrection – 16:1-8

Q. Post-Resurrection Appearances – 16:9-20

1. The Appearance to Mary Magdalene – 16:9-11
2. The Appearance to Two Disciples – 16:12-13
3. The Appearance to and Commission of the Eleven – 16:14-18
4. The Ascension and the Disciples' Mission – 16:19-20

BIBLIOGRAPHY

Aland, Barbara, Kurt Aland, Johannes Karavidopoulos, Carlo M. Martini, and Bruce M. Metzger. *The Greek New Testament.* Fourth Revised Edition. Stuttgart: Biblia-Druck, United Bible Societies, 1993.

Anderson, Hugh. *The Gospel of Mark.* New Century Bible Commentary. Grand Rapids: Eerdmans, 1976.

Batey, Richard, A. *Jesus and the Forgotten City: New Light on Sepphoris and the Urban World of Jesus.* Grand Rapids: Baker, 1991.

Bauer, Walter, William F. Arndt, and F. Wilbur Gingrich. *A Greek-English Lexicon of the New Testament and Other Early Christian Literature,* 2nd ed. Rev. by F. Wilbur Gingrich and Frederick W. Danker. Chicago: University of Chicago Press, 1979.

Beasley-Murray, G.R. *Baptism in the New Testament.* London: MacMillan, 1962.

__________. *Jesus and the Kingdom of God.* Grand Rapids: Eerdmans, 1986.

Best, Ernest. *Mark: The Gospel As Story.* Edinburgh: T. & T. Clark, 1983.

Blackburn, Barry. *Theios Aner and the Markan Miracle Traditions.* WUNT 2.40. Tübingen: J.C.B. Mohr, 1991.

Blomberg, Craig L. *Interpreting the Parables.* Downers Grove: InterVarsity, 1990.

__________. *The Historical Reliability of the Gospels.* Downers Grove: InterVarsity, 1987.

__________. *Matthew.* New American Commentary. Nashville: Broadman, 1992.

Bock, Darrell L. "Elijah and Elisha." *DJG* 203-206.

Bratcher, Robert G. and Eugene A. Nida. *A Translator's Handbook on the Gospel of Mark.* Leiden: E.J. Brill, 1961.

Brown, Raymond E. *The Death of the Messiah.* Anchor Bible Reference Library, 2 Volumes. New York: Doubleday, 1994.

Bruce, F.F. *The Canon of Scripture.* Downers Grove: InterVarsity, 1988.

Cargounis, C.C. "The Kingdom of God/Heaven." *DJG* 417-430.

Carson, Donald A., Douglas J. Moo, and Leon Morris. *An Introduction to the New Testament.* Grand Rapids: Zondervan, 1992.

Carson, Donald A. "Matthew." In *The Expositor's Bible Commentary*. Ed. Frank E. Gaebelein. Vol. 8. Grand Rapids: Zondervan, 1984.

Cranfield, C.E.B. *The Gospel according to Saint Mark.* Cambridge Greek Testament Commentary. Cambridge, England: University Press, 1959.

Davids, Peter. *Commentary on James.* New International Greek Testament Commentary. Grand Rapids: Eerdmans, 1982.

Dodd, C.H. "The Kingdom of God Has Come." *Expository Times* 48 (1936-37): 138-142.

__________. *The Parables of the Kingdom.* London: Nisbet, 1935.

Farmer, William R. *The Last Twelve Verses of Mark.* SNTSMS 25. Cambridge: Cambridge University Press, 1974.

Ferguson, Everett. *Backgrounds of Early Christianity.* 2nd edition. Grand Rapids: Eerdmans, 1993.

Fitzmyer, Joseph A. "The Aramaic Qorban Inscription from Jebel Hallet et-Turi and Mark 7:11/Matt. 15:5." *Journal of Biblical Literature* 78 (1959): 60-65.

__________. *The Gospel According to Luke I-IX.* Anchor Bible Commentary, Vol. 28A. Garden City, NY: Doubleday, 1981.

France, Richard T. *Jesus and the Old Testament.* Downers Grove: InterVarsity, 1971.

__________. *Matthew.* Tyndale New Testament Commentaries. Grand Rapids: Eerdmans, 1985.

Geldenhuys, Norval G. *Commentary of the Gospel of Luke.* New International Commentary on the New Testament. Grand Rapids: Eerdmans, 1983.

Green, Joel B. and Scot McKnight, eds. *Dictionary of Jesus and the Gospels.* Downers Grove: InterVarsity, 1992.

Guelich, Robert A. *Mark 1:1-8:26.* Word Biblical Commentary, Vol. 34A. Dallas: Word, 1989.

Gundry, Robert H. *Mark: A Commentary on His Apology for the Cross.* Grand Rapids: Eerdmans, 1993.

__________. *Matthew.* Grand Rapids: Eerdmans, 1982.

Hawthorne, Gerald F. "Amen." *DJG* 7-8.

Heard, Warren J. "Revolutionary Movements." *DJG* 688-698.

Helton, Stanley N. "Churches of Christ and Mark 16:9-20." *Restoration Quarterly* 36 (1994): 32- 52.

Hengel, Martin. *Crucifixion in the Ancient World and the Folly of the Message of the Cross.* London: SCM, 1977.

__________. *Studies in the Gospel of Mark.* Trans. John Bowden. Philadelphia: Fortress, 1985.

Herzog, William R., II. "Temple Cleansing." *DJG* 817-821.

Hoehner, Harold.W. *Herod Antipas.* Grand Rapids: Zondervan, 1972.

__________. "Herodian Dynasty." *DJG* 317-326.

Hooker, Morna. *The Gospel According to Saint Mark.* Black's New Testament Commentaries. Peabody, MA: Hendrickson, 1991.

Hurtado, Larry W. *Mark.* New International Biblical Commentary. Peabody, MA: Hendrickson, 1989.

Jeremias, Joachim. *The Central Message of the New Testament.* New York: Charles Scribner's Sons, 1965.

Judge, E.A. "The Regional Kanon for Requisitioned Transport." In *New Documents Illustrating Early Christianity.* Ed. G.H.R. Horsley. North Ryde, Australia: Macquarie University, 1976.

Juel, Donald. *Messianic Exegesis.* Philadelphia: Fortress, 1988.

Keck, Leander E. "The Introduction to Mark's Gospel." *New Testament Studies* 12 (1965-66): 352-372.

Lane, William L. *The Gospel according to Mark.* New International New Testament Commentary. Grand Rapids: Eerdmans, 1974.

Marcus, Joel. "The Jewish War and the Sitz im Leben of Mark." *Journal of Biblical Literature* 111 (1992): 443-446.

Marshall, I. Howard. *The Gospel of Luke.* New International Greek Testament Commentary. Grand Rapids: Eerdmans, 1978.

__________. *The Origins of New Testament Christology.* Updated ed. Downers Grove: InterVarsity, 1990.

McGarvey, J.W. "Biblical Criticism." *Christian Standard* 32 (1896): 1367.

__________. *The New Testament Commentary. Vol. 1: Matthew and Mark.* Delight, AR: Gospel Light, 1875.

McIver, Robert K. "One Hundred-Fold Yield – Miraculous or Mundane? Matthew 13.8, 23; Mark 4.8, 20; Luke 8.8." *New Testament Studies* 40 (1994): 606-608.

McRay, John. *Archaeology and the New Testament.* Grand Rapids: Baker, 1991.

Merriam-Webster's Collegiate Dictionary. 10th ed. Springfield, MA: Merriam-Webster, 1993.

Metzger, Bruce M. *A Textual Commentary on the Greek New Testament.* Second Edition. Stuttgart: Wurttemberg Bible Society, 1994.

Michaels, J. Ramsey. *1 Peter.* Word Biblical Commentary, Vol. 49. Dallas: Word, 1988.

Roads, David and Donald Michie. *Mark As Story.* Philadelphia: Fortress, 1982.

Rousseau, John J. and Rami Arav, eds. *Jesus and His World: An Archaeological and Cultural Dictionary.* Minneapolis: Fortress, 1995.

Sanders, E.P. *Judaism: Practice and Belief, 63BCE-66CE.* Philadelphia: Trinity Press International, 1992.

Schmidt, Thomas E. "Taxes." *DJG* 804-807.

Twelftree, G.H. "Blasphemy." *DJG* 75-77.

__________. "Demon, Devil, Satan." *DJG* 163-172.

__________. "Sanhedrin." *DJG* 728-732.

__________. "Scribes." *DJG* 732-735.

Westerholm, Stephen. "Pharisees." *DJG* 609-614.

Wilkins, Michael J. "Sinner." *DJG* 757-760.

Williamson, Lamar, Jr. *Mark.* Interpretation Commentary. Atlanta: John Knox, 1983.

Willis, Wendell, ed. *The Kingdom of God in 20th-Century Interpretation.* Peabody, MA: Hendrickson, 1987.

Wuellner, Wilhelm H. *The Meaning of "Fishers of Men."* The New Testament Library. Philadelphia: Westminster, 1967.

MARK 1

I. INTRODUCTION (1:1-15)

Mark's Gospel begins with an introduction that orients the reader to the story to follow.[1] The extent of the introduction is debatable, with different scholars arguing for setting the limit at the end of v. 8, v. 13, or v. 15.[2] However, even if one were to conclude that vv. 14-15 or even vv. 9-13 are not technically part of what Mark envisioned as an introduction to the book, they nevertheless clearly function to introduce the identity and mission of Jesus.[3]

It is important to read 1:1-15 carefully since these verses set the framework for the rest of the story.[4] They tell us that Mark's story will focus on Jesus; they identify him as the Christ, the Son of God; they sum up his message; they declare his story to be the fulfilment of the prophetic message

---

[1]As I have argued in the introduction to the commentary, Mark apparently assumes an audience of Christians who know much of the Christian story. For example, in 1:1-8, he assumes prior familiarity with John the Baptist and baptism in the Holy Spirit.

[2]E.g., for ending the introduction at v. 8 see Gundry, pp. 30-31; for v. 13 see Lane, pp. 39-40; and for v. 15 see Guelich, p. 4. The most popular position is to include vv. 1-15, with many scholars referring to Keck, "The Introduction to Mark's Gospel," pp. 352-370.

[3]In other words, those who argue that these paragraphs are not part of the introduction to the book must still recognize them as serving an introductory role as the first paragraphs of the body of the book.

[4]By using the terms "story" or "narrative" I do not intend to suggest any doubt about the historicity of Mark. One may, of course, "narrate" or "tell the story of" historical events (e.g., the Civil War). I accept the events Mark describes as actual historical occurrences.

concerning the coming one and his kingdom; and they indicate that the good news about Jesus calls for a response.

A. THE BEGINNING OF THE GOSPEL (1:1-8)

1 The beginning of the gospel about Jesus Christ, the Son of God.[a]

2 It is written in Isaiah the prophet:
"I will send my messenger ahead of you,
who will prepare your way"[b] –
3 "a voice of one calling in the desert,
'Prepare the way for the Lord,
make straight paths for him.'"[c]
4 And so John came, baptizing in the desert region and
preaching a baptism of repentance for the forgiveness of
sins. 5 The whole Judean countryside and all the people of
Jerusalem went out to him. Confessing their sins, they were
baptized by him in the Jordan River. 6 John wore clothing
made of camel's hair, with a leather belt around his waist,
and he ate locusts and wild honey. 7 And this was his mes-
sage: "After me will come one more powerful than I, the
thongs of whose sandals I am not worthy to stoop down and
untie. 8 I baptize you with[d] water, but he will baptize you with
the Holy Spirit."

[a] *1* Some manuscripts do not have *the Son of God.* [b] *2* Mal. 3:1 [c] *3* Isaiah 40:3
[d] *8* Or *in*

In 1:1-8, Mark begins with the preaching of John the Baptist, but he does so in a way that puts the focus on Jesus. Vv. 1 and 7-8 make this apparent, as does the description of John as one sent to "prepare the way." The first eight verses are in one sense primarily about John, but their more significant purpose is to set the stage for Jesus.

1. The first verse deserves a detailed examination. Some believe it refers to the opening section of the Gospel (whether

vv. 1-8, 1-13, or 1-15) while others argue it is Mark's title for the book as a whole.[5] The first view is more likely, especially in view of the opening phrase of v. 2, "as it is written."[6] In the other twenty-five New Testament occurrences of this phrase it comments on what has just preceded it, usually introducing an Old Testament quotation that is applied to the preceding statement.[7] If the same is true here, then the quotation in vv. 2-3 clarifies what Mark has in mind when he speaks of "the beginning of the gospel." He is thinking about the preparatory work of John.[8]

Yet there is a sense in which the rest of the first verse after "the beginning" describes the entire Gospel of Mark. All sixteen chapters are not "the beginning," but all sixteen chapters are concerned with "the gospel about Jesus Christ, the Son of God."

The word "gospel" (εὐαγγέλιον, *euangelion*) means "good news." In Mark's day it had a broad usage like the modern phrase "good news."[9] However, Mark's use of the term was based on its Christian use in which it referred to the saving message about Jesus.[10] Mark uses the word "gospel" (in 1:1, 14-15; 8:35; 10:29; 13:10; and 14:9)[11] to refer either to Jesus'

---

[5]See Guelich, pp. 6-7, for references to modern scholarly opinion.

[6]The NIV fails to translate the Greek word καθώς (*kathōs*, "as") at the beginning of v. 2.

[7]As correctly observed by Guelich, pp. 7, 10, and Gundry, p. 3.

[8]Gundry, pp. 30-31. Hos 1:2 LXX, "The beginning of the word of the Lord to Hosea," provides a parallel to Mark 1:1 in using "the beginning" to refer to the initial section of a book.

[9]E.g., Josephus, *The Jewish War* 4.618 describes Vespasian becoming the emperor and says "Every city kept festival for the good news (*euangelia*) and offered sacrifices on his behalf." All translations of Josephus are from the Loeb Classical Library edition of Josephus, *Works*, ed. and trans. H. St. J. Thackeray (vols. 1-5), Ralph Marcus (vols. 5-8), and Louis Feldman (vols. 9-10) (Cambridge, MA: Harvard University Press, 1926-65).

[10]Which, in turn, was probably based primarily on the LXX (the Septuagint, the ancient Greek translation of the Old Testament) uses of the cognate verb form to speak of proclaiming the good news of God's coming salvation (e.g., Isa 52:7; 61:1).

[11]"Gospel" also appears in the disputed ending of Mark at 16:15.

own message (as in 1:14-15) or to the message about Jesus (as in 13:10). The NIV translation "gospel about Jesus Christ" is probably correct in indicating the latter for v. 1, although the phrase could be translated "Jesus Christ's gospel" (that is, the gospel proclaimed by Jesus himself, as in 1:14-15).[12]

Jesus is identified in v. 1 as "Jesus Christ, Son of God."[13] "Christ" was the Greek translation of "messiah," a Hebrew word meaning "anointed one." Since Israel's kings were designated by anointing, the king many Jews expected God to send in the future was called the messiah.[14] By identifying Jesus as Christ, Mark indicates that he is the one who fulfilled the centuries old Jewish expectations of a coming messiah.[15]

The title "Son of God" is not part of v. 1 in several important ancient witnesses to the text. It may not belong to the original text of Mark 1:1, although Jesus' Sonship is clearly an important theme elsewhere in Mark (1:11; 3:11; 8:38; 9:7; 12:6; 13:32; 14:36, 61; 15:39). The prominence of this concept

---

[12]C.E.B. Cranfield, *The Gospel according to Saint Mark*, Cambridge Greek Testament Commentary (Cambridge, Eng.: University Press, 1959), pp. 35-36, prefers "Jesus Christ's gospel," although he concludes the other meaning is also intended to some extent.

[13]On the name "Jesus" see Cranfield, p. 37. Jesus is the Greek form of a popular Hebrew name. In the Old Testament several men have this name, which is there translated "Joshua." It appears in the New Testament not only for our Savior, but also for someone in his genealogy (Luke 3:29), for Bar-Jesus (Acts 13:6), and Justus (Col 4:11). It remained a popular name among Jews until the second century A.D. Etymologically, it meant "Yahweh is salvation" or "Yahweh saves."

[14]See, e.g., the first century B.C. Psalm of Solomon 17:32: "And he will be a righteous king over them, taught by God . . . and their king shall be the Lord Messiah." Brown, p. 474, cites the available references to the messiah from the period 200 B.C. to A.D. 100.

[15]Some believe that in v. 1 "Christ" is used more as a proper name than a title. (Cf. *BAGD*, pp. 886-887.) However, of Mark's seven uses of this term, all but two (here and 9:41) unquestionably point to "the Christ" of Jewish expectation. Even though, as *BAGD* suggests, Gentiles could easily understand "Christ" as a personal name, it is dubious whether the Jewish meaning is ever completely lost in any New Testament usage. The "proper name vs. title" distinction can easily be overdrawn.

in Mark favors its originality here.[16] In the Old Testament angels, Israel's kings, and the nation of Israel are described as being God's sons (e.g., Job 1:6; 2 Sam 7:14; Exod 4:22-23). In the New Testament the title "Son of God" is often associated closely with the term "Christ" (e.g., Mark 1:1; 14:61; Matt 16:16; Luke 4:41; Rom 1:1-4).[17] Of course Mark describes Jesus as God's Son in a sense that transcends what could be said of Israel, Israel's kings, or angels. Jesus is uniquely God's Son, as seen especially in his baptism (1:11) and his transfiguration (9:7). The importance of Jesus' divine sonship for Mark may be indicated by its appearance at the beginning of his Gospel in connection with Jesus' baptism (1:11), in the middle during the transfiguration scene (9:7), and at the end immediately after Jesus' death (15:39).

By the end of the first verse, Mark's readers know that the book will focus on the good news about Jesus Christ, the Son of God.

2-3. The next two verses also serve a valuable introductory function. This is the only occasion when Mark quotes a specific prophecy in an editorial comment. (The other fulfilment quotations in Mark are cited by people in the story.) However, coming at the very beginning of the book, this quotation sets the entire book of Mark in the framework of the fulfilment of Old Testament prophecy (cf. 1:15, "The time has come. . . . The kingdom of God is near"). Mark's story is the story of God fulfilling his promises about the coming messiah and kingdom.

The quotation in vv. 2-3 looks back to v. 1 to explain that the beginning of the gospel came about "as it is written in

---

[16]Guelich, p. 6.

[17]In light of such Old Testament texts as 2 Sam 7:14 and Ps 2:7 there is a prima facie case for pre-Christian descriptions of the messiah as the Son of God. The clearest evidence is a document from the Dead Sea scrolls (4Q Florilegium 1:10-12) which cites 2 Sam 7:14 ("I will be his father and he will be my son") with reference to the expected Davidic messiah. See Donald Juel, *Messianic Exegesis* (Philadelphia: Fortress, 1988), pp. 61-77.

Isaiah the prophet."[18] Although many ancient manuscripts of Mark read "as it is written in the prophets," the best manuscripts refer only to Isaiah.[19] Perhaps Mark wanted to focus on the citation of Isa 40:3 in v. 3.

V. 2 combines elements of Exod 23:20 and Mal 3:1.[20] Through the use of Mal 3:1 Mark implicitly identifies John the Baptist as the Elijah to come of Mal 4: 5, an identification that is later made overtly in Mark 9:11-13. In addition to combining Old Testament texts, Mark makes small but significant changes in wording. His use of "your" way rather than "my" way[21] points to Jesus as the one for whom the messenger prepares. V. 3 alters the Isa 40:3 citation in a similar way, speaking of making straight "his" (that is, Jesus') paths rather than the paths "of our God."

The point of the composite and edited citation is that the beginning of the gospel of Jesus Christ came about as it had been prophesied: God sent a messenger into the wilderness to prepare the way for the Christ. The following verses provide the specifics of the fulfilment. The messenger is John the Baptizer. The location of his preaching is the wilderness. He prepared the people by proclaiming a baptism of repentance and teaching them about the one who would come after him.

4-5. Although our manuscripts differ, the best attested reading of Mark's description of John is probably not the NIV's "John came, baptizing," but "John the baptizer came."[22] Mark is unique in describing John as "the baptizer" rather than "the baptist," but the meaning is basically the same. John was known for baptizing Jews in the Jordan river.

Before John, immersion rituals were already common in Palestine. Many Jews practiced repeated ritual (self-adminis-

---

[18]See the notes on v. 1 for the backward reference and for the observation that the NIV omits "as."

[19]Guelich, p. 6.

[20]Guelich, pp. 7, 11, makes a possible case that the LXX reflects a perceived relationship between these two Old Testament texts.

[21]Both the Hebrew and the LXX read "my."

[22]Guelich, p. 16.

tered) immersions to deal with uncleanness.[23] John's baptism differed in that it was a one time event, administered by another, and connected with repentance and forgiveness of sins. Unfortunately, we do not know for sure whether proselyte baptism (for initiating Gentiles into Judaism) was practiced before the ministry of John.[24] It would provide a more similar (one time only) precedent for John's baptism, although it was also self-administered.

In any case, John's baptism was not a repeated ritual immersion, but a one time event connected with repentance and confession of sins. It led, as does Christian baptism, to forgiveness of sins (compare Mark 1:4 and Acts 2:38 – although, of course there could be no thought in John's baptism of the parallel with the death, burial, and resurrection of Jesus or of the atoning value of Jesus' death).

Mark's statement that "the whole Judaean countryside and all the people of Jerusalem" were baptized by John is hyperbolic, but it indicates that John did have much success in preparing people for the one to come after him.[25]

6. Why does Mark tell us what John wore and ate? Probably he wants to underscore the point that John was a man of the wilderness (in fulfilment of Isa 40:3).[26] It is possible that

---

[23]E.P. Sanders, *Judaism: Practice and Belief, 63 BCE-66 CE* (Philadelphia: Trinity Press International, 1992), pp. 222-229. At Qumran immersion rituals were practiced daily (pp. 352-354).

[24]See the discussion in G.R. Beasley-Murray, *Baptism in the New Testament* (London: MacMillan, 1962), pp. 13-25. The existence of proselyte baptism in the late first century is attested by the philosopher Epictetus in his *Discourses* 2.9.9-21: "when he accepts the experience of the baptized and chosen, then he is in name and reality a Jew."

[25]V. 5 contains Mark's first use of καί (*kai*, "and") to begin a sentence or clause. Mark uses this word 1100 times, nearly 400 of which begin sentences. Most modern translations obscure Mark's heavy use of this conjunction by varying its translation, especially when it begins a sentence.

[26]Gundry, p. 37. Compare the parallel of Bannus in Josephus, *The Life* 2. Josephus says he became Bannus's disciple for three years. He describes Bannus as a man "who dwelt in the wilderness, wearing only such clothing as trees provided, feeding on such things as grew of themselves." See also the *Martyrdom of Isaiah* 2:8-12 (Lane, p. 51 n. 42).

John's garment of camel hair is mentioned to identify him as a prophet (cf. Zech 13:4; Heb 11:37) or that his leather belt relates him to Elijah (2 Kgs 1:8).[27]

7-8. John's teaching about the one who would follow him is that he will be more powerful than John. The statement that he is not worthy even to stoop and untie Jesus' sandals emphasizes the vast superiority that he grants to the coming one. One element of Jesus' superiority will be that he will baptize with (one could also translate ἐν as "in") the Holy Spirit.

Mark does not explain the meaning of John's description of Jesus as baptizing with the Holy Spirit. Presumably, he assumed his readers would know the meaning of this concept. Modern readers must turn to other New Testament texts. The reflections of John's statement in Acts 1:4-5 and 11:16 make it clear that for Luke John's prediction about Jesus baptizing in the Spirit was fulfilled in Acts 2 at Pentecost and in Acts 10 with Cornelius's household. It may be questioned, however, whether Luke intended to limit the fulfilment to these two events. The fact that John proclaimed this message to all who came out to him suggests a more general application. It can be argued from Acts 1:4-5; 2:16-21, 33, 38-39 that Peter equates being baptized with the Spirit, the pouring out of the Spirit on all flesh, and receiving the gift of the Holy Spirit. In that case being baptized in the Spirit would not be a special miracle-working measure of the Spirit granted only to some Christians and not others, but the common reception of the Spirit also referred to as receiving the gift of the Holy Spirit. This accords with Paul's usage in 1 Cor 12:13: "For we all were baptized by (or "with" or "in"–it is the same preposition ἐν Mark uses) the Holy Spirit." Thus John the baptizer probably speaks of the universal reception of the Spirit by all who are baptized with Christ's baptism.[28] John's baptism brought

---

[27]See especially Guelich, pp. 20-21, who doubts the leather belt alludes to Elijah.

[28]The New Testament knows no doctrine of a "second (Pentecostal) blessing," a baptism of the Spirit received by some Christians, but not all. To be

forgiveness of sins, but only Christ would fulfill the Old Testament promises that God would give his Spirit to all his people (Isa 32:15; 44:3; Ezek 36:27; 37:14; Joel 2:28-29).

B. JOHN BAPTIZES JESUS (1:9-11)

[9]At that time Jesus came from Nazareth in Galilee and was baptized by John in the Jordan. [10]As Jesus was coming up out of the water, he saw heaven being torn open and the Spirit descending on him like a dove. [11]And a voice came from heaven: "You are my Son, whom I love; with you I am well pleased."

In this paragraph Jesus is introduced into the story in a way that highlights who he is. Mark's account of John baptizing Jesus connects Jesus to the work of John. More importantly, it portrays the Spirit descending on Jesus and God identifying Jesus as his beloved Son. From this point forward Jesus is the main figure in every section of Mark except 6:17-29 (the description of John's death).

9. Note the parallel between v. 9 and v. 5. V. 9, of course, does not have a parallel to "confessing their sins." Jesus' hometown Nazareth is named only here in Mark. But in 1:24; 10:47; 14:67; and 16:6 he is identified as a Nazarene, that is, a man from Nazareth. Mark 6:1-6 takes place there. Nazareth

---

baptized by the Spirit is to receive the gift of the Spirit, a universal Christian experience connected with water baptism, an experience which was not universally accompanied by the ability to do signs and wonders (see, e.g., Acts 2:43). J.W. McGarvey (probably the most influential commentator on Mark in the Restoration tradition), although reticent to accept this position, describes it as follows: "Some have supposed that the baptism in the Spirit is not confined to those who received miraculous gifts, but is enjoyed by all who receive the Holy Spirit at all. This hypothesis, which I am not prepared to adopt, would very satisfactorily explain John's language." (*The New Testament Commentary*, Vol. 1: *Matthew and Mark* [Delight, AR: Gospel Light, 1875], p. 38.)

was a small village in the hills of lower Galilee. However, it is incorrect to think of it as completely isolated. It was only a few miles from ancient Sepphoris, which "in the decades following the birth of Jesus . . . was the chief city and capital of Galilee."[29]

10-11. Mark focuses attention on three things that happened as Jesus came up from being immersed.[30] The tearing open of the heavens and the Spirit's descent may echo Isa 64:1 (LXX Isa 63:19) where Isaiah petitions God to open the heavens and come down. Whether or not it reflects Isaiah, the heavens being opened suggests a revelation from God.[31] The two other things that happen should be thought of as coming out of the open heavens: the descent of the Spirit upon Jesus and the voice declaring Jesus to be God's Son.

It is questionable whether we can ascertain why the Spirit appeared in the particular form of a dove.[32] It is more significant to ask what his descent upon Jesus signified, although Mark does not provide a specific answer. It may indicate the

---

[29]Richard A. Batey, *Jesus and the Forgotten City: New Light on Sepphoris and the Urban World of Jesus* (Grand Rapids: Baker, 1991), p. 11. "The popular picture of Jesus as a rustic growing up in the relative isolation of a small village of four hundred people in the remote hills of Galilee must be integrated with the newly revealed setting of a burgeoning Greco-Roman metropolis [Sepphoris] boasting upwards of thirty thousand inhabitants" (p. 14).

[30]Although the NIV uses a variety of translations which often obscure its presence, v. 10 contains the first of Mark's forty-seven uses (more than half the New Testament occurrences) of the adverb εὐθύς (*euthus*) and its cognate εὐθέως (*eutheōs*). Mark uses these terms sometimes in a temporal way ("immediately, at once") and other times in a weaker sense ("then, so then").

[31]For the heavens opening see also Ezek 1:1; *Testament of Levi* 2:6; 5:1; 18:6; *Testament of Judah* 24:2; *2 Baruch* 22:1; 3 Maccabees 6:18; John 1:51; Acts 7:56; 10:11; Rev 19:11.

[32]Guelich, p. 33. Matt 10:16, "innocent as doves," may suggest the dove symbolizes purity. Cf. Gundry, 49, for this and other suggestions. Some have suggested that Mark uses "like a dove" adverbially to describe the manner of the Spirit's descent instead of adjectivally to describe the form taken by the Spirit. Guelich, pp. 32-33, rightly argues that since Jesus "saw" the Spirit, Mark must be using the phrase adjectivally, as the parallels in the other Gospels clearly specify (Matt 3:16; Luke 3:22; John 1:32-34).

point at which the Spirit came to dwell within Jesus (as long as one does not understand this in an adoptionistic sense as the point when the man Jesus is adopted as the Son of God).[33] It could be understood as a means of identifying Jesus as the one who will baptize in the Spirit (Mark 1:8; cf. John 1:33) or of commissioning him for his mission (cf. Isa 61:1-3).[34] Nor are these possible implications mutually exclusive.

The voice from heaven confirms Mark's previous identification of Jesus (in 1:1) as the Son of God.[35] That is its main purpose. It is probable that "You are my Son" reflects Ps 2:7 and that "whom I love; with you I am well pleased" reflects Isa 42:1.[36] However, what Mark provides are allusions, not quotations. It may be overinterpreting to argue that we are meant to think of the contexts of Ps 2 and Isa 42 and to interpret the statement from heaven as combining the concepts of the messianic king and the suffering servant.[37] The word ἀγαπητός (*agapētos*) translated "whom I love," (or preferably "beloved") generally means just that, but in a few cases (e.g., Gen 22:2 LXX) it designates an "only" son. It might have that connotation here (although the primary meaning "beloved" would still be present).[38] It is not clear whether "with you I am well pleased" is a response to Jesus' obedience in baptism in particular or simply a general declaration.[39]

Despite some uncertainty over details, the general importance of the incidents accompanying Jesus' baptism are clear. Jesus is the one John came to prepare for. He is God's beloved and pleasing Son.

---

[33]Cranfield, pp. 53-54.

[34]Larry W. Hurtado, *Mark*, New International Biblical Commentary (Peabody, MA: Hendrickson, 1989), p. 19.

[35]There is no indication in Mark that he has in mind the rabbinic concept of the "Bath Qol" ("the daughter of the voice," that is, an echo of God's voice). Cf. Gundry, pp. 51-52.

[36]See Guelich, pp. 33-35, and Gundry, pp. 49-50, 52-53, for details.

[37]As e.g., Guelich, pp. 34-35. But see Gundry, p. 53.

[38]Lane, p. 58; Guelich, p. 34; Gundry, p. 49.

[39]Gundry, p. 53.

C. TEMPTATION IN THE WILDERNESS (1:12-13)

[12]At once the Spirit sent him out into the desert, [13]and he was in the desert forty days, being tempted by Satan. He was with the wild animals, and angels attended him.

In contrast to Matt 4:1-11 and Luke 4:1-13, Mark's description of Satan tempting Jesus is extraordinarily brief. It is also somewhat enigmatic. We do not know how much Mark assumed his readers knew about this incident and it is not easy to determine what he would have wanted them to understand about its significance.

12. Coming immediately after the descent of the Spirit on Jesus at his baptism, this verse demonstrates that the Spirit was active in Jesus' life.[40] The wilderness experience of Jesus was according to divine plan.

13. Forty days is a common time period in Scripture. In Exod 34:28; Deut 9:9, 18; and 1 Kgs 19:8 it is a period of fasting. Unlike Matthew and Luke, Mark does not refer to Jesus fasting, but he may assume his readers know more of the story than he describes. In three brief clauses Mark tells what happened in the wilderness: Jesus was tempted by Satan, he was with the wild beasts, and the angels attended (διηκόνουν, *diēkonoun*, NRSV: "waited on") him. When he says Jesus was tempted by Satan, Mark expects the reader to assume that Jesus successfully resisted those temptations. The second clause – about being with the wild beasts – is unique to Mark. The point may be that the wild beasts would not harm him because of who he was.[41] The third item – that the angels attended to him – also seems to underscore his identity.

---

[40]The verb ἐκβάλλει (*ekballei*) translated "sent" is a strong verb, as indicated by the NRSV translation "drove."

[41]Guelich, pp. 38-39, argues that the reference to the wild beasts should be read against the background of the prophetic predictions of a paradisical time when the wild beasts would be peaceful (e.g., Isa 11:6-9; 65:25; Hos 2:18). But see Gundry, pp. 58-59.

Perhaps Mark's chief purpose in his brief account of Jesus' experiences in the wilderness is to continue his emphasis on Jesus' unique identity.[42]

D. THE GOSPEL JESUS PREACHED (1:14-15)

[14]After John was put in prison, Jesus went into Galilee, proclaiming the good news of God. [15]"The time has come," he said. "The kingdom of God is near. Repent and believe the good news!"

This brief paragraph locates Jesus' ministry in space and time. More importantly, it provides a brief summary of his message. Whether it is considered to be the last part of Mark's introduction or the first part of his description of Jesus' ministry it serves to introduce the reader to Jesus' gospel. Here "good news" does not refer to the message about Jesus, but to what Jesus himself preached.

14. Jesus began his ministry in Galilee after John's arrest. This region was the setting of most of Jesus' ministry. Located above Samaria and west of the Sea of Galilee, Galilee was a predominately Jewish area ruled by Herod Antipas. The Gospels name seven Galilean towns that Jesus entered: Cana, Capernaum, Chorazin, Gennesaret, Nain, Nazareth, and Tiberias.

15. Jesus' gospel centers on the coming of the kingdom of God. "The time has come" is clarified by "The kingdom of God is near." "The time" is the appointed time God had announced through the prophets. "Has come" (πεπλήρωται, *peplērōtai*) could be translated "is fulfilled" (as in the NRSV).[43] Jesus is announcing the fulfilment of the prophecies concerning the kingdom.

---

[42]So Gundry, p. 59.
[43]Guelich, p. 43.

The clause "The kingdom of God is near" is more problematic than it first appears to be.[44] The verb translated "is near" (ἤγγικεν, *ēngiken*) has been the subject of continuing debate throughout much of the twentieth century. In 1935 C.H. Dodd argued that Jesus was saying that the kingdom had already arrived in his ministry. Dodd argued that the saying ought to be translated "The kingdom of God has come."[45] The upshot of decades of debate is that few current scholars would agree with Dodd completely, but many believe that the verb in this clause is deliberately ambiguous as to whether the kingdom "is near" or "has come."[46] This understanding correlates with the widespread opinion that for Jesus the kingdom was both (in some sense) already present and (in its full sense) yet to come. The NRSV translation "The kingdom of God has come near" probably intends to indicate this ambiguity.

Whether in this instance one chooses "The kingdom is near" or "The kingdom has come near," there is ongoing debate concerning Jesus' overall teachings concerning the nature and the arrival of the kingdom of God.[47] The phrase "kingdom of God" (or Matthew's equivalent, "kingdom of heaven") is not defined in the Gospels and so our understanding must be developed from careful examination of every detail in Jesus' statements about it. One aspect which is quite clear in Mark and elsewhere is that Jesus sometimes has reference to the final, otherworldly, abode of the faithful. For example, in Mark 9:47 Jesus says, "It is better for you to enter the kingdom of God with one eye than to have two eyes and be thrown into hell." There can be no serious doubt that here and elsewhere Jesus is thinking of the eternal, heavenly kingdom.

---

[44]See Wendell Willis, ed., *The Kingdom of God in 20th-Century Interpretation* (Peabody, MA: Hendrickson, 1987).

[45]C.H. Dodd, *The Parables of the Kingdom* (London: Nisbet, 1935), p. 44; "The Kingdom of God Has Come," *Expository Times* 48 (1936-37): 138-142.

[46]E.g., G.R. Beasley-Murray, *Jesus and the Kingdom of God* (Grand Rapids: Eerdmans, 1986), pp. 72-74; Guelich, pp. 43-44.

[47]Willis, ed., *The Kingdom of God.*

On the other hand, it is not clear that Jesus always had heaven in mind when he spoke of the kingdom of God. On two occasions most interpreters believe Jesus was saying that in some sense the kingdom was already present in his ministry: Luke 17:21 and especially Matt 12:28 (=Luke 11:20).[48] In Matt 12:28 when Jesus says "But if I drive out demons by the Spirit of God, then the kingdom of God has come upon you," he uses a different verb than in the saying we are considering from Mark. He seems to be giving his authority over demons as evidence that the kingdom is already present. If the kingdom of God is understood as a dynamic concept with the general sense of the rule or reign of God, then it is possible to speak of the reign of God breaking into the world in a new way in Jesus' ministry and more fully after Jesus' death in the church, and yet to reserve the ultimate ideal for the all-encompassing reign of God in his heavenly kingdom.

The good news Jesus proclaims in Mark is that "The kingdom of God is (or has come) near." In response people need to repent and believe the good news. John had also called upon the people to repent (Mark 1:4-5).

II. THE GALILEAN MINISTRY, SECTION ONE (1:16-3:12)[49]

A. THE CALL OF THE FIRST DISCIPLES (1:16-20)

16As Jesus walked beside the Sea of Galilee, he saw Simon and his brother Andrew casting a net into the lake, for they were fishermen. 17Come, follow me," Jesus said, "and I will make you fishers of men." 18At once they left their nets and followed him.

48C.C. Caragounis, "The Kingdom of God/Heaven," in *DJG*, pp. 420-424, correctly analyzes the importance of these texts for the present consensus, although he disagrees with the usual view of their meaning.

49See the observations on Mark's structure in the Introduction to the commentary.

[19]When he had gone a little farther, he saw James son of Zebedee and his brother John in a boat, preparing their nets. [20]Without delay he called them, and they left their father Zebedee in the boat with the hired men and followed him.

The first event of Jesus' ministry in Mark is the call of the four fishermen. If one takes Mark 1:1-15 as an introduction, 1:16-20 begins the first half of the body of the book. In this half there are two major themes: 1) christology, with a strong emphasis on Jesus' authority, and 2) discipleship. The call of the fishermen brings the disciples into the picture. From this point forward they participate in almost every scene, becoming the most important characters other than Jesus. Mark presumably expected his readers to identify with the disciples as they sought to follow Jesus. We learn from both their successes and their failures. The four disciples called in this section are designated as part of the twelve in 3:13-19. Three of them–Peter, James, and John–become the inner circle of the twelve who are privileged on three special occasions (5:37; 9:2; 14:33). The first named, Peter, plays a central role among the twelve, coming to the forefront several times, including his famous confession (8:29) and denials (14:66-72) of Jesus.

16-18. This is the first of several scenes that take place on or near the Sea of Galilee.[50] Mark calls Peter "Simon" until 3:16 when he says Jesus gave Simon the name Peter.[51] Peter and his brother Andrew are fishermen. From Luke 5:1-11 we learn that Peter owned his own boat and that James and John were his partners. Combining this with the reference in Mark 1:20 to hired hands we should probably think of the two sets of brothers as successful entrepreneurs.[52]

The main points of the story concern christology and discipleship. Christologically, Mark's portrait of Jesus calling these

---

[50]The "Sea" of Galilee is a large inland fresh water lake, about 13 miles long and, at its widest point, about 7 miles wide.

[51]On one later occasion, 14:37, Jesus calls Peter "Simon."

[52]See Wilhelm H. Wuellner, *The Meaning of "Fishers of Men,"* The New Testament Library (Philadelphia: Westminster, 1967), pp. 45-63.

men in the midst of their work and receiving an immediate response highlights the authority of Jesus, a theme demonstrated repetitively in the first half of the book. Mark also suggests that Jesus' own mission is to fish for men, both through his successful catch of the four fishermen and through his definition of their task in following him.

As far as discipleship is concerned, we learn that discipleship involves "following," a concept repeated throughout Mark.[53] We learn that following may involve leaving something as important as one's occupation. And we learn that following leads to becoming another kind of fisherman, one who fishes for people. The imagery of fishing for people or nations is found in the Old Testament (Jer 16:16; Ezek 29:4-5; Amos 4:2; Hab 1:14-17) as a metaphor of God's punishment. Jesus apparently created the positive metaphor in connection with the occupation of the fishermen. Both Jesus and his disciples fish for people to bring them into the kingdom of God.

19-20. The second calling adds James and John. It indicates that in addition to making sacrifices with respect to occupation, discipleship may involve making sacrifices with respect to family ("they left their father Zebedee in the boat"). Peter will later say, "We have left everything to follow you!" (10:28) and Jesus will commend those who have "left home or brothers or sisters or mother or father or children or fields for me and the gospel" (10:29).

It is important not to misread Peter's declaration about leaving everything. In Mark 1:29 Peter still has a house and a mother-in-law, and in 1 Cor 9:5 Paul says that Peter took his wife around with him. The demands Jesus made should not be read as equivalent to the ancient Cynic's demand for

---

[53]E.g., Mark 1:20; 2:14; 8:34; 10:21. Most of the occurrences of "following" in Mark (other than 1:17, 20) use the word ἀκολουθέω (*akoloutheō*), which is used both for following in the metaphorical sense (following Jesus' teaching and example) and for following in a purely literal sense (e.g., Mark 3:7; 5:24). It is interesting that the metaphorical use of "following Jesus" as a way of defining what it means to be a disciple is not found in the New Testament outside of the Gospels.

renunciation of property and family.[54] It is also important to be cautious about applying the demands made on the twelve to Christian discipleship in general. The twelve had a special role for which they left their former work as fishermen, tax collectors, etc. Jesus did not ask everyone he taught to do this. Nevertheless, following Jesus sometimes involves sacrificing one's occupation or family relationships.

B. JESUS DEMONSTRATES HIS AUTHORITY IN CAPERNAUM (1:21-28)

21They went to Capernaum, and when the Sabbath came,
Jesus went into the synagogue and began to teach. 22The
people were amazed at his teaching, because he taught them as one who had authority, not as the teachers of the law.
23Just then a man in their synagogue who was possessed by
an evil spirit cried out, 24"What do you want with us, Jesus
of Nazareth? Have you come to destroy us? I know who you are – the Holy One of God!"

25"Be quiet!" said Jesus sternly. "Come out of him!"
26The evil spirit shook the man violently and came out of
him with a shriek.

27The people were all so amazed that they asked each
other, "What is this? A new teaching – and with authority! He
even gives orders to evil spirits and they obey him." 28News
about him spread quickly over the whole region of Galilee.

[a]*23* Greek *unclean*; also in verses 26 and 27

The call of the fishermen was the first event Mark describes from Jesus' ministry. The scene in the synagogue in

---

[54]Cf. Epictetus (c. A.D. 55-135) in his description of the Cynic philosopher's freedom from all ties in *Discourses* 3.22.45-49: "Look at me. I am without house, without home, without property, without slaves! I sleep on the ground, I have no wife, no children, no palace from which to rule but only the earth and sky and one rough coat. And what do I lack? Am I not without sorrow, am I not without fear, am I not free?" This is not Jesus' ideal.

Capernaum is the first public teaching event, accompanied by the first miracle. These verses open a section which presents a day in the life of Jesus (1:21-39). It is an unusual section in Mark because several different stories are tied together by the place (Capernaum) and by detailed time references (v. 29 "as soon as they left the synagogue," v. 32 "that evening after sunset," v. 35 "in the morning, while it was still very dark").

The synagogue scene emphasizes Jesus' authority (ἐξουσία, *exousia*, vv. 22 and 27) as demonstrated by both his teaching and his ability to command the unclean spirits. The evil spirit provides the correct understanding of Jesus' authority when he says, "I know who you are – the Holy One of God." Being a spirit with supernatural knowledge, he reaffirms what Mark (1:1) and God (1:11) have already affirmed about Jesus.

21. Capernaum was a lakeside town on the northwest shore of the Sea of Galilee. Peter and Andrew lived there (Mark 1:29). Jesus apparently spent a large amount of time there during his Galilean ministry. In Matt 9:1 (cf. Mark 2:1) it is described as "his (Jesus') own town." On the sabbath many Jews, including Jesus, went to the synagogue to worship.[55]

22. "Teachers of the law" is the NIV translation for the word γραμματεῖς (*grammateis*) traditionally translated "scribes." The scribes were professional interpreters and teachers of the Old Testament Law. They could be Pharisees, Sadducees, or Essenes, although the majority of those mentioned in the Gospels seem to be Pharisees (cf. 2:16). Mark mentions scribes twenty-one times as opponents of Jesus. They are sometimes mentioned alone (as here), sometimes associated with the Pharisees (e.g., 2:16; 7:5), and sometimes mentioned as part of the Sanhedrin in Jerusalem (e.g., 14:53).[56]

---

[55]Although the ancient synagogue remains which are currently visible at Capernaum probably date to a later century, the later synagogue was probably built on the site of the one Jesus entered to teach. See John McRay, *Archaeology and the New Testament* (Grand Rapids: Baker, 1991), pp. 162-164.

[56]For more on the scribes see G.H. Twelftree, "Scribes," in *DJG*, pp. 732-735.

Mark provides less of Jesus' teaching than the other Gospels, but he refers to the fact of Jesus' teaching (proportionately) more frequently.[57] The point he emphasizes here is that Jesus' teaching was different from that of the teachers of the scribes because he taught "as one who had authority." This may refer to Jesus' "You have heard . . . but I say" style (represented in the Sermon on the Mount and elsewhere) as opposed to the scribal tendency to cite the opinions of various rabbis. Or it may have more to do with the substance of his teaching (as in 2:5 when he forgives a man's sins). In either case Mark observes that the people in the synagogue were amazed at the authority of Jesus' teaching. This is the first of a series of references to Jesus' teaching or miracles creating amazement (1:27; 2:12; 5:20, 42; 6:2, 51; 7:37; 10:24, 26; 11:18).[58]

23-24. The first miracle Jesus performs in Mark's account involves an unclean spirit or demon. Mark uses the terms "unclean spirit" and "demon" interchangeably and roughly an equal number of times. The NIV prefers "evil spirit" rather than the more literal translation "unclean spirit." Mark does not call these beings "evil" spirits, although Luke does (7:21; 8:2).

This is the first of four exorcisms Mark selected from the many Jesus performed (5:1-20; 7:24-30; 9:14-29; cf. 1:34, 39). As a supernatural being, the demon knows Jesus, his hometown, his antagonism to demons, and his identity as "the Holy One of God." This is the first of many times in Mark that the demons identify Jesus (1:34; 3:11; 5:7; cf. 9:20).[59] The title

---

[57]Guelich, p. 55, observes "the frequency with which the evangelist refers to Jesus' 'teaching' (διδαχή, 5x), to Jesus as 'teacher' ([διδάσκαλος] 12x, and only in reference to Jesus), and to his use of 'to teach' ([διδάσκειν] 17x, 15x pertaining to Jesus)."

[58]On demons see G.H. Twelftree, "Demon, Devil, Satan," in *DJG*, pp. 163-172.

[59]It is possible that the demons are using their knowledge of Jesus' identity in a self-defense maneuver. See, e.g., Gundry, p. 83; and Barry Blackburn, *Theios Aner and the Markan Miracle Traditions*, WUNT 2.40 (Tübingen: J.C.B. Mohr, 1991), pp. 205-208. For counter arguments see Guelich, p. 57.

"Holy One of God" appears in the Gospels only here, in the parallel in Luke 4:34, and in John 6:69. It is used in the Old Testament for Aaron (Ps 106:16) and Elisha (2 Kgs 4:9). Like "Son of God," it developed a heightened meaning when applied to Jesus.

25-26. In this first instance, Jesus' silencing of the demon might be understood simply as his exerting his authority over it.[60] However, Mark 3:12, "But he sternly ordered them [the demons] not to make him known" (NRSV translation), suggests that the silencing of the demons is part of what is often called "the messianic secret."[61] In 8:30 Jesus instructs the disciples not to tell others that he is the Christ and in 9:9 he orders Peter, James, and John not to tell anyone about the transfiguration until after he is raised from the dead. Mark does not explain the reason for these instructions and there is not a concensus of opinion in contemporary scholarship. Jesus probably wanted to avoid misunderstandings of his identity and role based on various popular misconceptions of the messiah. It has often been argued that he wanted to avoid the possibility that the authorities would bring his ministry to an untimely end if they perceived him as claiming messiahship.[62] The most popular understanding today is that Jesus kept his messiahship secret because it would inevitably be misunderstood until it could be seen in the light of the cross and resurrection.[63] This point of view is supported by the way Jesus responds to Peter's confession with predictions of his death (8:27-31) and by the centurion's confession of Jesus as God's Son when he "saw how he died" (15:39). In the shadow of the cross the meaning of Jesus' identity could be seen more clearly.

---

[60]If the demon's identification of Jesus is meant to be a defense against him(see n. 59), then Jesus' silencing of the demon would assert his authority over the demon's defensive efforts.

[61]Cf. also Mark 1:34: "he would not let the demons speak because they knew who he was."

[62]E.g., Donald A. Carson, "Matthew," in *The Expositor's Bible Commentary*, ed. Frank E. Gaebelein, vol. 8 (Grand Rapids: Zondervan, 1984), p. 375.

[63]E.g., Lane, pp. 291-323; Hurtado, 57, 136, 146-147.

With a brief command, Jesus expelled the demon, which went out of the man in a visible and audible manner. Mark's point is that Jesus had authority over the demon.

27-28. At the beginning of the Capernaum synagogue scene Mark said that the people were amazed at the authority of Jesus' teaching. He concludes with another note about their amazement at Jesus' authority – this time at both his teaching and his power over the demon. Grammatically the phrase "with authority" can be taken with either "a new teaching" or "he even gives orders to evil spirits."[64] This grammatical problem underscores the fact that both features illustrate Jesus' authority.

The reference to Jesus' spreading fame is the first of many.[65]

C. HEALING SIMON'S MOTHER-IN-LAW (1:29-31)

29As soon as they left the synagogue, they went with James and John to the home of Simon and Andrew. 30Simon's mother-in-law was in bed with a fever, and they told Jesus about her. 31So he went to her, took her hand and helped her up. The fever left her and she began to wait on them.

The second miracle Mark records is a healing, the first of nine Mark has chosen to describe (1:29-31, 40-45; 2:12; 3:1-6; 5:21-43; 7:31-37; 8:22-26; 10:46-52). This story provides some incidental information about Simon: that he had a house in Capernaum,[66] a mother-in-law, and thus presumably a wife

---

[64]The NRSV text reads similarly to the NIV. The NRSV footnote provides the alternative: "A new teaching! With authority he commands even the unclean spirits."

[65]Before the entry into Jerusalem see 1:32, 36, 45; 2:2, 13; 3:7-10, 20; 4:1; 5:21, 24; 6:14, 31-4, 44, 54-6; 7:24, 36; 8:1, 9; 9:14; 10:1, 13, 46.

[66]John 1:44 identifies Bethsaida as the home of Simon and Andrew. Simon may have moved or as a commercial fisherman he may have had

(cf. 1 Cor 9:5). See the Introduction to this commentary for the early tradition that Mark's Gospel stems from the preaching of Peter.

The item Mark wanted to stress is no doubt the miraculous healing as another illustration of Jesus' authority.

D. OTHER HEALINGS AT CAPERNAUM (1:32-34)

32That evening after sunset the people brought to Jesus all the sick and demon-possessed. 33The whole town gathered at the door, 34and Jesus healed many who had various diseases. He also drove out many demons, but he would not let the demons speak because they knew who he was.

The people presumably waited until the sabbath ended at sundown to avoid violating the sabbath (by carrying the sick or by asking Jesus to heal). Mark uses hyperbole to underscore the popularity of Jesus ("the whole town gathered at the door").

This brief summary indicates that the exorcism and healing of 1:21-31 were just two of many miracles Jesus performed in Capernaum.[67] On Jesus' silencing of the demons see the comments on 1:25.

E. WHAT JESUS CAME TO DO (1:35-39)

35Very early in the morning, while it was still dark, Jesus got up, left the house and went off to a solitary place, where he prayed. 36Simon and his companions went to look for him, 37and when they found him, they exclaimed: "Everyone is looking for you!"

---

more than one house. See Guelich, p. 62. There is reasonably good evidence for the identification of one of the ancient houses discovered at Capernaum as Simon's house. See McRay, *Archaeology*, pp. 164-166.

[67]This is one of many texts that indicate that demon possession and illness were distinguished from each other by the Gospel writers.

[38]Jesus replied, "Let us go somewhere else – to the nearby villages – so I can preach there also. That is why I have come." [39]So he traveled throughout Galilee, preaching in their synagogues and driving out demons.

This is the first of three glimpses Mark provides into Jesus' prayer life (see also 6:46; 14:32-42). Jesus rose early and found a deserted place[68] partially because the crowds were always present. In fact, when Simon and the others find Jesus they tell him everyone is searching for him.

Jesus left Capernaum on the day after the events of 1:21-34. He began to travel throughout Galilee (cf. 1:14, 28). Although the summation in v. 39 includes exorcisms, Jesus' statement in v. 38 indicates where his emphasis was: he came in order to preach. The NIV translation "That is why I have come" hides an ambiguity apparent in the more literal NRSV translation "that is what I came out to do." Some argue that Jesus means to say why he left Capernaum, but Luke's "that is why I was sent" supports the more likely understanding (which the NIV has chosen). Jesus is stating the mission God sent him to accomplish. Vv. 38-39 should remind the reader of 1:14-15 and Jesus' message of good news about the kingdom of God's arrival. Perhaps v. 39 refers to the exorcisms because Jesus' victories over Satan's cohorts indicate the truth of his message about the arrival of the kingdom (cf. Matt 12:28).

F. HEALING A LEPER (1:40-45)

[40]A man with leprosy[a] came to him and begged him on his knees, "If you are willing, you can make me clean."

[41]Filled with compassion, Jesus reached out his hand and

---

[68]I would prefer the consistency of translating "desert" or "deserted place" for the nine occurrences of ἔρημος (*erēmos*) or ἔρημος τόπος (*erēmos topos*). The NIV uses "desert" for *erēmos* alone (1:3, 4, 12, 13) and "solitary place," "lonely place," "quiet place," or "remote place" for *erēmos topos* (1:35, 45; 6:31-32, 35).

touched the man. "I am willing," he said. "Be clean!"
[42]Immediately the leprosy left him and he was cured.
[43]Jesus sent him away at once with a strong warning:
[44]"See that you don't tell this to anyone. But go, show your-
self to the priest and offer the sacrifices that Moses com-
manded for your cleansing, as a testimony to them."
[45]Instead he went out and began to talk freely, spreading the
news. As a result, Jesus could no longer enter a town openly
but stayed outside in lonely places. Yet the people still came
to him from everywhere.

[a]*40* The Greek word was used for various diseases affecting the skin – not necessarily leprosy.

The one example Mark provides of Jesus' activity during the days after he left Capernaum is not an example of his preaching or exorcisms, but of his healings. Mark may have found the cure of a leper particularly impressive. He may have been especially interested in highlighting Jesus' obedience to the law (1:44) before the controversies of 2:1-3:6 in which Jesus is accused of disobedience. Whatever drew Mark to this particular incident, it is another example of Jesus' authority and another opportunity to highlight his growing popularity (v. 45).

40-42. The term "leper" (λεπρός, *lepros*) in Scripture is broader than it is in modern usage. But whatever skin disease was involved it would have put this man in a pitiable state; not only due to the disease, but also due to the social ostracizing that accompanied it (cf. Lev 13:45-46). Jesus had compassion on him.[69] He even touched him despite the leper's unclean-

[69]At the beginning of v. 41 a few manuscripts read "being angry" instead of "having compassion." Many commentators, including Guelich (p. 72) and Lane (p. 84 n. 141), believe this more difficult reading is the correct one. The support of the best manuscripts and the extreme difficulty of understanding a reference to anger in this context point mildly toward the originality of "having compassion." In the alternate reading, Jesus could be angry at what the leprosy had done to this man.

ness. The healing was immediate and impressive.[70]

43-45. The Greek words underlying both Jesus' "sending away" (ἐξέβαλον, *exebalon*) and his "strong warning" (ἐμβριμη-σάμενος, *embrimēsamenos*) to the leper are so strong that many wonder what motivated his intensity here. A good suggestion is that he foresaw the man's disobedience and the problems it would create for his ministry to the towns in Galilee (v. 45).[71] Mark's statement that the man's disobedient proclamation of his healing created a situation in which "Jesus could no longer enter a town openly" may provide the primary reason that on this and several other occasions Jesus instructed those whom he healed not to tell others (see 5:43; 7:36; 8:26). Jesus' reputation as a healer and exorcist created such enormous crowds of miracle seekers that he might have been hindered in his central mission, the preaching ministry.[72]

The instructions to go to the priest and to offer the sacrifices which Moses commanded for cleansing are in accordance with the instructions concerning leprosy in Lev 13-14. The priest would certify that the man was now clean and then the sacrifices would be offered. The phrase "as a testimony to them" is problematic. It could also be translated "as a testimony against them." But who are those who receive this testimony and what does it bear witness to? The recipients may be the priests (although Jesus only commands the man to show himself to one priest) or perhaps anyone who comes to know about the priest certifying the man's cleansing. The testimony is often thought to be a witness to Jesus' power in healing the leprosy or to his adherence to the Law in instructing the man to follow Mosaic regulations. However, since Jesus instructs

---

[70]Cf. 2 Kgs 5:7, the remark of the king of Israel when asked to cure Naaman, "Am I God? . . . Why does this fellow send someone to me to be cured of his leprosy?"

[71]So Lane, p. 87.

[72]Lane, pp. 88-89. If this view is correct, then these occasions (when Jesus instructs those whom he has healed not to tell) do not belong with the "messianic secret" theme.

the man not to tell about his involvement in the healing the point may simply be that the sacrifices offer testimony to others of the man's cleanness as certified by the priest.[73]

[73]See the discussions of this phrase in Lane, p. 88; Guelich, pp. 76-77; and Gundry, p. 97.

MARK 2

G. STORIES OF CONTROVERSY BETWEEN JESUS AND THE RELIGIOUS AUTHORITIES (2:1-3:6)

In 2:1-3:6 Mark provides five stories of controversy between Jesus and the religious authorities. These stories are not chronologically connected to each other and appear to be brought together primarily in a thematic rather than chronological way.[1] Their overall purpose is to introduce the conflict between Jesus and the religious authorities. By the end of these five stories Mark's readers know that many of the religious authorities are unbelieving antagonists who badger Jesus at every turn. The climax of these incidents is in 3:6: "Then the Pharisees went out and began to plot with the Herodians how they might kill Jesus."

1. Controversy over Forgiving Sins (2:1-12)

1A few days later, when Jesus again entered Capernaum,
the people heard that he had come home. 2So many gath-
ered that there was no room left, not even outside the door,
and he preached the word to them. 3Some men came, bring-
ing to him a paralytic, carried by four of them. 4Since they
could not get him to Jesus because of the crowd, they made
an opening in the roof above Jesus and, after digging
through it, lowered the mat the paralyzed man was lying on.

[1]Matthew places the first three controversy stories in chapter 9 and the last two in chapter 12.

**5When Jesus saw their faith, he said to the paralytic, "Son,
your sins are forgiven."**

**6Now some teachers of the law were sitting there, think-
ing to themselves, 7"Why does this fellow talk like that? He's
blaspheming! Who can forgive sins but God alone?"**

**8Immediately Jesus knew in his spirit that this was what
they were thinking in their hearts, and he said to them,
"Why are you thinking these things? 9Which is easier: to say
to the paralytic, 'Your sins are forgiven,' or to say, 'Get up,
take your mat and walk'? 10But that you may know that the
Son of Man has authority on earth to forgive sins . . . ." He
said to the paralytic, 11"I tell you, get up, take your mat and
go home." 12He got up, took his mat and walked out in full
view of them all. This amazed everyone and they praised
God, saying, "We have never seen anything like this!"**

The first controversy, 2:1-12, focuses in a dramatic way on the identity of Jesus. This story provides a fourth specific miracle performed by Jesus, which again underscores his authority. But this time the miracle is subordinated to an even more dramatic indication of Jesus' identity: he forgives sins. The scribes correctly conclude that forgiving sins implies a special relationship to God (v. 7), but they wrongly refuse to accept the correct conclusion. By healing the paralytic Jesus demonstrates "that the Son of Man has authority on earth to forgive sins."

In addition to this christological focus, Mark 2:1-12 also teaches an important lesson about discipleship. The four men who carried the paralytic to Jesus demonstrated not only ingenuity, but also – and more importantly – faith. Mark has already indicated the importance of faith in 1:15 ("Repent and believe the good news!"). He will underscore the point often (e.g., 4:40; 5:34, 36; 6:6; 9:23; 10:52). Faith is the proper response to Jesus' demonstrations of authority in his teaching and his miracles.

1-2. The scene returns to Capernaum, where the events of 1:21-35 took place. The NIV's "that he had come home" is a rather paraphrastic translation of a clause that might also be translated "that he was in a (or 'the') house." He was probably at Peter's house (1:29).[2] The intensity of the crowd resonates with Mark's previous descriptions of the crowds in 1:32-33, 37, and 45.

Jesus was teaching them "the word" (τὸν λόγον, *ton logon*). The word is presumably the message of 1:14-15 about the kingdom. The same expression is used in Mark 4:14-20, 33 for Jesus' parabolic message about the kingdom.[3]

3-4. When the four men could not get their paralyzed friend through the crowd to ask Jesus to heal him, they went up on the roof, opened up a hole, and lowered the paralytic on his pallet. [4] The point, of course, is that the five men went to great lengths because they believed in Jesus' ability to heal.

5-7. At the point when one would expect Jesus to heal the man, he instead declares the paralytic's sins forgiven. It is possible that in this particular case Jesus implies a connection between the man's infirmity and his sin.[5] Although in one case in John's Gospel Jesus explicitly denies that a particular man's blindness was caused by his sin (9:3), in another case (incidentally also involving paralysis) Jesus implies a connection between a man's sin and infirmity (John 5:14).[6]

Whatever motivated Jesus to declare this man's sins forgiven, the scribes recognize it as an implicit claim to a special relationship with God. Jesus' declaration of forgiveness does

---

[2]Guelich, p. 81; Gundry, p. 110.

[3]Guelich, p. 81.

[4]Mark's reference to the men "digging through" (ἐξορύξαντες, *exoryxantes*) the roof might be understood with reference to the typical Palestinian roof in which beams of wood were overlaid with thatch and mud, but Mark does not specify what the men dug through. (So I. Howard Marshall, *Luke*; contra Guelich, p. 85; Gundry, p. 117). Luke 5:19 speaks of lowering the man through "tiles." Tile roofs have been found on some houses in Palestine. John J. Rousseau and Rami Arav, eds., *Jesus and His World: An Archaeological and Cultural Dictionary* (Minneapolis: Fortress, 1995), pp. 128-129.

[5]So Lane, p. 94.

[6]See the treatment in Carson, *John*, pp. 245-246.

not necessarily involve more than Nathan's statement to David in 2 Sam 12:13: "The Lord has taken away your sin."[7] However, Jesus' subsequent statement that "The Son of Man has authority on earth to forgive sins" indicates that the scribes correctly understood Jesus to be claiming the ability not only to report God's forgiveness but also to grant it.[8] They accuse him of blasphemy because he claims to do what only God can do. The charge of blasphemy anticipates the trial of Jesus before the Sanhedrin where blasphemy is the basis for the sentence of death (14:64). Blasphemy could be narrowly defined in a way that involved specifically using God's name (Lev 24:15-16) or more broadly defined as "a word or act detracting from the power and glory of God."[9] This broad sense applies to Mark 2 and 14.

8-9. Jesus knows the thinking of the scribes and poses a counter-question, the first of several times he used this approach (3:4; 11:30; 12:37).[10] His question, "Which is easier . . . ?" probably refers to verifiability.[11] It seems easier to say "Your sins are forgiven" because it is not verifiable, but to say "Get up, take your mat and walk" is a statement subject to empirical verification.

10-12. Jesus intends to use the empirically verifiable, harder statement about healing to verify his authority to forgive sins. If he can heal the paralytic then his claim to forgive the paralytic's sins must be taken seriously.[12]

V. 10 introduces the enigmatic title "Son of Man," which is used again in 2:28 and then twelve times after Peter's confession at Caesarea Philippi. The Son of Man title has been studied vigorously, but there is no concensus concerning its

---

[7]Lane, p. 95.

[8]Gundry, p. 112.

[9]G.H. Twelftree, "Blasphemy," in *DJG*, p. 75, with references on pp. 75-77.

[10]Lane, p. 96.

[11]Guelich, p.88.

[12]Lane, pp. 96-98, incorrectly argues that Mark intends for the readers to see the first clause in v. 10 as Mark's own editorial comment and not a statement made by Jesus. Contra Lane, see Gundry, p. 118.

pre-Christian usage or precisely how Jesus used it. A few observations can be made with confidence: 1) Except for one case in the Gospels (John 12:34) and a few instances in the rest of the New Testament (Acts 7:56 and the probably non-titular uses in Heb 2:6; Rev 1:13; 14:14) the phrase "Son of Man" appears only on the lips of Jesus. Although it was Jesus' most common title for himself, the early Christians seem to have preferred other titles such as Lord and Christ. 2) Jesus' statement in Mark 14:62 alludes to Dan 7:13 and suggests that in using the title Son of Man he intended to identify himself as the "one like a son of man" in Daniel's vision. According to Daniel this figure was "coming with the clouds of heaven. He approached the Ancient of Days and was led into his presence. He was given authority, glory and sovereign power; all peoples, nations and men of every language worshipped him. His dominion is an everlasting dominion that will not pass away, and his kingdom is one that will never be destroyed." Jesus' claim to be this son of man was not simply a reference to his humanity, but an exalted claim with messianic overtones.

It is extremely difficult to establish whether Son of Man had been used as a title in association with Dan 7 before Jesus and whether anyone in Jesus' audiences would have recognized that connection or any messianic overtones.[13] An attractive but uncertain suggestion is that Jesus chose to emphasize this title partly because it was not a common messianic title and therefore he could use it (like the parables) not only to reveal the truth to some, but to conceal it from others.[14]

The story of the paralytic is an important one. It continues and heightens the emphasis on Jesus' authority. It introduces the teachers of the law as Jesus' antagonists. In contrast to the

---

[13]Cf. Brown, pp. 508-512, for a summary of research. Brown thinks it was a pre-Christian messianic title, but admits that the evidence is highly problematic.

[14]I. Howard Marshall, *The Origins of New Testament Christology*, updated ed. (Downers Grove: InterVarsity, 1990), pp. 77-78.

antagonism and disbelief of the teachers of the law, it highlights and illustrates the importance of faith by the actions of the five men and by Jesus' response to their faith.

2. Controversy over Eating with Tax Collectors and Sinners (2:13-17)

[13]Once again Jesus went out beside the lake. A large crowd came to him, and he began to teach them. [14]As he walked along, he saw Levi son of Alphaeus sitting at the tax collector's booth. "Follow me," Jesus told him, and Levi got up and followed him.

[15]While Jesus was having dinner at Levi's house, many tax collectors and "sinners" were eating with him and his disciples, for there were many who followed him. [16]When the teachers of the law who were Pharisees saw him eating with the "sinners" and tax collectors, they asked his disciples: "Why does he eat with tax collectors and 'sinners'?"

[17]On hearing this, Jesus said to them, "It is not the healthy who need a doctor, but the sick. I have not come to call the righteous, but sinners."

Vv. 13-14 could be separated from vv. 15-17 as the story of the calling of Levi. However, it is Matthew and not Mark who provides a connection with the rest of the story of Jesus by identifying Levi as Matthew the apostle. Mark seems content to treat Levi's call as an illustration of and introduction to Jesus' offensive companionship with the wrong sorts of people. He calls a tax collector to be one of his followers, he goes to the tax collector's house, and while there he eats a meal with other tax collectors and sinners.

13. This is another of Mark's many references to Jesus teaching the crowds. He has taught in the synagogue (1:21), at a house (2:2), and now beside the Sea of Galilee (2:13).

14. The call of Levi is similar to the previous call of the four fishermen: the call is to "follow," Jesus gives the call while Levi is working, and Levi responds on the spot. The critical difference noticeable to informed readers is that Levi was a tax collector. Tax collectors were widely despised for defrauding people to inflate their own commissions and for collusion with Rome.[15]

15-16. Levi invited Jesus to a meal at his house which was attended by other tax collectors and "sinners" (ἁμαρτωλοί, *hamartōloi*). Mark says that there were many of these who were following Jesus. The meaning of the term "sinners" in this and similar contexts is a point of continuing debate among contemporary scholars. Some argue that the term refers to those who did not follow the strict Pharisaic guidelines. Others argue that "sinners" were the wicked who sinned willfully and without repentance. I am inclined to agree with a third view which holds that this term refers to those who were opposed to God's will from the standpoint of the one who is using the term, whether Jesus or his opponents.[16]

It is clear from this passage and other New Testament texts (such as Acts 11:3 and Gal 2:12) that who one had table fellowship with was a matter of considerable importance for many first century Jews. The scribes who were Pharisees[17] find Jesus' table fellowship with tax collectors and sinners offensive, an obvious contradiction to his supposed status as a religious leader.

This is Mark's first reference to the Pharisees, who appear repeatedly during Jesus' Galilean ministry but only once by name in Jerusalem (12:13). The Pharisees were the leading sect or party among the Jews of Jesus' day. Although the Sadducees controlled the Sanhedrin,[18] the Pharisees probably had the most popularity among the people. Being a Pharisee

[15]Thomas E. Schmidt, "Taxes," in *DJG*, pp. 805-806.

[16]Michael J. Wilkins, "Sinners," in *DJG*, pp. 758-760.

[17]The Greek phrase is literally "the scribes of the Pharisees," an odd phrase occurring only here. The NIV translation is probably correct in suggesting that it means scribes who were Pharisees. There were scribes associated with other sects.

[18]On the Sanhedrin see the comments at 8:31.

was not a profession like being a scribe. Rather, people of various professions (including scribes) and classes could be Pharisees. Being a Pharisee was primarily a matter of commitment to Pharisaic norms of religious practice. They maintained a strong commitment to traditional beliefs and practices handed down from earlier generations. These traditions involved a strict interpretation of and supplement to the Old Testament Law. Examples would be their commitment to tithing (Matt 23:23) and ritual cleanliness (Mark 7:1-5).[19]

17. Jesus replies to their accusation with a common proverb using the imagery of doctors and their patients.[20] He does not defend the sinfulness of the tax collectors and sinners nor does he intend to imply that the Pharisees are truly righteous in God's sight, but he effectively makes the point that his task is to call sinners to God. Therefore he must be in their company.

3. Controversy over Fasting (2:18-22)

18Now John's disciples and the Pharisees were fasting. Some people came and asked Jesus, "How is it that John's disciples and the disciples of the Pharisees are fasting, but yours are not?"

19Jesus answered, "How can the guests of the bridegroom fast while he is with them? They cannot, so long as they have him with them. 20But the time will come when the bridegroom will be taken from them, and on that day they will fast.

21"No one sews a patch of unshrunk cloth on an old garment. If he does, the new piece will pull away from the old,

---

[19]On the Pharisees see Stephen Westerholm, "Pharisees," in *DJG*, pp. 609-614.

[20]E.g., Plutarch, *Sayings of the Spartans* 230-231. Plutarch, (c. A.D. 50-after 120) cites Pausanias (King of Sparta, 408-394 B.C.) as follows: "The physicians, he said, are not to be found among the well but customarily spend their time among the sick."

making the tear worse. [22]And no one pours new wine into old wineskins. If he does, the wine will burst the skins, and both the wine and the wineskins will be ruined. No, he pours new wine into new wineskins."

Like the previous story, this controversy centers on ancient Jewish traditions rather than on the clear demands of Mosaic law. The law itself required fasting only on the Day of Atonement (Lev 16:29-31). However, fasting is often commended in the Old Testament as a pious behavior (e.g., Deut 9:9; Dan 9:3; Esth 4:1-3). By the time of Jesus many pious Jews fasted twice each week (Luke 18:12).[21] Such traditions were held in high honor among the Pharisees.

18. Since weekly fasting was practiced not only by those who followed the Pharisees[22] but also by the followers of John the Baptist who baptized Jesus, many would naturally be surprised that Jesus and his disciples did not follow this common spiritual discipline. They may even have viewed the customary fasting as mandatory.

19-20. Jesus replied with three metaphors. The first one uses the image of a wedding feast. It would be inappropriate for the guests at a wedding feast to fast, for the bridegroom is there and they need to celebrate with him. Jesus implies that his presence among the disciples creates an analogous situation of celebration. V. 20 is an odd statement in the context of a wedding feast. It is an allusion to the death of Jesus and the mourning of his disciples concerning his death. It is the only reference to Jesus' death before Mark 8:31.

The rest of the New Testament indicates that the early Christians did fast on various occasions. Jesus' reference here,

---

[21]The Mishnah (c. A.D. 200) states that the weekly days of fasting were Monday and Thursday (*Taanith* 1.4-5). This may be true of the early first century.

[22]Technically, the Pharisees did not have "disciples." However, the text presumably refers to those who did not become Pharisees but did generally respect and follow their teachings.

however, probably refers to mourning over his death.[23]

21-22. The second two metaphors are parallel in meaning. The point of both is similar to the point of the bridegroom analogy. Jesus compares his presence to a new unshrunk piece of cloth and to new wine. The tradition of fasting is part of an old garment or an old wineskin. The new situation created by Jesus' presence makes the old form of fasting inappropriate for his disciples. The disciples need to act in a way that is appropriate for the new situation created by Jesus.

It is difficult to be sure what it was about fasting that made it inappropriate for Jesus' disciples. In the light of the bridegroom analogy, a good suggestion is that Jesus' coming and the inbreaking of the kingdom which accompanied him called for a joyful response, while fasting was associated primarily with mourning.[24]

4. Controversy over Picking Grain on the Sabbath (2:23-28)

23One Sabbath Jesus was going through the grainfields, and as his disciples walked along, they began to pick some heads of grain. 24The Pharisees said to him, "Look, why are they doing what is unlawful on the Sabbath?"

25He answered, "Have you never read what David did when he and his companions were hungry and in need? 26In the days of Abiathar the high priest, he entered the house of God and ate the consecrated bread, which is lawful only for priests to eat. And he also gave some to his companions."

27Then he said to them, "The Sabbath was made for man, not man for the Sabbath. 28So the Son of Man is Lord even of the Sabbath."

The fourth and fifth controversies in this series focus on interpreting the sabbath law. The grain picking incident

---

[23]Guelich, p. 114.
[24]Lane, pp. 109-110.

appears to modern readers to be tedious nit-picking on the part of the Pharisees. It may be, but modern readers are prone to swing to the other side of the pendulum and perhaps forget such texts as Num 15:32-36 in which a man was stoned for picking up wood on the sabbath.

23-24. As in 2:13-17 and 2:18-22, the chronological connection with the preceding story is loose, but the thematic connection is strong. Mark provides another illustration of the conflict between Jesus and the religious authorities.

The Pharisees are not suggesting that the disciples are stealing. The old gleaning laws certainly made it legitimate for the disciples to pick a few heads of grain. The problem is that they are doing this on the sabbath. The accusation is that they are violating the sabbath by working.[25]

25-26. We expect Jesus to argue (as he does in the case of 3:1-6) that such activity is not actually a violation of the sabbath. However, his approach to the subject seems to grant their accusation that the disciples are doing what is not lawful on the sabbath. Jesus argues that there are special circumstances in which some "break the sabbath and yet are guiltless."[26]

The story about David and the consecrated bread (1 Sam 21:1-6) is a parallel case. Under normal circumstances no one could eat this bread except priests. David's circumstances were special. He and his companions were hungry. Furthermore, and significantly, David was the anointed king of Israel. (Presumably, neither Jesus nor the Pharisees would grant just any hungry band of men the privilege of eating the consecrated bread without guilt.) Jesus and his disciples' situation was analogous.[27]

---

[25]Cf. the Mishnah *Shabbat* 7.2 which lists thirty-nine categories of work which must not be done on the sabbath, including reaping, threshing, and winnowing crops.

[26]This phrase is from the NRSV translation of Matthew's account of this story, Matt 12:5. There it applies to the priests serving in the temple on the sabbath, another example Jesus used in defending his disciples' behavior.

[27]The reference to Abiathar the high priest involves one of the most problematic statements in the Gospels. 1 Sam 21:1-6 says that Ahimelech was the high priest who gave David and his men the consecrated bread. There is a

27-28. The two-part pronouncement at the climax of the story highlights the special circumstances of both David and Jesus and their companions. First, "The Sabbath was made for man, not man for the Sabbath." Jesus would not approve of a legalistic approach to the sabbath in which no work could ever be done regardless of the circumstances. The sabbath law was created to help people, not to harm them. Second, "the Son of Man is Lord even of the Sabbath." If in the example of David, it was important that David was the anointed king, then in the case of Jesus an even greater one is involved. Jesus had already declared his authority to forgive sins. He now declares his authority to make judgments about the sabbath.[28]

The term translated "So" at the beginning of v. 28 ties the two statements together.[29] If there are circumstances in which the spirit of the sabbath law takes precedence over the letter, then the authoritative Son of Man surely has the right to make this determination. Jesus tries to get the Pharisees to recognize both that in some cases the sabbath law may be broken without guilt and that the Son of Man has the authority to determine such cases.

---

contextual connection, however, to Abiathar, Ahimelech's son. At the same time Ahimelech gave David the bread he let him take the sword of Goliath (1 Sam 21:8-9). Because of this Saul killed Ahimelech and all of his family except Abiathar who escaped and ran to David (1 Sam 22:6-23). The primary issue is whether Mark meant to say that Abiathar was high priest at the time of the bread incident. The debate centers on the translation of the preposition ἐπί (*epi*) which governs "Abiathar the high priest." The NRSV translation "*when* Abiathar was high priest" involves Mark in an error. The NIV translation "In the days of Abiathar the high priest" allows Mark to identify the incident by the more well known priest, but opens the possibility that Mark did not intend to say that he was high priest at the time. Lane, p. 116, and Gundry, pp. 141-142, are inclined to accept the proposal that *epi* should be translated something like "at the place about" Abiathar the high priest. They see it as a reference to where the story is found in the Old Testament, analogous to Mark 12:26 "in the account of (*epi*) the bush."

[28]In the Matthean parallel, Jesus declares "one greater than the temple is here" (Matt 12:6).

[29]"So" translates the Greek term ὥστε (*hōste*).

MARK 3

5. Controversy over Healing on the Sabbath (3:1-6)

**[1]Another time he went into the synagogue, and a man
with a shriveled hand was there. [2]Some of them were looking for a reason to accuse Jesus, so they watched him closely
to see if he would heal him on the Sabbath. [3]Jesus said to
the man with the shriveled hand, "Stand up in front of
everyone."**

**[4]Then Jesus asked them, "Which is lawful on the Sabbath:
to do good or to do evil, to save life or to kill?" But they
remained silent.**

**[5]He looked around at them in anger and, deeply dis-
tressed at their stubborn hearts, said to the man, "Stretch
out your hand." He stretched it out, and his hand was completely restored. [6]Then the Pharisees went out and began to
plot with the Herodians how they might kill Jesus.**

In the Gospels there are several occasions when Jesus is criticized for healing on the sabbath (Mark 3:1-6=Matt 12:9-14=Luke 6:6-11; Luke 13:10-17; 14:1-6; John 5:1-18; 7:21-24; 9:13-16). Among the Jews of Jesus' day there were differing opinions about what could be done on the sabbath with respect to the health of humans and animals. Luke 14:5 indicates that even Jesus' opponents would rescue a son if he fell into a well on the sabbath. Other Gospel passages indicate that many of them would accept watering a domestic animal on the sabbath (Luke 13:15) or rescuing a domestic animal who fell into a ditch or well (Matt 12:11; Luke 14:5). On the other hand, at Qumran the *Damascus Document* even forbids helping an animal give birth or rescuing one that falls into a pit or cistern.[1] The disputed healings of Jesus involved non-life threatening problems. As might be expected, some witnesses agreed with his actions and others did not.

1-5. As in 1:21-27 this healing takes place in a synagogue, a common place for Jesus to teach (1:39). As in 2:1-12, the focus of this incident is not so much on another illustration of Jesus' healing power as on other attendant circumstances. In this case the focus is on the conflict over healing on the sabbath. A withered hand is not life threatening and many would have agreed with the synagogue leader of Luke 13:14 who told the crowd "There are six days for work. So come and be healed on those days, not on the Sabbath." Jesus, however, considered it permissible to do good on the sabbath. There is irony in his alternatives "to do evil . . . . to kill," for v. 6 reveals that his opponents used the sabbath to plan his death.

6. This sentence is the climax of the five controversy stories that began at Mark 2:1. Jesus' opponents are ready to kill him. This murderous intent lies behind every subsequent reference to the Pharisees. The Herodians are not a well known group. They only appear here, in Mark 12:13, and in one reference in Josephus.[2] In Josephus the Herodians are supporters of Herod the Great. In Mark they are presumably supporters of Herod Antipas, ruler of Galilee. They would not seem to be natural allies of the Pharisees, but a common enemy often brings even former enemies together.

---

[1] *Damascus Document* 11.13-14: "No man shall assist a beast to give birth on the Sabbath day. And if it should fall into a cistern or pit, he shall not lift it out on the Sabbath." (Translation from Geza Vermes, *The Dead Sea Scrolls in English* [Middlesex, England: Penguin Books, 1962], p. 113.) During the second century B.C. Maccabean revolt a thousand Jewish men, women, and children allowed themselves to be slaughtered rather than fight a battle on the sabbath (1 Macc 2:29-38). Immediately afterward others resolved to defend themselves when attacked on the sabbath (1 Macc 2:39-41).

[2] Josephus, *War* 1.16.6.

H. SUMMARY STATEMENT ABOUT THE CROWDS AND HEALINGS (3:7-12)

[7]Jesus withdrew with his disciples to the lake, and a large crowd from Galilee followed. [8]When they heard all he was doing, many people came to him from Judea, Jerusalem, Idumea, and the regions across the Jordan and around Tyre and Sidon. [9]Because of the crowd he told his disciples to have a small boat ready for him, to keep the people from crowding him. [10]For he had healed many, so that those with diseases were pushing forward to touch him. [11]Whenever the evil[a] spirits saw him, they fell down before him and cried out, "You are the Son of God." [12]But he gave them strict orders not to tell who he was.

[a]*11* Greek *unclean*; also in verse 30

7-10. This time Jesus' return to the lake (cf. 1:16; 2:13) seems to be motivated at least partially by the plot in 3:6. Mark's emphasis in vv. 7-10 is on the extent of the crowds, a common theme in earlier statements (1:33, 45; 2:2, 13). The new factor is his description of the geographical regions the crowds were coming from. Brief examination of a map demonstrates that Jesus' fame had spread remarkably.[3]

11-12. Exorcisms were a routine part of Jesus' healing ministry. On the silencing of the demons see the comments on 1:25. At this point in the story Jesus' identity as the Son of God is unknown to humans, but has been declared by Mark (1:1), God (1:11), and demons (1:24, 34; 3:11).

[3]"The regions across the Jordan" refers to regions on the east side of the Jordan river. On the map it is especially important to note the geographical extent represented by Sidon (to the northwest), the regions beyond the Jordan (to the east), and Idumea (to the south).

III. THE GALILEAN MINISTRY, SECTION TWO (3:13-6:6a)

A. THE APPOINTMENT OF THE TWELVE APOSTLES (3:13-19)

**[13]Jesus went up on a mountainside and called to him
those he wanted, and they came to him. [14]He appointed
twelve – designating them apostles[a] – that they might be
with him and that he might send them out to preach [15]and
to have authority to drive out demons. [16]These are the
twelve he appointed: Simon (to whom he gave the name
Peter); [17]James son of Zebedee and his brother John (to
them he gave the name Boanerges, which means Sons of
Thunder); [18]Andrew, Philip, Bartholomew, Matthew, Thomas,
James son of Alphaeus, Thaddaeus, Simon the Zealot [19]and
Judas Iscariot, who betrayed him.**

[a]14 Some manuscripts do not have *designating them apostles.*

13-15. From a large entourage of followers Jesus chose twelve to be apostles.[4] The number twelve has significance because of Israel's twelve tribes.[5] Jesus appointed the twelve to be with him and to be sent out to extend his ministry of preaching and driving out demons. The Greek word for "send" (ἀποστέλλω, *apostellō*) is the verb form of the noun for "apostle" (ἀπόστολος, *apostolos*). He designated them "apostles" because he planned to send them to represent him and extend his ministry.

16-19. The first four apostles listed are the fishermen called in 1:16-20. Peter is listed first. Mark speaks about Peter

---

[4]Some manuscripts do not contain the phrase "designating them apostles." Whether the phrase was written by Mark is a difficult judgment.

[5]In Luke 22:30 and Matt 19:28 this significance is made explicit in the reference to the twelve sitting on twelve thrones judging the twelve tribes. In Acts 1:15-22 the eleven fill Judas's place so that there will still be twelve apostles.

more often than any other apostle. Peter's prominence in Mark may be related to the tradition that Mark's Gospel essentially came from Peter's preaching.[6] As is indicated in later parts of Mark (5:37; 9:2; 14:33; cf. 13:3) Peter, James, and John are a special group that Jesus occasionally selected from among the twelve. In Mark's list Jesus gives special names only to these three. Simon was a popular Jewish name in the first century. The Greek "Peter" (Πέτρος, *Petros*) is unknown as a name before Jesus gave it to Peter, although the Aramaic equivalent "Cephas" existed already as a name.[7] Both mean "rock."[8] Mark says Boanerges means "Sons of Thunder." Andrew is listed fourth, after the two sons of Zebedee. He is also the only one of the four not given a new name by Jesus.

From Matt 9:9 we learn that Matthew is the tax collector known in Mark 2:14 as Levi. Luke 6:16 suggests that Thaddaeus was also know as Judas son of James. In translating Simon "the Zealot" the NIV uses the language of Luke 6:15. Matthew and Mark call him Simon "the Cananaean," from an Aramaic word which means enthusiast or zealot.[9] It may be that even Luke used "zealot" as "a characterizing name (namely, Simon was zealous), rather than a technical term identifying his affiliation with a revolutionary party."[10] Judas Iscariot is presumably deliberately listed last because, as Mark observes, he betrayed Jesus.[11]

---

[6]See the authorship section in the Introduction to this commentary.

[7]Guelich, p. 161.

[8]*BAGD*, pp. 654-655. Versus the argument that "Peter" means "stone" not "rock" see Carson, "Matthew," pp. 367-368.

[9]*BAGD*, p. 402.

[10]Warren J. Heard, "Revolutionary Movements," in *DJG*, p. 696. Heard agrees with many scholars who argue that "the Zealot party per se was not formed until the winter of A.D. 67-68."

[11]Iscariot perhaps means "Man of Kerioth," identifying Judas' hometown. But this meaning is uncertain. See Guelich, p. 163.

B. JESUS ACCUSED OF LUNACY AND BEING POSSESSED (3:20-35)

**20 Then Jesus entered a house, and again a crowd gath-
ered, so that he and his disciples were not even able to eat.
21 When his family heard about this, they went to take charge
of him, for they said, "He is out of his mind."**

**22 And the teachers of the law who came down from
Jerusalem said, "He is possessed by Beelzebub[a]! By the prince
of demons he is driving out demons."**

**23 So Jesus called them and spoke to them in parables:
"How can Satan drive out Satan? 24 If a kingdom is divided
against itself, that kingdom cannot stand. 25 If a house is
divided against itself, that house cannot stand. 26 And if
Satan opposes himself and is divided, he cannot stand; his
end has come. 27 In fact, no one can enter a strong man's
house and carry off his possessions unless he first ties up
the strong man. Then he can rob his house. 28 I tell you the
truth, all the sins and blasphemies of men will be forgiven
them. 29 But whoever blasphemes against the Holy Spirit will
never be forgiven; he is guilty of an eternal sin."**

**30 He said this because they were saying, "He has an evil
spirit."**

**31 Then Jesus' mother and brothers arrived. Standing out-
side, they sent someone in to call him. 32 A crowd was sitting
around him, and they told him, "Your mother and brothers
are outside looking for you."**

33 "Who are my mother and my brothers?" he asked.

**34 Then he looked at those seated in a circle around him
and said, "Here are my mother and my brothers! 35 Whoever
does God's will is my brother and sister and mother."**

[a]22 Greek *Beezeboul* or *Beelzeboul*

The structure of Mark's Gospel has been compared to a string of pearls.[12] Most of the stories are told as individual units. However, on a few occasions Mark tells two stories that are structured like a sandwich, with the first story forming the two pieces of bread around the second story. In most, if not all of these "sandwich" sections, the two stories have an overlapping theme which ties them together.[13] The first of these units is 3:20-35.

20-21. Jesus again enters a house and Mark again emphasizes the crowds Jesus attracts. V. 21 contains two difficulties for translators. The phrase translated "his family" is literally something like "the ones close to him." In varying contexts it could refer to Jesus' friends, neighbors, or family.[14] The NIV is probably correct in this instance, for in v. 21 "the ones close to him" "went to take charge of him" and in v. 31 we are told "Jesus' mother and brothers arrived." One objection that might be raised to this is that Jesus' family would not have thought he might be out of his mind. However, in John 7:5 we learn that Jesus' brothers did not believe in him.[15] Jesus' mother could have gone with them at this point due to general concerns about what would happen – or perhaps, like John the Baptist, she too had come to doubt.[16]

In any event someone was spreading the idea that Jesus was out of his mind. The other translation difficulty in this text is to decide who that was. Those who were saying, "He is out of his mind," could be the family (as suggested in the NIV) or some anonymous group of people (as suggested by the NRSV's "people were saying"). Wherever the idea originated, the family of Jesus was concerned about it.

---

[12]Hugh Anderson, *The Gospel of Mark*, New Century Bible Commentary (Grand Rapids: Eerdmans, 1976), p. 6, with reference to K. L. Schmidt.

[13]Lane, p. 137; David Rhoads and Donald Michie, *Mark As Story* (Philadelphia: Fortress, 1982), p. 51. See 3:20-32; 5:21-43; 6:6b-44; 11:12-25; 14:1-11.

[14]Lane, p. 138 n. 75.

[15]Although James and Jude later believed after Jesus' death.

[16]On John the Baptist's doubt see Matt 11:2-3.

22. If v. 21 represents one possible unbelieving response to Jesus, the second story introduced in v. 22 represents another. The scribes from Jerusalem accused Jesus of being possessed by the prince of demons, Beelzebub.[17] They could not deny that he cast out demons, but they would not accept the conclusion that Jesus was empowered by God.

23-26. Using the analogy of human kingdoms Jesus easily demonstrated the foolishness of the scribes' blasphemous suggestion. Satan would not war against himself. Note that Mark designates these metaphorical sayings "parables." The writers of the Gospels use the term "parable" to include virtually any metaphorical saying or proverb, whether or not it takes story form. Modern usage is generally more restricted to metaphorical stories.

27. Moving to the offensive, Jesus argues that in fact his exorcisms show his triumph over Satan. In another "parable" he compares casting out demons to robbing a strong man (Satan) of his possessions. To be able to do this Jesus must be able to bind Satan or else Satan would stop him from plundering his possessions. In Matthew's more lengthy account of the same incident, Jesus explains that his ability to cast out demons by the Spirit of God is evidence that the kingdom of God has come (Matt 12:28; cf. Luke 11:20). Mark's less detailed account implies the same thing. Jesus' exorcisms are evidence of his victory over Satan and the inbreaking of the kingdom.

28-30. As we have seen in connection with Mark 2:7, the term "blasphemy" could be loosely used to refer to any "word or act which detracts from the power and glory of God."

---

[17]The Greek text has Beelzebul rather than Beelzebub. The NIV translation accords with the ancient Vulgate and Syriac translations which apparently took the name to be the same as the ancient god of Ekron mentioned in 2 Kgs 1:2-3, 6, 16. But that may be a false identification. Beelzebul does not occur elsewhere in Jewish literature and may have been created for this occasion from two words meaning "Lord of the heaven." See the arguments in Guelich, pp. 174-175. In any case, the scribes were referring to Satan, the prince of demons.

V. 30 indicates that Jesus made his remarks about blasphemy against the Holy Spirit because the scribes had called the Spirit by which Jesus worked his miracles "an evil spirit."[18] What the scribes had done either was or was dangerously close to blasphemy against the Spirit.

Jesus says that blasphemy against the Spirit is different from other sins and blasphemies. "Whoever blasphemes against the Spirit will not be forgiven; he is guilty of an eternal sin." This is one of several biblical texts that raise the difficult question of unforgivable sins (cf. Num 15:30-31; Heb 6:4-6; 10:26-31; 12:16-17; 1 John 5:16-17). The other texts I have listed do not mention blasphemy against the Holy Spirit, but they do raise the uncomfortable prospect of a sin that cannot be forgiven. Many interpreters argue that these texts refer to sins that cannot be forgiven so long as one continues in them.[19] However one solves the theological problem raised by these texts, it is clear that they mean to provide a serious warning. Jesus wanted the scribes to know they were on dangerous ground.

The NIV's "I tell you the truth" translates the first occurrence of a two word phrase, ἀμὴν λέγω (*amēn legō*), which is used thirteen times in Mark.[20] It is a characteristic phrase used by Jesus to emphasize the truth and significance of a statement. The word "amen" was found frequently in the Hebrew Old Testament to mean something like "Yes, this is true" or "May it be as you say." A Greek transliteration of amen is often used in the same manner in the New Testament. However, in the Gospels "amen" always appears on the lips of Jesus and at the beginning of a statement. In Jesus' usage it means something like "truly." No other New

---

[18]McGarvey, p. 109: "Whether a man can commit this blasphemy in any other way, does not appear from the text. . . . It is best in this, as in all other matters, to be content with what is clearly taught."

[19]McGarvey, p. 110, disagrees: "If it be answered that a man might do this at one period of his life, and subsequently be convinced and repent, we reply that this is precisely what the Savior, in effect, says he can not do."

[20]Mark 3:28; 8:12; 9:1, 41; 10:15, 29; 11:23; 12:43; 13:30; 14:9, 18, 25, 30.

Testament person or author uses it this way.[21]

31-35. These verses complete the story begun in vv. 20-21 when Jesus' family set out to take charge of him because some were saying he was out of his mind. The family arrived while Jesus was commenting on the scribes' accusations against him. Because of the crowd they sent a messenger in to summon Jesus.

When the crowd realized Jesus' mother and brothers were outside, they told Jesus.[22] His response is strong: "Here are my mother and my brothers! Whoever does the will of God is my brother and sister and mother." Jesus often used striking, even shocking, ways of expressing an important concept. This type of rhetoric makes a deep impression on us and helps us to see how serious Jesus is about the will of God.

---

[21]Gerald F. Hawthorne, "Amen," in *DJG*, pp. 7-8.

[22]According to some ancient manuscripts the crowd told Jesus his mother, brothers, *and sisters* were outside. It is difficult to decide whether to include "and sisters" as in the NRSV or to omit "and sisters" as in the NIV.

MARK 4

C. JESUS TEACHES IN PARABLES (4:1-34)

There are two chapters in Mark that focus on Jesus' teaching. Chapter 13 contains his private teaching to the disciples concerning the destruction of Jerusalem and the second coming. Chapter 4:1-34 is a "sampler" of his public teaching in parables. It contains the parable of the Sower, the parable of the Growing Seed, and the parable of the Mustard Seed. Since Mark used the term "parable" to refer to various figurative sayings (cf. 3:23), he would also include the sayings in vv. 21-25 as parables. V. 35 suggests that this parable section is all from one day of teaching.

There has been and continues to be significant discussion and debate over the proper principles for interpreting Jesus' parables.[1] In the twentieth century interpreters have rightly turned away from the allegorizing interpretations that characterized previous centuries, although many also correctly conclude that there are allegorical elements in many of the parables. Mark's account of Jesus' interpretation of the parable of the Sower (vv. 14-20) clearly indicates that the parables may contain allegorical elements. However, it is important not to "allegorize" the parables and give them meanings that neither Jesus nor Mark would have had in mind. In general, we should acknowledge those allegorical elements that are clearly present in the story and its context, but remain skeptical of further allegorization. For example, the church father

---

[1]See especially Craig L. Blomberg, *Interpreting the Parables* (Downers Grove: InterVarsity, 1990).

Augustine erred in his allegorizing of the parable of the Good Samaritan in which he taught that the man going down to Jericho represented Adam, the priest and the Levite represented the Old Testament Law, the Samaritan represented Christ, the inn represented the church, and the innkeeper represented Paul.[2]

1. The Parable of the Sower (4:1-9)

1Again Jesus began to teach by the lake. The crowd that gathered around him was so large that he got into a boat and sat in it out on the lake, while all the people were along the shore at the water's edge. 2He taught them many things by parables, and in his teaching said: 3"Listen! A farmer went out to sow his seed. 4As he was scattering the seed, some fell along the path, and the birds came and ate it up. 5Some fell on rocky places, where it did not have much soil. It sprang up quickly, because the soil was shallow. 6But when the sun came up, the plants were scorched, and they withered because they had no root. 7Other seed fell among thorns, which grew up and choked the plants, so that they did not bear grain. 8Still other seed fell on good soil. It came up, grew and produced a crop, multiplying thirty, sixty, or even a hundred times."

9Then Jesus said, "He who has ears to hear, let him hear."

The longest and most allegorical parables in Mark are the Sower and the Tenants (12:1-12). The Sower is the only Markan parable with a detailed explanation (4:14-20). I will reserve comments on the interpretation of the story for vv. 14-20.

1-2. The setting for Jesus' teaching recalls ("again") Mark

---

[2]Augustine *Quaestiones Evangeliorum* 2.19.

3:7-10. With immense crowds following him and trying to touch him, it was convenient for him to teach from a boat. The crowd could gather on the land and listen. Jesus used parables for reasons that are discussed later in the chapter. Apparently, the parable was his primary mode of teaching (see 4:34).

3-8. The opening word, "Listen!", corresponds to the concluding comment in v. 9: "He who has ears to hear, let him hear."[3] Jesus is not trying to get the crowd to stop talking. He is calling for understanding. He wants the audience to do more than simply hear words. His meaning is similar to a parent who tells a child, "Now I want you to listen to what I am saying."

The story fits primitive agricultural practices in which a sower casts the seed on the ground. The first three soil types are fairly easily understood even by modern city dwellers. The yield of the fourth soil type needs some clarification. The thirty, sixty, and one hundred-fold yield were quite remarkable by ancient standards. The seeds produced thirty, sixty, and one hundred times the number sowed. According to the careful research of Robert McIver, yields of four or five-fold would have been typical.[4] Gen. 26:12 says that Isaac reaped one hundred-fold, but only because the Lord blessed him to become rich. Jesus' audience would have been amazed at such high yields.

9. Jesus urges his listeners to hear with understanding. The same saying is found in v. 23.[5] V. 24, "Pay attention to what you hear; the measure you give will be the measure you get, and still more will be given you," could be viewed as Jesus' own commentary on this saying.

---

[3]"Listen" and "hear" translate the same Greek word, ἀκούω (*akouō*).

[4]Robert K. McIver, "One Hundred-Fold Yield – Miraculous or Mundane? Matthew 13.8, 23; Mark 4.8, 20; Luke 8.8," *New Testament Studies* 40 (1994): 606-608. "Yields of thirty-fold have been achieved in modern Israel, using sophisticated farming technology and fertilizers, but even so this happens only in good years" (p. 607).

[5]And Matt 11:15; 13:43; Luke 14:35; Rev 2:7, 11, 17, 29; 3:6, 13, 22; 13:9.

2. The Purpose of the Parables (4:10-12)

[10]When he was alone, the Twelve and the others around him asked him about the parables. [11]He told them, "The secret of the kingdom of God has been given to you. But to those on the outside everything is said in parables [12]so that,

"'they may be ever seeing but never perceiving,
and ever hearing but never understanding;
otherwise they might turn and be forgiven!'[a]"

[a]*12* Isaiah 6:9,10

Most Bible readers think of the parables as aids to understanding, as stories which use the familiar to teach about the unfamiliar. They are surprised to read that Jesus spoke in parables so that some of his listeners would not be able to understand. It is true that Jesus called upon his listeners to listen and understand (see 4:3, 9, 23). But it is also true that these appeals were for those with "ears to hear." Some of Jesus' listeners were spiritually deaf.

10. This is the first of many indications that the disciples, even the twelve, often failed to understand Jesus. In some ways the parables are easier for us to understand than they were for their original hearers. We know more than they did about Jesus' identity and intentions.

11-12. It is not clear what "the secret (μυστήριον, *mystērion*; Matt 13:11 and Luke 8:10 say secret*s*) of the kingdom of God" means. The most common view of Mark's meaning is that it is the secret that the kingdom of God was dawning in Jesus.[6] If so, then in Matthew and Luke the secret*s* may be multiple elements bound up with this basic concept.[7]

"Those on the outside" surely include the opponents of Jesus (3:6, 22, 30), and might be basically limited to them. For them the parables are meant to conceal the message so that

---

[6]Guelich, p. 206; Lane, p. 158.
[7]Carson, "Matthew," p. 308.

they would not understand, turn, and be forgiven. The words of v. 12 come from Isa 6:9-10 where the Lord gave Isaiah a mission of wrath against his disobedient child, Israel. Part of Jesus' mission was also one of divine recompense.

3. The Interpretation of the Sower (4:13-20)

[13]Then Jesus said to them, "Don't you understand this parable? How then will you understand any parable? [14]The farmer sows the word. [15]Some people are like seed along the path, where the word is sown. As soon as they hear it, Satan comes and takes away the word that was sown in them. [16]Others, like seed sown on rocky places, hear the word and at once receive it with joy. [17]But since they have no root, they last only a short time. When trouble or persecution comes because of the word, they quickly fall away. [18]Still others, like seed sown among thorns, hear the word; [19]but the worries of this life, the deceitfulness of wealth and the desires for other things come in and choke the word, making it unfruitful. [20]Others, like seed sown on good soil, hear the word, accept it, and produce a crop – thirty, sixty or even a hundred times what was sown."

13. The questions Jesus asked about the Sower and the other parables may imply that Jesus thought the Sower was one of the easier parables to understand or, less probably, that he considered understanding the Sower to be foundational for understanding the others.

14-20. The primary point of the Sower parable is to encourage people to hear the word, accept it, and let it bear fruit in their lives. The reactions of the seed in the four types of soil represent different ways in which people receive the word of God. Like the seed on the path which the birds ate, some people never respond to the word. Satan turns them against it from the beginning. A second group is like the seed that fell on rocky ground. They initially receive the word, but they do not have much depth. They fall away at the first sign of trouble or persecution. Like the seed sown among thorns, the third group receives the word, but spiritual thorn bushes – "the worries of this life, the deceitfulness of wealth, and the desire for other things" – choke it out.

Only the fourth group, the good soil group, bears fruit. Fruit bearing may represent the life of discipleship, the outcome of obedience to the word.[8] As documented in the above comments on v. 8, the yield Jesus proposed is exceptionally high by ancient standards. Wherever the word takes hold and stays in a life, that life is changed enormously.

In addition to the purpose of exhorting those who listen to hear and accept the word, the great outcome of the fourth soil may indicate that Jesus was also seeking to encourage those who sow (like his disciples). Many hearers may not receive the word, or may quickly fall away, but those who sow may rest assured that the word will bear great fruit in many lives.

4. The Parable of the Lamp (4:21-23)

21He said to them, "Do you bring in a lamp to put it under a bowl or a bed? Instead, don't you put it on its stand? 22For whatever is hidden is meant to be disclosed, and whatever is concealed is meant to be brought out into the open. 23If anyone has ears to hear, let him hear."

The parable of the Lamp does not fit the modern definition of a parable, but it does fit Mark's understanding. As noted above, Mark 3:23 exemplifies the Gospel writers' use of the term to apply to any figurative saying.

The sayings in vv. 21-25 are extraordinarily difficult to understand. Some of them occur in other contexts in Matthew or Luke (Matt 7:2; 10:26; 25:29; Luke 6:38; 12:2;

[8]Gundry, p. 206.

19:26), but of course the same saying may have differing meanings in different contexts. What is needed in interpreting Mark is close attention to the context of Mark 4. One important consideration is the question of Jesus' audience for vv. 21-25. Even though the NIV translation "he continued" in v. 24 obscures the parallel, in the Greek text both v. 21 and v. 24 begin "And he was saying to them." Vv. 10-13 suggest that "them" means the disciples in private rather than the crowds. It clear from vv. 33-34 that at some point in the chapter Jesus returns to addressing the crowds. I take that to be in v. 26 with the parable of the Seed Growing Secretly.

Another contextual clue to understanding vv. 21-25 is also partially obscured by the NIV. In the Greek text both v. 22 and v. 25 begin with "for," which suggests that in each pair of sayings (vv. 21-22 and 24-25) the second saying is meant to explain the first. Even though the explanatory sayings are somewhat parabolic themselves, the fact that Jesus offers an explanation supports the understanding (see the previous paragraph) that these sayings were addressed to the disciples in private. Vv. 33-34 say that Jesus' method was to teach in parables and explain everything privately to his disciples.

21. It is not difficult to understand the literal meaning of this one sentence parable. Lamps are put on lamp stands to provide light. People do not bring in lamps in order to hide their light under a bowl (the Greek term [μόδιον, *modion*] refers to a bowl or basket used to measure a peck of grain) or a bed.[9] The problem is to decide what the lamp stands for.

22. The opening "for" (γάρ, *gar*) indicates that this saying is explanatory. The lamp stands for something which is hidden or concealed, but is meant to be disclosed and brought out into the open. It is often suggested that the lamp refers to the kingdom of God as it is present in the ministry of Jesus. The

---

[9]Lane, p. 165, makes a point of Mark's somewhat unusual use of ἔρχομαι (*erchomai*) and suggests that Mark means the lamp "comes" rather than "is brought." However, *BAGD*, p. 311, provides ancient parallels which use *erchomai* with various objects to mean "be brought."

lesson would be that even though the kingdom in its present state during Jesus' ministry seems hidden or obscure, it will be brought out into the open in the future.[10]

The context, however, suggests another understanding. If vv. 21-22 are directed to the disciples in the context of their question about the meaning of the parables, then the lamp may refer to the meaning of Jesus' parabolic teaching. Although Jesus teaches in a form that obscures his message for those outside (vv. 11-12), his message is meant to be made known and will be made known to the disciples through his explanations. His message is not meant to be hidden under a bowl or a bed, but set up on a lamp stand as a source of light.[11]

23. See the comments on v. 9.

5. The Parable of the Measure (4:24-25)

24"Consider carefully what you hear," he continued. "With the measure you use, it will be measured to you – and even more. 25Whoever has will be given more; whoever does not have, even what he has will be taken from him."

24-25. As explained in the introductory comments on vv. 21-22, these verses also seem to be private teaching to the disciples. In this case the parable of the Measure is introduced by a non-parabolic explanatory comment ("Consider carefully what you hear") and followed by a parabolic explanatory comment (see again the introductory comments on vv. 21-22 for the observation that in the Greek text v. 25 begins with the word "for" [γάρ, *gar*], which indicates that it is an explanatory comment on v. 24).

The parable is about how one hears the parables. It fits well the context which has explained that the parables are

---

[10]So, e.g., Guelich, pp. 231-232.
[11]See Gundry, p. 212.

meant to conceal the message from those outside, but that those inside have been given the secret to understanding. The difference between those outside and those inside is the measure they give in the way they hear the parables. The disciples who consider carefully what they hear will be given more. They even receive private explanations (vv. 13-20, 33-34). But "those on the outside" do not listen discerningly and the parables are meant to obscure the message to them. They have no knowledge of Jesus' meaning and are not supposed to. The saying in v. 25 can be considered in economic terms: "The rich get richer and the poor get poorer." Jesus is speaking of the economics of spirituality. Those who are open to his teaching will learn more, those who are spiritually obstinate will never learn.[12]

6. The Parable of the Growing Seed (4:26-29)

**[26]He also said, "This is what the kingdom of God is like.
A man scatters seed on the ground. [27]Night and day, whether
he sleeps or gets up, the seed sprouts and grows, though he
does not know how. [28]All by itself the soil produces grain –
first the stalk, then the head, then the full kernel in the
head. [29]As soon as the grain is ripe, he puts the sickle to it,
because the harvest has come."**

I have argued above that with the two last parables Mark returns to Jesus' public teaching. In both cases Jesus says that the parables are about the kingdom of God.

26-28. Apparently, the seed is the kingdom. The bottom line is that the seed will produce. The kingdom of God dawning in Jesus' ministry is like seed which will grow into a full field to be harvested. It will become a great kingdom ready for the judgment.

---

[12]Similarly, Gundry, pp. 216-218.

The last words of v. 27 ("though he does not know how") and the first word of v. 28 (αὐτομάτη, *automatē*, "all by itself") may add their own special significance. Their meaning may be that it does not matter whether those who observe or participate in Jesus' ministry can visualize or understand the development of the kingdom. The maturation of the kingdom is God's work.

29. The conclusion of the parable adds a reference to judgment. The use of harvesting as an image for judgment has Old Testament precedents (Joel 3:12-13). In Matt 13:39-43 (in connection with another parable of the kingdom) Jesus uses harvesting as an image for the final judgment.

7. The Parable of the Mustard Seed (4:30-32)

[30]Again he said, "What shall we say the kingdom of God is like, or what parable shall we use to describe it? [31]It is like a mustard seed, which is the smallest seed you plant in the ground. [32]Yet when planted, it grows and becomes the largest of all garden plants, with such big branches that the birds of the air can perch in its shade."

30. The Mustard Seed parable is also about the kingdom of God.

31-32. Once again the kingdom is represented as a growing seed. The mustard seed was known for its tiny size (cf. Matt 17:20). The shrub it produces is not huge (c. 8-10 feet high),[13] but the point lies in the contrast. Jesus assures his listeners that the kingdom will achieve greatness. This parable speaks to either supporters or detractors who might view what they saw in Jesus' ministry as inappropriate for the great kingdom of God.[14]

[13]Lane, p. 171 n. 76.

[14]Blomberg, *Parables*, pp. 284-286.

8. Teaching in Parables (4:33-34)

[33]With many similar parables Jesus spoke the word to them, as much as they could understand. [34]He did not say anything to them without using a parable. But when he was alone with his own disciples, he explained everything.

These verses indicate that Jesus' standard procedure was to teach in parables. "As they were able to hear it" indicates that he sought to use parables so as to be understood by those who had ears to hear. He taught according to their ability to understand. Just as parables had the ability to conceal the word (vv. 11-12), so they also had the ability to reveal it (vv. 3, 9, 23, 33). In addition to his public teaching in parables, Jesus gave private explanations to his disciples. (If Mark had recorded all of these, the need for some of the above comments would be considerably lessened.)

D. JESUS' AUTHORITY OVER NATURE, DEMONS, DISEASE, AND DEATH (4:35-5:43)

Mark follows his "sampler" of Jesus' teaching in parables with a "sampler" of Jesus' miraculous powers. The next four stories portray Jesus' authority over nature, demons, disease, and death. At the end of the first of these miracles, the disciples ask "Who is this? Even the wind and the sea obey him!" The following stories add more dimensions to the question: even a legion of demons obey him; a severely ill woman was healed by touching his garment; he raised a young girl from the dead. "Who is this?" This section of Mark is his best overview of the range of Jesus' miraculous power. It underscores what the reader already knows about Jesus' identity. He is the Christ, the Son of God.

Furthermore, these stories provide important lessons on discipleship. The first, third, and fourth focus attention on the importance of faith and the need to overcome fear. Faith and fear are directly contrasted in each of these three stories. Discipleship involves faith, and faith overcomes fear. The second story, the Gerasene demoniac, contains a similar contrast in a less overt way.

1. Authority Over Nature (4:35-41)

35That day when evening came, he said to his disciples, "Let us go over to the other side." 36Leaving the crowd behind, they took him along, just as he was, in the boat. There were also other boats with him. 37A furious squall came up, and the waves broke over the boat, so that it was nearly swamped. 38Jesus was in the stern, sleeping on a cushion. The disciples woke him and said to him, "Teacher, don't you care if we drown?"

39He got up, rebuked the wind and said to the waves, "Quiet! Be still!" Then the wind died down and it was completely calm.

40He said to his disciples, "Why are you so afraid? Do you still have no faith?"

41They were terrified and asked each other, "Who is this? Even the wind and the waves obey him!"

This is the first of three scenes in Mark (4:35-41; 6:45-52; 8:13-21) in which the disciples have a special learning experience with Jesus while crossing the Sea of Galilee.[15] The lake was one place where Jesus and the disciples could be alone – although in this first instance, there were other boats with them (4:36).

35-36. The teaching segment in vv. 1-34 must have taken place on the western shores of the lake. Jesus' request to go to the other side may be motivated by a desire to retreat from the crowds, as in 6:31-32. They set out in the evening.

15In Mark 4-8 Jesus travels on the lake five times (4:35; 5:21; 6:32; 7:53; 8:10).

37-39. The storm that arose must have been a major storm to strike fear into even experienced Galilean fishermen. Yet Jesus was able to calm the storm by his command. Although it cannot be seen in the NIV translation, Jesus' rebuking of the wind in 4:39 is reminiscent of his rebuking of a demon in 1:25. In both cases Mark describes Jesus' comments as "rebuking" (ἐπιτιμάω, *epitimaō*) and in both cases Jesus says "Be silent!" (φιμάω, *phimoō*).[16] Not only did the wind cease, but there was a great calm on the lake.

40-41. Most readers probably find the disciples' fear understandable. Jesus did not. If they had had faith, they would not have been afraid. Presumably he meant faith in his identity as the Christ, the Son of God. If they knew who it was that accompanied them in the boat, they would not have feared death in the waves. The last verse underscores the fact that they did not know Jesus' true identity. They were now filled with a new kind of fear or terror – awe at the marvelous power of Jesus. In the four miracles of 4:35-5:43, Mark seeks to lead the reader into deeper faith and less fear.

---

[16]See Gundry, p. 240, vs. the frequent claim that Mark portrays the storm as literally demonic.

MARK 5

2. Authority over Demons (5:1-20)

[1]They went across the lake to the region of the Gerasenes.[a]
[2]When Jesus got out of the boat, a man with an evil[b] spirit
came from the tombs to meet him. [3]This man lived in the
tombs, and no one could bind him any more, not even with
a chain. [4]For he had often been chained hand and foot, but
he tore the chains apart and broke the irons on his feet. No
one was strong enough to subdue him. [5]Night and day
among the tombs and in the hills he would cry out and cut
himself with stones.

[6]When he saw Jesus from a distance, he ran and fell on
his knees in front of him. [7]He shouted at the top of his
voice, "What do you want with me, Jesus, Son of the Most
High God? Swear to God that you won't torture me!" [8]For
Jesus had said to him, "Come out of this man, you evil spirit!"

[9]Then Jesus asked him, "What is your name?" "My name
is Legion," he replied, "for we are many." [10]And he begged
Jesus again and again not to send them out of the area.

[11]A large herd of pigs was feeding on the nearby hillside.
[12]The demons begged Jesus, "Send us among the pigs; allow
us to go into them." [13]He gave them permission, and the evil
spirits came out and went into the pigs. The herd, about two
thousand in number, rushed down the steep bank into the
lake and were drowned.

[14]Those tending the pigs ran off and reported this in the
town and countryside, and the people went out to see what

had happened. [15]When they came to Jesus, they saw the man who had been possessed by the legion of demons, sitting there, dressed and in his right mind; and they were afraid. [16]Those who had seen it told the people what had happened to the demon-possessed man – and told about the pigs as well. [17]Then the people began to plead with Jesus to leave their region.

[18]As Jesus was getting into the boat, the man who had been demon-possessed begged to go with him. [19]Jesus did not let him, but said, "Go home to your family and tell them how much the Lord has done for you, and how he has had mercy on you." [20]So the man went away and began to tell in the Decapolis how much Jesus had done for him. And all the people were amazed.

[a]*1* Some manuscripts *Gadarenes*; other manuscripts *Gergesenes* [b]*2* Greek *unclean*; also in verses 8 and 13

This is the most dramatic exorcism story. Jesus' later statement in 9:29 "This kind (of demon) can come out only by prayer," indicates that there are differences between one demon and the next. The Gerasene demoniac was an extreme case involving social ostracization (v. 3), superhuman powers (vv. 3-4), howling and masochistic behavior (v. 5), and thousands of demons (vv. 9, 13). Jesus' ability to control these demons was awe inspiring.

1. The reference to the Gerasenes creates a difficult geographical problem. One would presume Mark was speaking of the inhabitants of Gerasa, one of the cities of the Decapolis. The problem is that the exorcism clearly takes place at the edge of the lake and yet Gerasa was some thirty miles southeast of the lake. One possible solution is to accept one of the other readings found in the ancient witnesses to the text. In addition to "Gerasenes" there is ancient manuscript support for "Gadarenes" or "Gergesenes."[1] "Gedarenes"

[1]The decision is a difficult one. The United Bible Societies Greek New

(the best attested reading for Matthew) would point to Gedara, a city about five miles southeast of the lake which had a harbor on the lake. "Gergesenes" is the alternative supported by Origen in the third century.[2] Some scholars who accept this reading believe Gergesa should be associated with a small village on the northeastern shores of the lake now known as the ruins of Kursi.[3] In any case the region Jesus entered was part of the Decapolis (the "Ten Cities"), a largely Gentile region east of the lake.

2-5. Mark describes the demon possessed man in some detail. He had superhuman strength so that he could not be restrained by shackles or chains. He lived with the dead (unclean according to the cleanliness laws) among the tombs in some region near the lake. He was forever howling and cutting (or "bruising" as in the NRSV) himself with stones.

6-8. This pitiable man (who had never seen Jesus) recognized Jesus immediately, even at a distance. The demon knew Jesus' identity as "Son of the Most High God." When Jesus commanded him to come out he objected, calling on God's name in an effort to implore Jesus not to torment him.

9. A legion was a military division, which in Jesus' time numbered "about 6000 soldiers, usually with approximately an equal number of auxiliary troops."[4] The name Legion and the subsequent possession of two thousand pigs suggests that the demoniac was possessed by thousands of spirits.

10-13. Jesus only appears to aid the demons by permitting them to enter the pigs. The pigs rush into the lake and are drowned, leaving the demons without a host. Jews do not eat or raise pigs. But this lakeside scene was in the Decapolis, a predominately Gentile region.

Testament gives their decision for "Gerasenes" a "C" rating, indicating significant uncertainty. (The rating system ranges from "A" to "D," with "A" indicating a high degree of confidence that they have chosen correctly.) See *UBS*[4], p. 135.

[2]Origen, *Commentary on John* 5.41.

[3]E.g., Gundry, pp. 255-257.

[4]*BAGD*, pp. 467-468.

14-17. The people of the town and countryside apparently knew about the demon-possessed man. They were surprised to find him sitting still, dressed, and clear-headed. The statement that they were afraid translates the same verb used of the disciples in 4:41. However, in this case it seems to have a negative connotation, since their fear led them to ask Jesus to leave. They were afraid for a man of such remarkable powers to remain among them.[5]

18-20. The actions of the former demoniac contrast sharply with those of the crowd. It seems surprising that Jesus would encourage him to tell about his experience, since he had strongly warned the leper of 1:40-45 not to tell anyone. Perhaps the distinction is to be sought in the region and the reaction of the people. In Galilee, Jesus could not even enter a town due to the immense crowds that followed him everywhere. But in the Decapolis his first miracle was greeted with rejection and with appeals for him to leave the region. Jesus did not need an ambassador to spread the word in Galilee, but the Decapolis was a different situation. The former demoniac's story of God's mercy through Jesus' power evoked the same reaction that many in Galilee had had – they were amazed (cf. 1:27).

3. Authority over Disease and Death (5:21-43)

[21]When Jesus had again crossed over by boat to the other side of the lake, a large crowd gathered around him while he was by the lake. [22]Then one of the synagogue rulers, named Jairus, came there. Seeing Jesus, he fell at his feet [23]and pleaded earnestly with him, "My little daughter is dying. Please come and put your hands on her so that she will be healed and live." [24]So Jesus went with him.

A large crowd followed and pressed around him. [25]And a woman was there who had been subject to bleeding for

[5]Lane, p. 187.

**twelve years. 26She had suffered a great deal under the care
of many doctors and had spent all she had, yet instead of
getting better she grew worse. 27When she heard about
Jesus, she came up behind him in the crowd and touched
his cloak, 28because she thought, "If I just touch his clothes,
I will be healed." 29Immediately her bleeding stopped and
she felt in her body that she was freed from her suffering.**

**30At once Jesus realized that power had gone out from
him. He turned around in the crowd and asked, "Who
touched my clothes?"**

**31"You see the people crowding against you," his disci-
ples answered, "and yet you can ask, 'Who touched me?'"**

**32But Jesus kept looking around to see who had done it.
33Then the woman, knowing what had happened to her,
came and fell at his feet and, trembling with fear, told him
the whole truth. 34He said to her, "Daughter, your faith has
healed you. Go in peace and be freed from your suffering."**

**35While Jesus was still speaking, some men came from
the house of Jairus, the synagogue ruler. "Your daughter is
dead," they said. "Why bother the teacher any more?"**

**36Ignoring what they said, Jesus told the synagogue ruler,
"Don't be afraid; just believe."**

**37He did not let anyone follow him except Peter, James
and John the brother of James. 38When they came to the
home of the synagogue ruler, Jesus saw a commotion, with
people crying and wailing loudly. 39He went in and said to
them, "Why all this commotion and wailing? The child is
not dead but asleep." 40But they laughed at him.**

**After he put them all out, he took the child's father and
mother and the disciples who were with him, and went in
where the child was. 41He took her by the hand and said to
her, "Talitha koum!" (which means, "Little girl, I say to you,
get up!"). 42Immediately the girl stood up and walked
around (she was twelve years old). At this they were completely astonished. 43He gave strict orders not to let anyone
know about this, and told them to give her something to eat.**

Once again (cf. 3:20-35) two of Mark's stories create a sandwich, with one complete within the other. As usual there are clear thematic relationships between the two. Both illustrate Jesus' authority and together they complete the four realms of authority illustrated in 4:35-5:43. Both involve the conflict between faith and fear (see vv. 33-34, 36).

21-24a. Jesus crossed back to the western shores of the lake, where most of his ministry took place. Once again there were large crowds around Jesus. As a ruler of the synagogue, Jairus was presumably a man of some prominence. The synagogue he served is not identified. Since he encountered Jesus by the lake (v. 21) and they then walked to his house, he presumably served a synagogue in a village near the lake, such as Capernaum or Tiberias. Jairus pleaded with Jesus to heal his twelve year old daughter, who was near death.

24b-26. Mark sets up the story of the woman touching Jesus by noting that the crowd was large and pressed upon him as he walked toward Jairus's house. Just as Mark explained in more than his usual depth the nature of the Gerasene demoniac's problem, he does the same for the woman with the hemorrhage. She had been sick for twelve years, had spent all her money on many different doctors, but had only gotten worse. Mark wants to emphasize the extent of the woman's problem to highlight the power of Jesus.

27-29. Not only could Jesus heal this woman, he could do it simply by her touching his cloak. Jesus may have healed in this way before (3:10 "those with diseases were pushing forward to touch him") and he certainly did so afterwards (6:56 "They begged him to let them touch even the edge of his cloak, and all who touched him were healed"). The woman's depth of faith is illustrated by her belief that if she could simply touch his clothes she would be healed. She knew immediately that her plan had worked.

30-32. Remarkably, so did Jesus. From v. 24a and from the disciples' remark in v. 31, it is apparent that many people were touching Jesus as the crowd pressed around him. And yet in this case he was aware that "power had gone out from him."

33-34. The woman's fear of Jesus may have been enhanced by her awareness of the laws of cleanliness (cf. Lev 15:25-33). Touching or being touched by someone with a flow of blood caused uncleanness. She may have been concerned about how Jesus would react to her touching him. In saying she told him "the whole truth," Mark may mean even the specific nature of her disease as involving a flow of blood. But instead of rebuking her, Jesus commended her for her faith – another of the many instances in Mark which emphasize the importance of faith. The woman was both fearful and faithful, but her faith overcame her fear, and for that she was blessed.

35-36. The thematic relationship between the story of the woman and the story of Jairus's daughter is made plain in these verses. The messengers from Jairus's house obviously did not know Jesus could raise the dead. The NIV says Jesus "ignored" what they said. The Greek verb used here (παρακούω, *parakouō*) is difficult to translate,[6] but the context points more toward the NRSV translation that Jesus "overheard" what they said. Having overheard it, he exhorted Jairus, "Don't be afraid; just believe." The woman with the hemorrhage had just demonstrated faith and how faith can conquer fear. Jairus needed to follow her example.

37. For the first of three special occasions in Mark (cf. 9:2; 14:33) Jesus singled out Peter, James, and John as an inner circle among the twelve.

38-40a. The grieving people at the house testify to the truth of the message of the little girl's death. Jesus said she was sleeping because he planned to raise her from the dead. It is not clear whether the mourners laughed at his implication that he would raise her or at his supposed foolishness in saying she was sleeping. In either case the laughter reinforces the fact that they were confident that she was indeed dead.

40b-42. The great miracle was performed simply and with few words. Mark preserves the Aramaic statement ("Talitha koum"), which he translates into Greek ("Little girl, I say to

---

[6]*BAGD*, p. 619.

you, get up!"). Some argue that Mark preserves the Aramaic here and in the healing at 7:34 as examples of foreign words used as magical incantations (similar to "abracadabra"). However, Mark's translation of the Aramaic weighs against that understanding. So does the fact that most of Mark's uses of Aramaic terms are not connected with working miracles (3:17; 7:11; 11:9-10; 14:36; 15:22, 34).[7]

Those who witnessed the miracle were "completely astonished." Astonishment, amazement, or fear are the common reactions to the miracles of Jesus (cf. 1:27; 2:12; 4:41; 5:15, 20). In Mark's Gospel this is the only time Jesus raised someone from the dead (cf. Luke 7:11-17; John 11:1-44).

43. It is not clear what Jesus did not want anyone to know. Eventually, the young girl would be seen alive. Perhaps he was concerned that the miracle be kept secret until he left the town where the synagogue ruler lived. Perhaps he did not want anyone to know how the miracle happened. Eventual public knowledge that the girl was raised from the dead seems inevitable.

---

[7]Guelich, p. 302.

MARK 6

E. REJECTION AT NAZARETH (6:1-6a)

[1]Jesus left there and went to his hometown, accompanied by his disciples. [2]When the Sabbath came, he began to teach in the synagogue, and many who heard him were amazed.

"Where did this man get these things?" they asked. "What's this wisdom that has been given him, that he even does miracles! [3]Isn't this the carpenter? Isn't this Mary's son and the brother of James, Joseph,[a] Judas and Simon? Aren't his sisters here with us?" And they took offense at him.

[4]Jesus said to them, "Only in his hometown, among his relatives and in his own house is a prophet without honor." [5]He could not do any miracles there, except lay his hands on a few sick people and heal them. [6]And he was amazed at their lack of faith.

[a]*3* Greek *Joses*, a variant of *Joseph*

The first five chapters of Mark are replete with huge crowds that flock to see and hear Jesus. However, there are those who oppose him. In Mark 2:1-3:6 we find Jesus attacked by the religious leadership and the Herodians. In 3:20-30 he is again criticized by the religious leaders and his family comes to take charge of him because of charges that he is out of his mind. In 5:17 the Gerasenes ask Jesus to leave their region. Opposition continues in 6:1-6 when Jesus visits Nazareth and is rejected by pious Jews from his own hometown.

1. Mark does not identify Jesus' hometown by name here, but he has already indicated it in 1:9 and 24. For information on Nazareth see the comments on 1:9.

2-3. When Jesus taught in the synagogue at Capernaum the audience was amazed at his teaching and his ability to heal (1:21-28). In 6:2 Mark uses the same word as in 1:22 to describe the amazement in the synagogue at Nazareth. However, the amazement at Capernaum had positive connotations and resulted in Jesus performing many miracles there (1:32-34). The Nazareth crowd was offended. In Capernaum they spoke about his teaching; in Nazareth they spoke about his wisdom. In both places they spoke about his miraculous powers. But in Nazareth they remembered him as the carpenter (τέκτων, *tektōn*)[1] whose mother, brothers, and sisters they knew.[2] They were offended at the hometown boy who seemed to them to be claiming too much for himself.

4. The reality of life Jesus' proverb expresses has been widely recognized throughout human history.[3]

5-6a. There is quite a contrast between the many miraculous healings and exorcisms Jesus performed after his appearance in the synagogue at Capernaum (1:32-24) and the few healings he performed at Nazareth. The reason Jesus could not do many miracles there was their unbelief. Rather than amazing the citizens of Nazareth with his many miracles, Jesus was himself amazed at their unbelief. Once again Mark stresses the importance of belief.

IV. THE GALILEAN MINISTRY, SECTION THREE (6:6b-8:30)

All of the events in 1:16-3:12 took place in Galilee. The sec-

---

[1]Matt 13:55 identifies Jesus as "the carpenter's son." He apparently took up the trade of his father.

[2]The fact that Jesus is identified by his mother and his father is not mentioned has elicited several hypotheses. Perhaps the most common is that Joseph was no longer alive. See Guelich, pp. 309-310.

[3]*BAGD*, p. 637, cites several ancient parallels which comment on how philosophers got no respect in their home areas.

ond section of the Galilean ministry (3:13-6:6b) contains one event in the Decapolis (the Gerasene demoniac), but the citizens of Gerasa asked him to leave. The third section of the Galilean ministry contains several events which occur in the surrounding regions in every direction except south. After the mission of the twelve, Jesus apparently seeks out other regions where he can spend more time with them alone, trying to lead them to the correct conclusion concerning his own identity.

A. THE MISSION OF THE TWELVE (6:6b-13)

Then Jesus went around teaching from village to village.
7Calling the Twelve to him, he sent them out two by two and
gave them authority over evil[a] spirits.
8These were his instructions: "Take nothing for the jour-
ney except a staff – no bread, no bag, no money in your
belts. 9Wear sandals but not an extra tunic. 10Whenever you
enter a house, stay there until you leave that town. 11And if
any place will not welcome you or listen to you, shake the
dust off your feet when you leave, as a testimony against
them."
12They went out and preached that people should repent.
13They drove out many demons and anointed many sick peo-
ple with oil and healed them.

[a]7 Greek *unclean*

Like the call of the four fishermen and the selection of the twelve, the sending of the twelve is a convenient dividing point in the Galilean ministry. Each of these represents a significant stage in Jesus' work with those who would become his chief representatives. When he called the four, he called them to share his mission of fishing for people. When he selected the twelve he named them "apostles" (see notes on 3:14) because he planned to send them out to preach. Now they are ready to begin.

6b. Teaching from village to village was the essence of Jesus' ministry in Galilee. This verse echoes the previous statements in 1:14 ("Jesus went into Galilee, proclaiming the good news of God") and 1:38 ("'Let us go somewhere else – to the nearby villages – so I can preach there also. That is why I have come.' So he traveled throughout Galilee, preaching in their synagogues and driving out demons.").[4]

7. The twelve shared not only in Jesus' teaching ministry, but also in healing and exorcism. Like their message, their authority over the unclean spirits came from Jesus. They would extend both Jesus' teaching and healing ministries. The use of pairs in mission work is reflected later in Acts (e.g., 13:1-3). "The background may lie in Jewish legal practice where two witnesses established the evidence (Deut 17:6; 19:15; cf. Matt 18:16; John 8:17; 2 Cor 13:1; 1 Tim 5:19), but it also may reflect the travel conditions and the need for personal and moral support."[5]

8-9. The disciples were not allowed to take food, money, or a change of clothing. Perhaps the reason for these prohibitions was that the twelve were to depend upon God to provide the needs for their journey.[6]

10-11. The primary means by which God would provide for the twelve in their traveling was through the hospitality of individuals in various places. The exhortation to stay in any house they enter until they leave the area was perhaps designed to oppose moving up to finer quarters if offered by another supporter.[7] On the other hand, in some places they would not be welcome at all. As they leave they should shake off the dust of their feet as a witness against that location.

---

[4]Mark does not differentiate between preaching and teaching.

[5]Guelich, p. 321.

[6]Ibid., p. 322. Gundry, pp. 308-309, lists seven hypotheses concerning why Jesus made the prohibitions listed in vv. 8-9. He concludes that there is no clear answer.

[7]Guelich, p. 322.

This was a symbolic act of separation and condemnation.[8] Luke 10:5 provides the accompanying explanation to be given by the missionaries: "Even the dust of your town that sticks to our feet we wipe off against you."

12-13. The ministry of the twelve is portrayed as parallel to the ministry of Jesus. Like him they preach repentance and they heal the sick and cast out demons.

In interpreting the disciples' use of anointing with oil it would be unwise to overlook the common use of oil as a medical potion in antiquity.[9] Nonetheless, the context makes it clear that the healings brought about by the disciples were miraculous in nature. The oil may have been viewed both as a symbol of God's healing power and as a medical potion.[10] The widespread recognition of oil's medicinal value may have suggested its usefulness as a symbol in connection with miraculous healings. In both respects there may be a parallel in Jesus' use of spittle in Mark 7:33 and 8:23.

B. HEROD HEARS ABOUT JESUS (6:14-16)

[14]King Herod heard about this, for Jesus' name had become well known. Some were saying,[a] "John the Baptist has been raised from the dead, and that is why miraculous powers are at work in him."

[15]Others said, "He is Elijah."

And still others claimed, "He is a prophet, like one of the prophets of long ago."

---

[8]See Acts 13:51 and the similar act of shaking one's clothes in Neh 5:13 and Acts 18:6.

[9]Cf. Isa 1:6; Luke 10:34. Josephus, *Jewish Antiquities* 17.172 reports that Herod the Great's physicians "seated him in a tub of (warm) oil" in an effort to treat his terminal illness. See the list of ancient texts in Peter Davids, *Commentary on James*, New International Greek Testament Commentary (Grand Rapids: Eerdmans, 1982), p. 193.

[10]In non-healing situations anointing with oil clearly could have symbolic value. For example, it was used ceremonially in the appointment of kings.

[16]But when Herod heard this, he said, "John, the man I beheaded, has been raised from the dead!"

[a]*14* Some early manuscripts *He was saying*

Although less clearly so than 3:20-35 and 5:21-43, 6:6b-44 could be considered one of the sandwich sections in Mark. The sending of the twelve can be considered a complete story by itself, but to some extent it is continued in 6:30 when the twelve return from their mission and begin to tell Jesus about it. Between the sending of the twelve and their return Mark reports concerning Herod hearing about Jesus, which leads him to describe the death of John the Baptist (since Herod's own opinion is that Jesus might be John raised from the dead). Some connect the sandwiched material thematically, noting that there is a sense in which John the Baptist's encounter with and persecution by Herod foreshadow both the experiences of Jesus and the twelve (cf. 13:9-13) with respect to governing authorities.

Herod Antipas, son of Herod the Great, was born in 20 B.C.[11] He ruled Galilee and Perea from 4 B.C. (the date of his father's death) to A.D. 39. He was never officially designated "king" by the Romans. However, he was one of the tetrarchs who ruled over a part of the former kingdom of his father and Mark's reference to him as "king" reflects popular, unofficial usage.[12] During Jesus' childhood and early manhood Antipas ruled from Sepphoris, a city only a few miles from Nazareth. During the ministries of John the Baptist and Jesus he ruled from Tiberias on the shores of Galilee, a city he founded and named after the emperor Tiberius.

14-15. Mark continues to provide various reactions to Jesus and assessments of him by friend and foe. The three assessments provided in these verses apparently come from those who considered it possible that Jesus was not a false teacher,

---

[11]On Antipas (and the rest of the Herodian dynasty) see H.W. Hoehner, "Herodian Dynasty," *DJG*, pp. 317-326.

[12]*BAGD*, p. 136.

an ally of Satan, or a lunatic, but was perhaps a prophetic man of God. Only those who, like Herod, believed that John was "a righteous and holy man" would conclude that Jesus might be John raised from the dead. Since there is no reference to John working any miracles they apparently concluded that the miraculous powers were given to him in his resurrected state.

Mal 4:5-6 created a widespread expectation that Elijah would return in the last days (see Mark 9:11; John 1:21).[13] Jesus' miraculous powers could easily be associated with the miracles of Elijah the Tishbite. Of course, Jesus himself considered John the Baptist to be Elijah (cf. Mark 9:13).

Moses had predicted in Deut 18:17-20 that God would raise up a prophet like himself to lead the people. It was a natural conclusion for many that Jesus was a prophet like the ancient prophets of Israel.

16. It may very well be true that a guilty conscience and superstitious thinking led Antipas to seriously consider the possibility that John had been raised from the dead. It is also possible that Herod made this statement with a note of irony or mockery.[14]

C. HEROD HAS JOHN BEHEADED (6:17-29)

[17]For Herod himself had given orders to have John arrested, and he had him bound and put in prison. He did this because of Herodias, his brother Philip's wife, whom he had married. [18]For John had been saying to Herod, "It is not lawful for you to have your brother's wife." [19]So Herodias nursed a grudge against John and wanted to kill him. But

---

[13]Sirach 48:10 (c. 180-200 B.C.) says of Elijah, "At the appointed time, it is written, you are destined to calm the wrath of God before it breaks out in fury, to turn the hearts of parents to their children, and to restore the tribes of Jacob" (NRSV). Cf. 4 Ezra 6:26.

[14]Harold W. Hoehner, *Herod Antipas* (Grand Rapids: Zondervan, 1972), pp. 189-191.

she was not able to, [20]because Herod feared John and protected him, knowing him to be a righteous and holy man. When Herod heard John, he was greatly puzzled[a]; yet he liked to listen to him.

[21]Finally the opportune time came. On his birthday Herod gave a banquet for his high officials and military commanders and the leading men of Galilee. [22]When the daughter of Herodias came in and danced, she pleased Herod and his dinner guests.

The king said to the girl, "Ask me for anything you want, and I'll give it to you." [23]And he promised her with an oath, "Whatever you ask I will give you, up to half my kingdom."

[24]She went out and said to her mother, "What shall I ask for?"

"The head of John the Baptist," she answered.

[25]At once the girl hurried in to the king with the request: "I want you to give me right now the head of John the Baptist on a platter."

[26]The king was greatly distressed, but because of his oaths and his dinner guests, he did not want to refuse her. [27]So he immediately sent an executioner with orders to bring John's head. The man went, beheaded John in the prison, [28]and brought back his head on a platter. He presented it to the girl, and she gave it to her mother. [29]On hearing of this, John's disciples came and took his body and laid it in a tomb.

[a]*20* Some early manuscripts *he did many things*

Mark now explains what Herod meant when he referred to "John, the man I beheaded." This is the only incident in Mark that does not mention Jesus. However, it is tied to the speculation that Jesus was John raised from the dead. Mark may also have seen this story as a precursor of Jesus' death.[15] Both

[15]So, e.g., Lane, p. 215.

men died by the order of Roman rulers who were reluctant to have them executed. John's death may also be viewed as a precursor of the fate of Jesus' disciples (cf. 13:9-13), especially if this story is viewed as sandwiched by the story of the mission of the twelve (see the introductory remarks on 6:14-16).[16]

The Jewish historian Josephus (c. A.D. 37-120) also commented on Antipas's marriage to Herodias and on his execution of John. According to Josephus, Antipas had been married to his first wife for a long time when he fell in love with Herodias, his half-brother's wife (and Antipas' own niece).[17] He "brazenly broached to [Herodias] the subject of marriage," and she accepted on the condition that he divorce his first wife.[18] Josephus does not mention John's criticism of the marriage, but does discuss the fact that "Herod had put [John] to death, though he was a good man and had exhorted the Jews to lead righteous lives . . ."[19] According to Josephus, Antipas feared the possibility that John's work might lead to an uprising. Therefore he had John brought in chains to, and then put to death in, Machaerus – a Herodian fortress in Perea on the eastern side of the Dead Sea.[20]

17-18. Mark does not identify the place where John was imprisoned and finally executed. He does mention the presence of "the leading men of Galilee," but they could have been invited to the fortress at Machaerus (in accord with Josephus). Josephus's opinion that Antipas had John imprisoned because of fear of an uprising is also consistent with Mark's account, although Mark emphasizes the particular conflict over the marriage.[21] The Philip Mark identifies as

---

[16]Anderson, *Mark*, p. 170.

[17]Hoehner, *Herod Antipas*, p.138 n. 4, observes that there were several uncle-niece marriages in the Herodian family. He discusses the differing opinions among the ancient Jews about the legitimacy of such marriages. Neither the Gospels nor Josephus address this issue with respect to Antipas and Herodias.

[18]Josephus, *Antiquities* 18.110.

[19]Ibid., 18.117.

[20]Ibid., 18.119.

[21]On these matters see Lane, pp. 215-217.

Herodias's former husband is apparently not Philip the tetrarch, who ruled the region north and east of Antipas's territory. Philip the tetrarch was a different half brother, who later married Herodias's daughter Salome. The three men involved in this discussion – Antipas, Philip the tetrarch, and Philip the first husband of Herodias – were all sons of Herod the Great, but had three different mothers.[22] The different mothers explains how two half brothers could both bear the name Philip.[23]

John offended Antipas by telling him, "It is not lawful for you to have your brother's wife." Although the Mosaic levirate marriage laws involved marrying a dead brother's widow, the law was quite explicit about the shame of marrying a living brother's wife (Lev 18:16; 20:21). Josephus does not report what John said about the marriage of Herodias and Antipas, but Josephus himself disapproved of marrying a living brother's wife: "Herodias, taking it into her head to flout the way of our fathers, married Herod, her husband's brother by the same father, who was tetrarch of Galilee; to do this she parted from a living husband."[24] That John exhibited great bravery in criticizing Antipas is clear from the eventual outcome.

19-20. Herodias's desire to kill John fits well with two other events that reveal her character, or lack of it. First, she had, of course, conspired with Antipas to leave their current spouses

---

[22]Herod the Great had many wives. For discussion of the two Philips see Hoehner, "Herodian Dynasty," pp. 322-324.

[23]Ibid.

[24]Josephus, *Antiquities* 18.136. Josephus would disapprove both of the fact that a woman initiated the divorce (*Antiquities* 15.259-60) and that she married her husband's brother. In another case Josephus (*Antiquities* 17.341) observes that Archelaus, one of Antipas's brothers, married the widow of a half brother named Alexander. Even though in this case Alexander was deceased (cf. Josephus, *War* 2.114-116) the marriage was still against Mosaic law because the levirate statute only applied if there were no children born to a brother before he died. Alexander had children and so Josephus remarks "And [Archelaus] transgressed ancestral law in marrying Glaphyra, . . . who had been the wife of his brother Alexander and had borne him children, for it is abhorrent to the Jews to marry the wife of a brother."

for each other, a matter made worse by the fact that Antipas was Philip's half brother. Second, when Herodias's own brother Agrippa was later made ruler over adjoining territories and was given the title "king," she was filled with envy and pushed Antipas, against his will, into going to Rome to pursue the same title.[25] These two incidents demonstrate the selfish and opportunistic character of Herodias.

Antipas, however, feared John because he knew John was righteous and holy. Although he arrested him, he initially spared his life, protecting him from Herodias. It is quite interesting that Antipas liked to listen to John and that what John said perplexed[26] him.

21-23. The birthday banquet was probably held at the fortress in Machaerus. Josephus tells us that Herodias had a daughter from her previous marriage named Salome.[27] She was thus Herodias's daughter, but not Antipas's. The term "girl" (v. 22) and Salome's appeal to her mother for advice (v. 24) suggest that Salome was young.[28] Although the dance is usually portrayed as a sensual dance, it might have been a respectable kind of dancing.[29]

Concerning Antipas's oath, it is noteworthy that Josephus records an incident years later in which the emperor Caligula

---

[25]Josephus, *Antiquities* 18.240-252. The result was the deposition and banishment of Antipas.

[26]According to *BAGD*, p. 97, the word ἀπορέω (*aporeō*) means "to be at a loss, in doubt, uncertain." For this text Bauer suggests "he was very much disturbed." UBS[4] provides a variant reading here with a "C" rating, meaning they are uncertain which reading is correct. The NIV footnote translates the alternative "he did many things." It is hard to understand what it might mean to say "When Herod heard John, he did many things; yet he liked to listen to him."

[27]According to some ancient witnesses to v. 22, Herodias's daughter is here named Herodias. The UBS[4] text chooses this reading, but gives their choice a "C" rating indicating their uncertainty. Since Josephus, *Antiquities* 18.136 says Herodias had a daughter named Salome from her previous marriage, it seems best not to adopt the reading which identifies the dancing girl as being named Herodias. See Hoehner, *Herod Antipas*, pp. 151-154.

[28]Hoehner, *Herod Antipas*, pp. 154-156, suggests twelve to fourteen.

[29]Ibid., pp. 156-157.

made a somewhat similar oath to Agrippa I at a banquet in Rome. According to Josephus, "while he was relaxed with wine and while his mood was unusually genial," Caligula offered to Agrippa "any service that can add its weight in the scale of prosperity."[30] Both promises were rash and led their makers to do something they did not want to do.

24-28. With the incredible possibility of asking for virtually anything, Herodias advised her daughter to ask for the head of the Baptist. Lane suggests that the idea of putting John's head on a platter was "an expression of black humor inspired by the banquet yet in progress."[31]

Antipas's need to fulfill his rash oath because of the witnesses (v. 26) is paralleled in the Josephus story of Caligula's promise to Agrippa I: "Furthermore, if he repented quickly of his offer, he regarded it as unseemly to break his word before so many witnesses."[32]

29. Mark completes the story with John's burial. Antipas allowed John's disciples to take the body for burial.

D. FEEDING THE FIVE THOUSAND (6:30-44)

30The apostles gathered around Jesus and reported to him all they had done and taught. 31Then, because so many people were coming and going that they did not even have a chance to eat, he said to them, "Come with me by yourselves to a quiet place and get some rest."

32So they went away by themselves in a boat to a solitary place. 33But many who saw them leaving recognized them and ran on foot from all the towns and got there ahead of them. 34When Jesus landed and saw a large crowd, he had compassion on them, because they were like sheep without a shepherd. So he began teaching them many things.

30Josephus, Antiquities 18.293.
31Lane, p. 222.
32Josephus, Antiquities 18.299-300.

35By this time it was late in the day, so his disciples came to him. "This is a remote place," they said, "and it's already very late. 36Send the people away so they can go to the surrounding countryside and villages and buy themselves something to eat."

37But he answered, "You give them something to eat."

They said to him, "That would take eight months of a man's wages[a]! Are we to go and spend that much on bread and give it to them to eat?"

38"How many loaves do you have?" he asked. "Go and see."

When they found out, they said, "Five – and two fish."

39Then Jesus directed them to have all the people sit down in groups on the green grass. 40So they sat down in groups of hundreds and fifties. 41Taking the five loaves and the two fish and looking up to heaven, he gave thanks and broke the loaves. Then he gave them to his disciples to set before the people. He also divided the two fish among them all. 42They all ate and were satisfied, 43and the disciples picked up twelve basketfuls of broken pieces of bread and fish. 44The number of the men who had eaten was five thousand.

[a]*37* Greek *take two hundred denarii*

The initial part of this section, vv. 30-32, could be considered the conclusion of the story of the mission of the twelve, which was begun in vv. 7-13. However, the focus quickly shifts to the crowd and to the miraculous feeding.

Mark gives considerable emphasis to the two miraculous feedings (6:30-44; 8:1-10) and to the disciples' responses to them (6:35-37, 51-52; 8:4, 14-21). In each case the disciples do not see how the crowd can be fed – even on the second occasion when they have already seen Jesus feed a larger crowd. Furthermore, each case is followed by a boat scene in which the disciples' failure to understand the import of the miraculous feedings is brought out.

The disciples' failure to understand has already been identified in Mark in 4:10-13 (concerning the meaning of the parables) and in 4:41 (concerning the identity of one who could command the wind and the waves). But in connection with the feeding narratives this theme reaches a heightened intensity when Mark says "their hearts were hardened" (6:52) and portrays Jesus as upbraiding them for their lack of understanding (8:17-21).

The importance of the story of the feeding of the five thousand is underscored by the fact that it appears in all four Gospels (Matt 14:13-21; Luke 9:10-17; John 6:1-13). John especially focuses attention on it by providing a lengthy discussion of its aftermath (6:14-15, 22-71).

There is a parallel to the miraculous feedings in 2 Kings 4:42-44: "A man came from Baal Shalishah, bring the man of God [Elisha] twenty loaves of barley bread baked from the first ripe grain, along with some heads of new grain. 'Give it to the people to eat,' Elisha said. 'How can I set this before a hundred men?' his servant asked. But Elisha answered, 'Give it to the people to eat. For this is what the Lord says: 'They will eat and have some left over.'' Then he set it before them, and they ate and had some left over, according to the word of the Lord." Of course, the miracle performed by Jesus was on a much grander scale.

30-32. Except for 3:14, where there is some question due to a textual variant, v. 30 is the only place in Mark in which "the twelve" (a designation used in 4:10; 6:7; 9:35; 10:32; 11:11; 14:10, 17, 20, 43) are identified as "the apostles." Perhaps the term "apostle" seems especially appropriate to Mark in these two contexts, one in which Jesus chooses those who will be "sent" (3:14, ἀποστέλλω, *apostellō*), and one in which they return from being "sent" (6:7, using the same Greek verb).

As Mark has frequently indicated on previous occasions (1:33, 45; 2:2, 13; 3:7-10, 20; 4:1; 5:24), Jesus was again inundated with crowds. As in 3:20, the crowds were even keeping him and the twelve from finding time to eat. Therefore, Jesus and the apostles left in a boat to find a deserted place along the shores of the lake (cf. v. 35), a place where they might rest.

33-34. These verses once again indicate the tremendous crowds following Jesus. Mark says they ran from all the towns. Jesus had compassion on them because they were like sheep without a shepherd, an image that would be familiar to ancient readers. Sheep were not kept in fenced plots of land, but were herded in open territory. Without a shepherd to herd them, lead them to food and water, and protect them, they would be in serious trouble. Despite Jesus' efforts to find a place of solitude for rest, his compassion (cf. 1:41; 8:2) compelled him to teach the crowds.

35-37. As darkness drew near the disciples became concerned about the crowd's need for food (and perhaps their own – see v. 31). They suggested Jesus dismiss the crowd so that they could go to find food. It is understandable on this first occasion before Jesus had performed a feeding miracle that the disciples were baffled by his suggestion that they provide the food. They presumed he was suggesting they go somewhere and buy it. They estimated that it would take two hundred denarii worth of bread to feed such a crowd. One denarius was a day's wages for a common laborer, and so the NIV translators estimate two hundred denarii at eight months of a man's wages.

38-41. According to John 6:9 the five loaves of bread and two fish came from a boy in the crowd. Jesus instructed his disciples to seat the people in groups of hundreds and fifties, apparently to facilitate the distribution of the food. Some consider Mark's statements "taking the five loaves . . . gave thanks and broke the loaves. Then he gave them to his disciples to set before the people" to be deliberate parallels to the description of the inauguration of the Lord's Supper in Mark 14:22, when he "took bread, gave thanks and broke it, and gave it to his disciples."[33] The language is similar, but so is the

---

[33]See the list in Guelich, p. 342.

language of Acts 27:35 where Paul encouraged the men on board a ship in a storm to eat and "took some bread and gave thanks to God in front of them all. Then he broke it and began to eat." Giving thanks before a meal and breaking loaves of bread for eating were common activities that do not necessarily have overtones of the Lord's Supper.[34]

42-44. According to Matt 14:21 the number five thousand includes only the men and does not include the women and children who were present. Mark, Luke, and John are consistent with this because in each case they use the term usually used for males in particular (ἀνήρ, *anēr*) rather than the generic term (ἄνθρωπος, *anthrōpos*) which often includes women. The term used here for the twelve baskets (κόφινος, *kophinos*) differs from the term used for the seven baskets (σπυρίς, *spyris*) in the account of the feeding of the four thousand.[35] In both cases the point of referring to the baskets is to emphasize that after everyone had plenty to eat there was still food left over.

E. WALKING ON THE WATER (6:45-52)

45Immediately Jesus made his disciples get into the boat and go on ahead of him to Bethsaida, while he dismissed the crowd. 46After leaving them, he went up on a mountainside to pray.

47When evening came, the boat was in the middle of the lake, and he was alone on land. 48He saw the disciples straining at the oars, because the wind was against them. About the fourth watch of the night he went out to them, walking on the lake. He was about to pass by them, 49but when they saw him walking on the lake, they thought he was a ghost. They cried out, 50because they all saw him and were terrified.

[34]Guelich, p. 342.

[35]*BAGD*, p. 447, cites Juvenal 3.14; 6.542 as providing evidence that *kophinoi* were typical for the Jews.

Immediately he spoke to them and said, "Take courage! It is I. Don't be afraid." [51]Then he climbed into the boat with them, and the wind died down. They were completely amazed, [52]for they had not understood about the loaves; their hearts were hardened.

This is the second major boat scene in which the disciples have a significant encounter with Jesus (cf. 4:35-41; 8:14-21). This story appears in Matthew (14:22-33), Mark, and John (6:16-21), but not in Luke. The focal point of the story is the disciples' failure to understand Jesus' identity.

45-46. Jesus made his disciples go on ahead to Bethsaida, although according to Mark 6:53 they did not go to Bethsaida, but to Gennesaret. Bethsaida was located somewhere close to where the Jordan enters the northeast portion of the Sea of Galilee.[36] Gennesaret may refer to a plain on the west shore (southwest of Capernaum)[37] or to a small village (probably ancient Chinnereth, Josh 19:35) located on the plain. Presumably the storm had something to do with their altered destination.

Jesus went alone to pray on a mountain. This is the second portrayal of Jesus praying alone in Mark. In the first, Mark 1:35, he sought solitude in a desert place early in the morning. Now he seeks solitude once again, but on a mountain, and in the late evening. The reference in v. 48 to the fourth watch of the night indicates that Jesus prayed extensively – the fourth watch was from 3:00 to 6:00 A.M.[38]

47-50. Mark says that Jesus saw the disciples struggling to row against the wind and that he "went towards them" (NRSV). It therefore seems strange for him to say that Jesus

---

[36]The exact location of Bethsaida is unknown. Some argue that there were two Bethsaidas: Bethsaida-Julias (Mark 8:23; Luke 9:10) and Bethsaida of Galilee (Mark 6:45 and other Gospel references). See McRay, *Archaeology*, p. 169; Rousseau and Arav, *Jesus and His World*, pp. 19-22.

[37]Gundry, p. 344.

[38]E.g., Guelich, p. 349. Cf. Brown, p. 606.

"intended to pass by them" (v. 48, NRSV).[39] Many recent interpreters do not interpret "he intended to pass them by" in a literal sense. Instead, they understand Mark to be using language based upon the appearances of God in Exod 33:19-23; 34:6; and 1 Kgs 19:11. In these cases God "passes by" Moses and then Elijah as part of a revelation of himself to them. It is argued that this phrase as well as Jesus' walking on the water is intended to draw a parallel between Jesus and God.[40] Interestingly, Job 9:8, 11 also juxtaposes the ideas of God "passing by" and "treading on the waves." In my opinion the reference to Jesus walking on water is intended as a parallel to God's sovereignty over the waves (Job 9:8; 38:16; Ps 77:20; Sir 24:5-6). But the reference to Jesus' intention to "pass them by" is more problematic. I am inclined to agree with some of the older commentators who took the phrase literally.[41] Jesus knew the disciples would weather the storm and he did not plan to stop at the boat.

The fourth watch of the night begins at 3:00 A.M. When the disciples saw Jesus, it was dark and the wind and the waves were up. Their guess that they were seeing a ghost is probably what many modern people would suppose in similar circumstances. It was not easy to dismiss as a figment of the imagination, for they all saw it.

The middle portion of Jesus' assurance, "It is I" (ἐγώ εἰμι, *egō eimi*), could be translated "I am." It is commonly interpreted as an allusion to God's declaration of his identity in Exod 3:14: "I AM WHO I AM. This is what you are to say to the Israelites: 'I AM has sent me to you.'"[42] However, "It is I" is a perfectly natural reply to the supposition that he was a

---

[39]The NIV's "He was about to pass by them" obscures the intentional aspect of ἤθελεν (*ēthelen*), he "wanted or wished or intended" to pass by them.

[40]Guelich, pp. 350-351; Gundry, p. 336.

[41]E.g., McGarvey, p. 305: "[Mark] pictures Jesus as walking in a direction which would have missed the vessel."

[42]Lane, p. 237; Gundry, p. 337.

ghost.[43] "It's not a ghost," Jesus implied. No, "it is I."

51-52. In 4:39, Jesus rebuked the wind and it ceased. Here, it ceased when he entered the boat. Presumably the disciples' amazement concerned both the walking on water and the wind ceasing. On the prior occasion, when Jesus calmed the storm, they were terrified and asked, "Who is this? Even the wind and waves obey him!" In this second boat scene Mark seems to expect them to know the answer and not to be so astounded. He explains that they were astounded because "they had not understood about the loaves." As indicated in the introductory comments to the feeding of the five thousand, Mark gives special importance to the miraculous feedings as particularly important pointers to Jesus' identity.

Instead of understanding, "their hearts were hardened." In 3:5, Mark writes concerning the scribes who opposed Jesus that "he was grieved at their hardness of heart." But it is not only Jesus' opponents who suffer from this malady. Here in chapter 6 (cf. 8:17) it is also the disciples. In 10:5 Jesus attributes Moses' permission of divorce to "your hardness of heart," indicating that this condition existed in many from Moses' day to his own. Mark's reference to the disciples' hardness of heart is his strongest indication yet of their failure to understand Jesus.

F. HEALING AT GENNESARET AND BEYOND (6:53-56)

53When they had crossed over, they landed at Gennesaret and anchored there. 54As soon as they got out of the boat, people recognized Jesus. 55They ran throughout that whole region and carried the sick on mats to wherever they heard he was. 56And wherever he went – into villages, towns or countryside – they placed the sick in the marketplaces.

---

[43]Although Gundry, p. 337, supports the view that Jesus' statement is to be associated with the name of God, he questions "whether Mark's original readers understood, or were expected to understand, this association."

They begged him to let them touch even the edge of his cloak, and all who touched him were healed.

Once again Mark provides a brief summary of a portion of Jesus' ministry (cf. 1:39, 45; 3:7-12; 6:6). Again, there is a strong emphasis on the crowds and on Jesus' power to heal.

53. The boat did not land at Bethsaida but at Gennesaret (cf. v. 45).

54-55. The description in these verses is quite similar to v. 33. Jesus was a public person known especially for his power to heal. Wherever he was recognized, crowds flocked to him and brought the sick to be healed.

56. On Jesus' healing those who touched him see 3:10 and 5:25-34. These healings may be compared with those of Peter in Acts 5:15 ("people brought the sick into the streets and laid them on beds and mats so that at least Peter's shadow might fall on some of them as he passed by") and Paul in Acts 19:11-12 ("God did extraordinary miracles through Paul, so that even handkerchiefs and aprons that had touched him were taken to the sick, and their illnesses were cured and the evil spirits left them").

MARK 7

G. THE CONTROVERSY OVER EATING WITH UNWASHED HANDS (7:1-23)

[1]The Pharisees and some of the teachers of the law who had come from Jerusalem gathered around Jesus and [2]saw some of his disciples eating food with hands that were "unclean," that is, unwashed. [3](The Pharisees and all the Jews do not eat unless they give their hands a ceremonial washing, holding to the tradition of the elders. [4]When they come from the marketplace they do not eat unless they wash. And they observe many other traditions, such as the washing of cups, pitchers and kettles.[a])

[5]So the Pharisees and teachers of the law asked Jesus, "Why don't your disciples live according to the tradition of the elders instead of eating their food with 'unclean' hands?"

[6]He replied, "Isaiah was right when he prophesied about you hypocrites; as it is written:

" 'These people honor me with their lips,
but their hearts are far from me.
[7]They worship me in vain;
their teachings are but rules taught by men.'[b]

[8]You have let go of the commands of God and are holding on to the traditions of men."

[9]And he said to them: "You have a fine way of setting aside the commands of God in order to observe[c] your own traditions! [10]For Moses said, 'Honor your father and your mother,'[d] and, 'Anyone who curses his father or mother

must be put to death.'[e] [11]But you say that if a man says to his father or mother: 'Whatever help you might otherwise have received from me is Corban' (that is, a gift devoted to God), [12]then you no longer let him do anything for his father or mother. [13]Thus you nullify the word of God by your tradition that you have handed down. And you do many things like that."

[14]Again Jesus called the crowd to him and said, "Listen to me, everyone, and understand this. [15]Nothing outside a man can make him 'unclean' by going into him. Rather, it is what comes out of a man that makes him 'unclean.'"[f]

[17]After he had left the crowd and entered the house, his disciples asked him about this parable. [18]"Are you so dull?" he asked. "Don't you see that nothing that enters a man from the outside can make him 'unclean'? [19]For it doesn't go into his heart but into his stomach, and then out of his body." (In saying this, Jesus declared all foods "clean.")

[20]He went on: "What comes out of a man is what makes him 'unclean.' [21]For from within, out of men's hearts, come evil thoughts, sexual immorality, theft, murder, adultery, [22]greed, malice, deceit, lewdness, envy, slander, arrogance and folly. [23]All these evils come from inside and make a man 'unclean.'"

[a]*4* Some early manuscripts *pitchers, kettles and dining couches* [b]*6,7* Isaiah 29:13 [c]*9* Some manuscripts *set up* [d]*10* Exodus 20:12; Deut. 5:16 [e]*10* Exodus 21:17; Lev. 20:9 [f]*15* Some early manuscripts *'unclean.' [16]If anyone has ears to hear, let him hear.*

Mark 2:1-3:6 contained a series of five controversies between Jesus and the religious authorities which culminated in their decision to plot Jesus' death. His opponents appeared again in 3:22 to accuse Jesus of being possessed and working miracles through the power of Beelzebub. Now they appear with another criticism.

1-4. As in 3:22 the religious authorities in this case had come from Jerusalem. They obviously came looking for a fight. They found it in the issue of ritual handwashing.

The Old Testament is deeply concerned with religious cleanliness. Although it does not command ritual handwashing for the people in general, it does require the priests to wash their hands and feet before entering the tabernacle (Exod 30:17-21). It takes the matter quite seriously, commanding them to "wash their hands and feet so that they will not die," and saying "this is to be a lasting ordinance for Aaron and his descendants for the generations to come" (30:21). At some point before the first century this practice was expanded beyond its original setting of tabernacle worship and beyond the original focus on the priests. Mark explains in vv. 3-4 that handwashing had become quite popular among the Jews along with washing a variety of objects.[1]

Mark (v. 3), the Pharisees and scribes (v. 5), and Jesus (vv. 6-9, 13) regard the handwashing rules as part of the "tradition of the elders." All parties recognized that these rules were not commanded in the law. But it would be a mistake to take this as a indication that the practice was not viewed with great seriousness. The Pharisees took ancient traditions seriously. Josephus explains that this was one of the chief hallmarks of the Pharisees and a basic point of dispute between them and the Sadducees:

> the Pharisees had passed on to the people certain regulations handed down by former generations and not recorded in the Laws of Moses, for which reason they are rejected by the Sadducaean group, who hold that only those regulations should be considered valid which were written down (in Scripture), and that those which had been handed down by former generations need not be observed. And concerning these matters the two parties came to have controversies and serious differences . . . [in which] the Pharisees have the support of the masses.[2]

---

[1]See Sanders, *Judaism*, pp. 222-230, for a fine summary of the widespread evidence of the use of immersion pools *(miqva'ot)* among the Jews. Many Jews of Jesus' time participated not only in washing hands or objects, but also in ritual immersions.

[2]Josephus, *Antiquities* 13.297.

(The last comment by Josephus indicates that many Jews would be sympathetic with the Pharisees' criticisms of Jesus.) There is continuing scholarly debate over whether the Pharisees of Jesus' day believed that the traditions could be traced to Moses and thus had equal status to the written word of Moses.[3] But there is no debate that they considered the traditions of the elders to be ancient and to be quite important.

There are several technical difficulties in vv. 3-4. In v. 3 the phrase translated "give their hands a ceremonial washing" cannot be translated precisely, although it certainly has to do with handwashing.[4] In v. 4a translational difficulties make it hard to decide whether to accept the NIV's "When they come from the marketplace they do not eat unless they wash" or the NRSV's "and they do not eat anything from the market unless they wash it."[5] At the end of v. 4, some ancient witnesses to the text add "and dining couches" (which could be translated – as in the NRSV note – "and beds") as the final item in the list of items which were washed.

5. As in 2:23-24 the religious authorities expected Jesus to instruct his disciples and took their behavior as indicative of his views. This assumption was correct on both occasions. Concerning the tradition of the elders see the comments above on v. 3.

6-8. Jesus did not begin by replying to their specific criticism, but began with a critique of their emphasis on the tradition of the elders. He argued that they had come to adhere to their traditions even to the point of contradicting the will of God. He supported his claim by a quotation from Isaiah and an illustration from scribal tradition.

The quotation is from the LXX of Isa 29:13. Like Isaiah's contemporaries, some of the Pharisees and scribes gave only lip service to honoring God, because instead of doing God's will they followed "rules taught by men." Therefore, their

---

[3]See Sanders, *Judaism*, pp. 423-424, who argues that they did not.

[4]Guelich, pp. 364-365.

[5]Ibid., p. 365.

claim to honor God was hypocritical. Sincere worshippers of God do his commandments.

9-13. Jesus now illustrates the point by using the tradition of the Corban oath. Josephus speaks of this oath twice, on one occasion speaking of "those who describe themselves as 'Corban' to God – meaning what Greeks would call 'a gift'," [6] and on the other occasion describing "the oath called 'Corban'" as "found in no other nation except the Jews, and, translated from the Hebrew, one may interpret it as meaning 'God's gift.'" [7] The Corban vow seems to have been used both for persons and for possessions and it declared them to be a gift to God. At least in some cases possessions which were declared Corban could still be used, but could not be given to others.[8]

The first citation in v. 10 is the fifth of the ten commandments as found in Exod 20:12 and Deut 5:16. The second is from either Exod 21:17 or Lev 20:9. The significance Moses gave to these commandments is indicated by the fact that "Honor your father and mother" is one of the ten fundamental commandments and that cursing father or mother brings the death penalty (Exod 20:12; 21:15, 17). Jesus understood the command to honor one's parents to imply more than verbal commendations or even obedience. In his understanding honoring included taking care of one's parents. The Corban tradition, when applied to parents, prohibited a man from caring for his father or mother.[9] Therefore it led to violations of the commandments given by Moses.

---

[6]Josephus, *Antiquities* 4.73.

[7]Josephus, *Against Apion* 1.167. See also Philo, *Special Laws* 2.16-17.

[8]Joseph A. Fitzmyer, "The Aramaic Qorban Inscription form Jebel Hallet et-Turi and Mark 7:11/Matt. 15:5," *Journal of Biblical Literature* 78 (1959): 60-65, cites an inscription on a Jewish ossuary from near the time of Jesus: "All that a man may find-to-his-profit in this ossuary (is) an offering to God from him who is within it." The items in the ossuary were to be left there because they had been declared Corban.

[9]Although there are dating problems in applying the Mishnah (c. A.D. 200) to Jesus' time, there is an interesting parallel in the Mishnah *Nedarim* 5:6 which speaks of "a man at Beth Horon, whose father was forbidden by

Jesus' main point is clear from v. 9 and v. 13. The Corban illustration was one of many in which the religious authorities kept their traditions and in so doing violated the commands of God.

14-15. Vv. 6-13 are addressed to the Pharisees and the teachers of the law. Jesus now addresses the crowd and replies to the specific objection concerning handwashing. The reply is a metaphorical saying characterized in v. 17 as a parable. It is explained in vv. 18-23. V. 16 ("If anyone has ears to hear, let him hear") is omitted from the NIV because it is missing from the best ancient witnesses and was probably added to Mark by a scribe.

17-23. As in 4:10 the disciples asked Jesus to explain the parable. In his explanation the emphasis falls on the contrast between that which enters and goes out from a person's digestive tract vs. that which goes out from a person's heart. The handwashing rules focus on the food that enters and departs from the stomach. Jesus is concerned with what originates in and departs from the heart.

To identify the things that are truly unclean Jesus provides a list of vices. The NRSV translation is probably correct in taking the first item, translated "evil thoughts" in the NIV, as an umbrella term that includes all the following items.[10] Most of the items are easily understood from the NIV translation. The second word in v. 22, "malice," translates a broad Greek word (πονηρία, *ponēria*) that could be translated "wickedness" or "sinfulness."[11] The fourth word, "lewdness," translates the word traditionally translated "licentiousness" (ἀσέλγεια, *aselgeia*). Another possibility would be "sensuality."[12] "Envy" translates an idiom (ὀφθαλμὸς πονηρός, *ophthalmos ponēros*), literally "the evil eye." As in most such lists, some items are

---

vow to have any benefit from him." All translations of the Mishnah are from Herbert Danby, *The Mishnah* (Oxford, Eng.: Clarendon Press, 1933).

[10]"For it is from within, from the human heart, that evil intentions come: fornication, theft, murder . . . ."

[11]*BAGD*, p. 690.

[12]*BAGD*, pp. 114-115.

vague or broad (e.g., wickedness) and some are overlapping (e.g., sexual immorality and adultery).

Mark's editorial observation in v. 19b, "In saying this, Jesus declared all foods 'clean,'" raises a question. Did Jesus intend for the crowd addressed in vv. 14-15 or even the disciples addressed in vv. 18-23 to quit observing the Old Testament dietary laws? This conclusion seems unlikely on at least three grounds. First, it is not consistent with Jesus' attitude toward the law as expressed in Matt 5:19: "Anyone who breaks one of the least of these commandments and teaches others to do the same will be called least in the kingdom of heaven." Second, the disciples did not know that Christians do not have to observe the dietary laws until well after Jesus' death (see, e.g., Acts 10:15 where Peter tells the Lord, "I have never eaten anything impure or unclean"). Third, the issue raised by the religious authorities was one even they recognized to be part of the traditions of the elders and not part of the law. The context suggests that Jesus' remarks should be applied primarily to traditions and not the law. In this very context he upholds the law vs. the traditions (vv. 6-13).

How, then, is Mark's comment to be understood? His remark that Jesus declared all foods "clean" clearly undermines the Old Testament dietary laws. The best understanding is probably that Mark sees the fuller implications of Jesus' words from the standpoint of later revelation.[13] In the original context Jesus was specifically addressing the traditions of the elders. But the principle he advocated had implications for the dietary laws and eventually God revealed to the church that the dietary laws were optional for Christians. Jewish Christians could and did continue to observe them. But they were not to be bound upon Gentile Christians. In the light of this further revelation, Mark correctly observes the ultimate implications of Jesus' principle contrasting the stomach and the heart.

---

[13]Lane, pp. 255-256.

H. THE SYROPHOENICIAN WOMAN (7:24-30)

[24]Jesus left that place and went to the vicinity of Tyre.[a]
He entered a house and did not want anyone to know it; yet
he could not keep his presence secret. [25]In fact, as soon as
she heard about him, a woman whose little daughter was
possessed by an evil[b] spirit came and fell at his feet. [26]The
woman was a Greek, born in Syrian Phoenicia. She begged
Jesus to drive the demon out of her daughter.

[27]"First let the children eat all they want," he told her,
"for it is not right to take the children's bread and toss it to
their dogs."

[28]"Yes, Lord," she replied, "but even the dogs under the
table eat the children's crumbs."

[29]Then he told her, "For such a reply, you may go; the
demon has left your daughter."

[30]She went home and found her child lying on the bed,
and the demon gone.

[a]*24* Many early manuscripts *Tyre and Sidon* **[b]*25* Greek *unclean***

In the predominantly Gentile region of the Decapolis Jesus encountered swineherds who must have been Gentiles and a demoniac who probably was (5:1-20). Now he goes to another predominantly Gentile area and encounters a woman that Mark explicitly describes as a Gentile. Part of Mark's purpose in identifying her background is to set the stage for the woman's remarkable display of faith. The woman's Gentile status is the obstacle her faith must overcome.

24. Jesus went to the region of Tyre[14] in a deliberate attempt to get away from the crowds in Galilee. Tyre was a coastal city in Phoenicia, which was at that time part of the Roman province of Syria. As when he entered the Decapolis, he was once again leaving the predominantly Jewish territory of Galilee. He wanted to keep his presence in Phoenicia a

[14]Or, "Tyre and Sidon."

secret, but again (cf. 6:31-33) his plans were thwarted.

25-26. The woman who learned of Jesus' presence was a Greek born in Phoenicia in the Roman province of Syria. Mark wants to make it clear that she was a Gentile (see vv. 27-30). She had a young daughter who was possessed by an unclean spirit (v. 25) or demon (v. 26). She had obviously heard of Jesus' miraculous powers and she bowed at his feet hoping he would cast the demon from her daughter.

27-28. Jesus' response takes the form of a proverb. The Matthean parallel (Matt 15:24 "I was sent only to the lost sheep of the house of Israel") makes it clear that in the proverb the children represent the Jews and the dogs represent the Gentiles. But this is not the same as using the term "dogs" as a racial slur.[15] The form of his statement is proverbial.[16] And the basis of the proverb is not an antipathy for Gentiles, but the necessary Jewish focus of Jesus' earthly ministry. Of course the eventual outcome of his ministry was meant to include the Gentiles.

Surprisingly, the woman not only seems to have understood the basic import of the proverb,[17] but she overcame the obstacle it presented. She replied by extending it. She recognized the priority of feeding the children, but all she wanted was a crumb from the table.

29-30. Jesus was impressed by her response. It was, after all, extraordinary. It demonstrated both insight ("For such a reply") and faith (as explicitly mentioned in Matt 15:28

---

[15]The word translated "dogs" is the diminutive form of the word (κυνάριον, *kynarion*) rather than the form that would typically be used in calling someone a "dog" as a derogatory term (κύων, *kyōn*). Lane, p. 262. *BAGD*, p. 457, observes that the diminutive form can be used to identify "a house-dog or lap-dog in contrast to a dog of the street or farm" or it can be used "with no diminutive force at all." The woman's reply shows that she understood Jesus' use here to have diminutive force.

[16]Perhaps an illustration would be helpful. Suppose one man (Mr. A) asks another (Mr. B) whether to bring up a touchy issue with his wife. Mr. B replies with the proverb, "Let sleeping dogs lie." Mr. B has not thereby called Mrs. A a dog.

[17]Although she may have erroneously viewed Jesus as a racist.

"Woman, you have great faith!"). It is presumably the woman's demonstration of faith that attracted Mark to this story. The importance of faith has already been emphasized repeatedly (1:15; 2:5; 4:40; 5:34, 36; 6:6). The miracle itself is also rather striking. Jesus exorcised the demon without going to the woman's house.

I. HEALING A DEAF MAN WITH A SPEECH IMPEDIMENT (7:31-37)

**31Then Jesus left the vicinity of Tyre and went through
Sidon, down to the Sea of Galilee and into the region of the
Decapolis.[a] 32There some people brought to him a man who
was deaf and could hardly talk, and they begged him to
place his hand on the man.**

**33After he took him aside, away from the crowd, Jesus put
his fingers into the man's ears. Then he spit and touched
the man's tongue. 34He looked up to heaven and with a deep
sigh said to him, "Ephphatha!" (which means, "Be
opened!"). 35At this, the man's ears were opened, his tongue
was loosened and he began to speak plainly.**

**36Jesus commanded them not to tell anyone. But the
more he did so, the more they kept talking about it. 37People
were overwhelmed with amazement. "He has done everything well," they said. "He even makes the deaf hear and the
mute speak."**

[a]*31* That is, the Ten Cities

This, the ninth specific healing (including exorcisms) recorded by Mark, is the first miraculous healing found in Mark alone.

31. The route Jesus took when he left the region of Tyre is unusual. Sidon is a coastal Phoenician city twenty miles north of Tyre – not south as one would expect if Jesus was going to the Decapolis or the Sea of Galilee. Unfortunately, it is not clear from the Greek text of Mark exactly how the references to the Sea of Galilee and to the Decapolis relate to each other.[18] The NRSV translation "towards the Sea of Galilee, in the region of the Decapolis" is possible, but it is problematic to describe the Sea as "in the region of the Decapolis," since the Decapolis only borders the southern and eastern shores of the Sea. The NIV translation proposes that the Decapolis was Jesus' ultimate destination, but the Greek text (εἰς τὴν θάλασσαν τῆς Γαλιλαίας, *eis tēn thalassan tēs Galilaias*) appears to favor the Sea as the ultimate destination. The best translation is perhaps that of the RSV: "[he] went through Sidon to the Sea of Galilee, through the region of the Decapolis." This route to the Sea would avoid the province of Galilee and its crowds.[19]

32. The NIV translation "there" suggests "there in the Decapolis." This translation assumes the NIV's questionable translation of the last part of v. 31. It is actually not a translation because there is no word meaning "there" in the Greek text. As is customary for Mark he simply begins the sentence with "and." Since the last part of v. 31 probably indicates that Jesus passed through the Decapolis to the Sea, the location of the healing in 7:32-37 is simply left unspecified.

The man they brought to Jesus was deaf. The Greek term μογιλάλος (*mogilalos*) may mean that he was mute, completely unable to speak, or, more probably, that he had a speech impediment and spoke with difficulty.[20] The people were apparently familiar with Jesus healing by laying his hand on the person (cf. 6:5).

33-34. Mark does not explain why Jesus took the man away from the crowd. It is possible that the motivation is revealed in v. 36 when Mark says "Jesus commanded them not to tell anyone." If Jesus did not want the crowd to know that he healed the man, this is another case of his intentions being thwarted (vv. 36-37).

---

[18]See the discussion in Guelich, p. 392.

[19]Lane, p. 265.

[20]*BAGD*, p. 525.

Touching the man's ears and tongue seems natural enough to modern readers since he was deaf and had a speech impediment. We know from other miracles that Jesus could heal without touching, but that he often touched those whom he healed. The touching here is appropriate to the problems. Modern readers are surprised by the use of saliva,[21] but ancient readers would probably have found this technique appropriate. Ancient parallels suggest two relevant uses of saliva. First, saliva was understood by some to have medicinal properties.[22] Second, saliva was sometimes used in miraculous healings.[23] There may be a parallel between the use of saliva in 7:33 and 8:23 and the use of oil in 6:13.

Jesus' looking up into heaven is paralleled in 6:41 when he blessed the loaves. His sighing is paralleled in 8:12 when he expresses frustration with the Pharisees. Here it seems to be a natural expression of emotion.[24] His use of the Aramaic "Ephphatha!" ("Be Opened!") is similar to the use of Aramaic in 5:41 in raising Jairus's daughter from the dead.

35. Mark spells out the results of the miracle. The man could now hear and he could speak plainly.

36-37. It is difficult to determine the antecedent of "them" in Mark's description of Jesus' command. Since Jesus took the man aside, away from the crowd, one could suppose that "them" meant this man and others like him – that is, those whom Jesus healed in private. On the other hand, the reference to the crowd in v. 37 suggests that Jesus might have been

---

[21]Jesus also used saliva to heal the blind man in Mark 10:22-26, this time on his eyes.

[22]E.g., the first century author Pliny the Elder (*Natural History* 28.7.37) considered human saliva to be an effective eye ointment against ophthalmia.

[23]E.g., Tacitus (c. A.D. 55-120) describes an incident in which the emperor Vespasian (who ruled from A.D. 69-79) supposedly healed a blind man with his saliva. Tacitus, *Histories* 4.81. For additional material on the use of saliva in antiquity see Blackburn, *Theios Aner*, pp. 218-219.

[24]See Blackburn, *Theios Aner*, pp. 216-218, vs. those who use materials from over three centuries later to argue that sighing was a common healing technique.

instructing them. But why would Jesus tell "crowds" not to tell about his healings? In that case it would seem that crowds of people already know. I am inclined to take "them" in v. 36 to refer to the deaf man and others healed in private. Despite Jesus' command to the healed man and others like him, they told the crowds, who marveled at Jesus' power. The last part of v. 37 alludes to Isa 35:5-6 ("Then will the eyes of the blind be opened and the ears of the deaf unstopped. Then will the lame leap like a deer, and the mute tongue shout for joy.")

MARK 8

J. FEEDING THE FOUR THOUSAND (8:1-10)

[1]During those days another large crowd gathered. Since they had nothing to eat, Jesus called his disciples to him and said, [2]"I have compassion for these people; they have already been with me three days and have nothing to eat. [3]If I send them home hungry, they will collapse on the way, because some of them have come a long distance."

[4]His disciples answered, "But where in this remote place can anyone get enough bread to feed them?"

[5]"How many loaves do you have?" Jesus asked.

"Seven," they replied.

[6]He told the crowd to sit down on the ground. When he had taken the seven loaves and given thanks, he broke them and gave them to his disciples to set before the people, and they did so. [7]They had a few small fish as well; he gave thanks for them also and told the disciples to distribute them. [8]The people ate and were satisfied. Afterward the disciples picked up seven basketfuls of broken pieces that were left over. [9]About four thousand men were present. And having sent them away, [10]he got into the boat with his disciples and went to the region of Dalmanutha.

See the comments on 6:30-44 for the importance Mark gives to the two feeding miracles. All four Gospels provide an account of the feeding of the five thousand. Mark and Matthew also record the feeding of the four thousand. The two stories are largely parallel, although this second account is briefer because it provides less detail. This is the fourth of the nature miracles of Mark (cf. 4:35-41; 6:30-52).

1-3. "During those days" is a fairly weak chronological link used by Mark here and in 1:9. In 8:9, Mark will be more specific about how large the crowd was. It is not clear from Jesus' comments whether the crowd had been totally without food for three days or perhaps had run out of whatever food was available. In any event they had little food at that time. The NIV translation suggests that the comment about collapsing on the way home applied only to those who had come from a long distance. However, the word translated "because" is Mark's favorite conjunction καί (*kai*) which should probably be translated as in the NRSV "*and* some of them have come from a great distance." Jesus was concerned about all of the crowd being weak from hunger. This is Mark's third reference to Jesus' compassion (1:41; 6:34).

4. On the occasion of the first feeding miracle it seemed quite natural for the disciples to ask how the crowds could be fed (6:37). Now that they have seen Jesus feed five thousand their question is surprising. But in 6:52 Mark said that "they had not understood about the loaves; their hearts were hardened." That statement in its context apparently applied primarily to the disciples' failure to understand the implications of the miraculous multiplication of the loaves for the identity of Jesus. But perhaps it also has some applicability to their failure to immediately consider Jesus' ability to feed the four thousand in light of his previous feeding of five thousand.

5-7. At the feeding of the five thousand there were five loaves. This time there are seven. The difference is insignificant as further indicated by Mark's lack of concern to specify the number of fish involved in the second feeding miracle. Concerning the improbable suggestion that the language of vv. 6-7 alludes to the Lord's Supper see the comments on 6:41.

8. This time seven basketfulls were collected.[1] Some com-

---

[1]Concerning the differing terms for baskets for the two miraculous feedings see the comments on 6:42-44.

mentators have allegorized the twelve baskets as referring to the Jews (the twelve tribes) and the seven as referring to the Gentiles (the number seven signifying the completion achieved by including the Gentiles with the Jews). This allegorizing is based upon the unlikely suggestion that the four thousand were predominately Gentiles.[2] It would be difficult to decide where to stop this allegorizing. Does Mark also have allegorical intent for the five vs. four thousand, or the five vs. seven loaves?

9-10. Matt 15:38 says that the count of four thousand included only the men and not the women and children (cf. Matt 14:21). Evidently the "remote place" (ἐρημία, *erēmia*) or "desert" (NRSV) where the crowd was gathered (v. 4) was near the Sea of Galilee. Jesus and the disciples again entered a boat on the Sea. There is a textual variant in the ancient witnesses to Mark's text concerning where they went. The best supported reading is the region of Dalmanutha, a place unknown outside of Mark's Gospel. Some ancient witnesses to Mark support Magadan or Magdala,[3] the readings attested for the parallel in Matt 15:39. The best witnesses to Matthew have Magadan, while others read Magdala. The locations of Dalmanutha and Magadan are unknown. Magdala was on the western shore of the Sea near Tiberias. A location on the west shore fits the subsequent references in Mark which indicate that Bethsaida, a city northeast of the Sea, was on the other side (8:13, 22).

K. THE PHARISEES DEMAND A SIGN (8:11-13)

11The Pharisees came and began to question Jesus. To test him, they asked him for a sign from heaven. 12He sighed

---

[2]Which in turn is based on the assumption that this miraculous feeding occurred in the Decapolis. This is an uncertain assumption (see the comments on 7:31-32). Furthermore, although the Decapolis was predominantly a Gentile region, many Jews lived there (Lane, p. 266).

[3]The evidence is complicated and involves several different spellings of Magadan.

deeply and said, "Why does this generation ask for a miraculous sign? I tell you the truth, no sign will be given to it."
13Then he left them, got back into the boat and crossed to the other side.

The Pharisees return to oppose Jesus once again (see 2:16, 24; 3:6; 7:5). Their question raises a problem of interpretation because Jesus' miracles are referred to as "signs" in John's Gospel and Acts 2:22, and the apostolic miracles are referred to as "signs" in Mark 16:17, 20 and often in the book of Acts. So how can the Pharisees, who have seen Jesus perform miracles, ask for a sign? And how can Jesus say that he will not provide one?

Apparently in this context the word "sign" (σημεῖον, *sēmeion*) has a special sense. Perhaps the Pharisees are asking for a sign such as God opening the heavens and declaring Jesus to be his Son. Such a sign would be more convincing than Jesus' miracles because it would require less interpretation. Such a sign was perhaps seen by a few at Jesus' baptism (John 1:32-34), was seen by three disciples at the transfiguration (Mark 9:7), and was seen in a vague and misunderstood way by a crowd in Jerusalem during the last week of Jesus' life (John 12:28-29). But no such sign was provided for Jesus' generation in general or the Pharisees in particular.

L. THE YEAST OF THE PHARISEES AND HEROD (8:14-21)

14The disciples had forgotten to bring bread, except for one loaf they had with them in the boat.
15"Be careful," Jesus warned them. "Watch out for the yeast of the Pharisees and that of Herod."

16They discussed this with one another and said, "It is because we have no bread."

17Aware of their discussion, Jesus asked them: "Why are you talking about having no bread? Do you still not see or

**understand? Are your hearts hardened? 18Do you have eyes
but fail to see, and ears but fail to hear? And don't you
remember? 19When I broke the five loaves for the five thousand, how many basketfuls of pieces did you pick up?"**

"Twelve," they replied.

**20"And when I broke the seven loaves for the four thou-
sand, how many basketfuls of pieces did you pick up?"**

They answered, "Seven."

21He said to them, "Do you still not understand?"

In this, the third boat scene with Jesus and the disciples, Mark once again portrays the disciples' lack of understanding about the feeding miracles. Immediately after the feeding of the five thousand, in connection with Jesus walking on the water, Mark says that "they had not understood about the loaves; their hearts were hardened" (6:52). Then, at the feeding of the four thousand they reveal their lack of insight by asking how anyone could feed so many people in the desert (8:4). Now, shortly after the feeding of the four thousand, they misunderstand Jesus' saying about yeast and think he is concerned about having enough bread.

14. The opening sentence of the story sets the stage for the disciples' misinterpretation of Jesus' saying. They had forgotten to bring bread to eat and had only one loaf. One loaf would not be nearly enough for everyone.

15. Jesus' metaphorical saying (which Mark would call a parable) is contextually connected to the Pharisees testing him in vv. 11-12. Along with the yeast of the Pharisees he includes the yeast of Herod Antipas.[4] The contextual connection of this saying to the Pharisees' question suggests that in some way their question might illustrate what the yeast of the Pharisees symbolized. In Luke 12:1 there is a parallel statement (in another setting) which says, "Be on your guard against the yeast of the Pharisees, which is hypocrisy." This explanation would seem to fit well in Mark's context as well.

---

[4]On Antipas see the commentary on 6:14-29.

The Pharisees asked questions, but they did not truly seek answers, except those that could be used against Jesus. Herod could presumably also be accused of hypocrisy. In Luke 13:32, Jesus refers to Herod as a "fox," a widely recognized epithet for a crafty individual.[5]

16. The disciples' misunderstanding of Jesus' saying perplexes the reader of Mark – and, as is revealed in the subsequent verses, Jesus.

17-18. The questions "Do you not see or understand?" and "Do you have eyes but fail to see, and ears but fail to hear?" recall the language of 4:12. There Jesus cited Isa 6:9-10 concerning why he spoke to outsiders in parables, "so that 'they may be ever seeing but never perceiving, and ever hearing but never understanding.'" The questions imply that the disciples are like outsiders. The question between these two, "Are your hearts hardened?" recalls Mark's specific statement in 6:52 that the disciples' hearts were hardened.

19-20. The last question of v. 18, "And don't you remember?" leads into two questions that summarize the basic facts about the miraculous feedings. Jesus first fed five thousand with five loaves and the disciples took up twelve baskets of leftovers. Then he fed four thousand with seven loaves and they took up seven baskets.

21. The point of the two review questions emerges in v. 21 through another question, "Do you still not understand?" The question Mark's reader must ask is what Jesus wanted the disciples to understand. Matthew provides an answer which seems consistent with Mark's contextual clues. According to Matt 16:11 Jesus asked, "How is it you don't understand that I was not talking to you about bread?" And Matt 16:12 adds "then they understood that he was not telling them to guard against the yeast used in bread, but against the teaching of the Pharisees." In Mark one might suppose that the larger context leading up to Peter's confession at Caesarea Philippi indicates that Jesus was speaking of understanding his identi-

[5]Fitzmyer, *Luke*, 2:1031.

ty. But the immediate context of the misunderstood parable about the yeast supports the same understanding made explicit in Matthew. Ultimately, however, the disciples' failure to understand about the loaves (which gave birth to their literalistic understanding of the yeast parable) was based on a misunderstanding about Jesus' identity as the Christ.

M. THE BLIND MAN AT BETHSAIDA (8:22-26)

22They came to Bethsaida, and some people brought a blind man and begged Jesus to touch him. 23He took the blind man by the hand and led him outside the village. When he had spit on the man's eyes and put his hands on him, Jesus asked, "Do you see anything?"

24He looked up and said, "I see people; they look like trees walking around."

25Once more Jesus put his hands on the man's eyes. Then his eyes were opened, his sight was restored, and he saw everything clearly. 26Jesus sent him home, saying, "Don't go into the village.[a]"

[a]*26* **Some manuscripts** ***Don't go and tell anyone in the village***

Like the healing of the deaf man with a speech impediment (7:31-35) the healing of the blind man at Bethsaida is found only in Mark. It is extraordinary in involving two acts of healing on Jesus' part in which the first is only partially effective. The clue to understanding this mysterious two-part healing is to be found in the context of Mark. This miracle, which at first appears to be merely another example of Jesus' healing ability, is actually an acted out parable of the disciples' stages of understanding.

22. This time the boat landed at Bethsaida (cf. 6:45, 53). The opening words of the story parallel those of the deaf man with a speech impediment. In both cases unidentified people bring a man to Jesus and beg Jesus to touch him (cf. 7:32).

23-24. The parallel to the final story of chapter 7 continues as Jesus takes the man outside the village (cf. 7:33, "away from the crowd") and makes use of saliva and touching (cf. 7:33, "Jesus put his fingers into the man's ears. Then he spit and touched the man's tongue.")[6] From v. 25 it is clear that Jesus put his hands on the blind man's eyes.

But then the story diverges from all other Gospel healings. When Jesus asked the blind man if he could see, the answer is surprising. He could see, but only vaguely. The healing was incomplete. People looked like walking trees.

25. After Jesus laid his hands upon the man's eyes a second time, he could see clearly. The mystery is in the rationale for a second act of healing. It is not in keeping with the rest of the New Testament to suppose Jesus had some sort of "power failure" on the first attempt. It might be possible to suppose that the blind man was afflicted by a failure in his faith (cf. 6:5-6), but there is a better explanation.

As noted in the commentary introduction, Mark's Gospel divides rather clearly into two sections. The first half[7] leads up to Peter's confession at Caesarea Philippi. The second half begins with Peter's acknowledgment that Jesus was the Christ and fills out the meaning of that title. Jesus is not the Christ many expected, but he has come to serve and to give his life for others. The confession of Peter, the beginning of the teachings about Jesus' suffering and death, and the beginning of the disciples' lack of understanding of a suffering Christ are found in the remainder of chapter 8, immediately after the healing of the blind man. Jesus healed the blind man in two stages as a living metaphor of the two stages through which the disciples opened their eyes to his identity and mission. In 8:27-29, when the disciples opened their eyes to see that Jesus was the Christ, they were like the blind man when

---

[6]On the use of saliva and on touching the place to be healed see the comments on 7:31-37.

[7]I am using the term "half" loosely. 1:1-8:30 is less than fifty percent of the book.

he saw men who looked like trees walking. Their eyes were opened, but they did not see clearly. Only after Jesus' death would they come to see him clearly.

N. PETER'S CONFESSION AT CAESAREA PHILIPPI (8:27-30)

27Jesus and his disciples went on to the villages around Caesarea Philippi. On the way he asked them, "Who do people say I am?"
28They replied, "Some say John the Baptist; others say Elijah; and still others, one of the prophets."
29"But what about you?" he asked. "Who do you say I am?"
Peter answered, "You are the Christ.[a]"
30Jesus warned them not to tell anyone about him.

[a]*29* Or *Messiah*. "The Christ" (Greek) and "the Messiah" (Hebrew) both mean "the Anointed One."

This story is the climax of the first half of Mark's Gospel. Although the readers of Mark know from the very first verse that Jesus is the Christ, the disciples have to come to this conclusion. Prior to Peter's confession only supernatural beings knew the complete identity of Jesus. He had revealed his identity through his proclamation of the kingdom of God, through his authoritative teaching that was not like that of the scribes, and through his miraculous powers over nature, demons, disease, and even death. But he had not proclaimed his stature as the Christ and had forbidden the demons who wanted to reveal who he was.

Peter's and the disciples' acknowledgment that Jesus was the Christ marked a significant turning point in his work with them. The second half of Mark begins as Jesus starts to teach them about his coming suffering, death, and resurrection.

27-28. Caesarea Philippi was about twenty-five miles north of Bethsaida. It was the capital city and place of residence of

Herod Philip (half brother of Herod Antipas), who ruled from 4 B.C. to A.D. 34 over the northeastern portion of what had been Herod the Great's kingdom. Philip built Caesarea Philippi and named it after himself and the emperor.[8]

When Jesus asked about who the people said he was, the disciples' description echoed the opinions expressed in 6:14. See the comments there for discussion of the identification of Jesus as John the Baptist, Elijah, or one of the prophets. It is striking that in both cases the public speculation does not include the notion that Jesus was the Christ.

29. Jesus solicited the correct answer from the disciples. Peter, speaking for the group, said "You are the Christ."[9] He was identifying Jesus as the long-awaited Messiah who would reign over the coming kingdom of God.

30. Although the identification was correct, Jesus ordered the disciples not to tell anyone. This is the clearest instance of the "messianic secret" concept in Mark (cf. the comments on 1:25-26). The "secret" includes this text, Jesus ordering the demons not to make him known (1:25, 34; 3:12), and his instruction to Peter, James, and John not to tell about the transfiguration until after he had been raised from the dead (9:9). The last of these provides a time limit for the secret. After Jesus' resurrection he could be proclaimed to all as the Christ. As indicated in the comments on 1:25-26, although the rationale for the secret is not stated by Mark and must remain uncertain, I am inclined toward the proposal that Jesus wanted his messiahship kept a secret until it could be seen in the light of the cross. Only in the light of the cross could one truly understand what it meant to Jesus to be the Christ. The misunderstandings likely before the cross are demonstrated immediately in Peter's reaction to Jesus in 8:31-32.

---

[8]Hoehner, "Herodian Dynasty," in *DJG*, p. 322.
[9]See the comments on the term Christ at Mark 1:1.

V. THE JOURNEY TO JERUSALEM (8:31-10:52)

A. JESUS PREDICTS HIS DEATH AND RESURRECTION (8:31-33)

31He then began to teach them that the Son of Man must suffer many things and be rejected by the elders, chief priests and teachers of the law, and that he must be killed and after three days rise again. 32He spoke plainly about this, and Peter took him aside and began to rebuke him.

33But when Jesus turned and looked at his disciples, he rebuked Peter. "Get behind me, Satan!" he said. "You do not have in mind the things of God, but the things of men."

On the one hand, it is problematic to divide the book of Mark in such a way as to split the connected story line of 8:27-9:1. On the other hand, 8:31-9:1 clearly marks a new beginning in terms of geography, christology, and discipleship. Geographically, the first passion prediction begins the journey to Jerusalem. Jerusalem is not spelled out as the destination, but it is implicit in the reference to the elders and chief priests who reside in Jerusalem. It becomes more explicit at the time of the second passion prediction, "They left that place and passed through Galilee" (9:30), and is fully expressed at the time of the third prediction, "See, we are going up to Jerusalem" (10:32). The geographical mode of 8:31-10:52 is the mode of a journey toward Jerusalem and the cross of Golgotha. Christologically, the new section is characterized by an emphasis on Jesus' death and resurrection. As soon as the disciples concluded that Jesus was the Christ, he began to teach them about the cross and the resurrection, concepts which were completely foreign to their ideas about the Christ (see 8:31-32; 9:9-12, 30-32; 10:32-45). In terms of the discipleship theme, there is a shift in this section to an emphasis on following Jesus in the path of suffering servanthood (8:34-35; 9:35; 10:42-45). This shift in the discipleship theme corresponds to and flows from the emphasis on a suffering servant christology. All of these thematic shifts justify seeing 8:31 as the turning point in the book.

31. In Mark's gospel the verb "began" (ἤρξατο, *ērxato*) is often used without the intention of indicating the first time something occurred. However, in this instance the fact that there is only a single vague reference to Jesus' death prior to this point (cf. 2:20), and Mark's declaration that "He spoke plainly about this" (8:32, suggesting he had not spoken plainly before) lead to the conclusion that this is the beginning of a new stage in Jesus' teaching of the disciples. He now begins to teach them about his death and resurrection. They had opened their eyes half way, but they yet needed to learn more about who he really was.

It is notable that in each of the predictions of his death and/or resurrection, Jesus uses the title Son of Man (8:31; 9:9, 12, 31; 10:33, 45; 14:21).[10] He does not use the title Christ, although he accepts it (8:29-30; 14:61-62).

Jesus clearly believed that the death and resurrection of the Son of Man were matters of prophecy (cf. 9:12; 14:21). That is presumably the sense of "must" (δεῖ, *dei*) here in 8:31. This does not mean that there must be a specific Old Testament prophecy that uses the phrase "Son of Man" in connection with suffering, although some would see that possibility in Dan 7. In that chapter, which Jesus clearly used with respect to the Son of Man title (cf. Mark 14:62), the "one like a son of man" in 7:13 is interpreted as a reference to "the saints of the Most High" (7:18). Then the fourth beast is said to "speak out against the Most High and oppress his saints" who "will be handed over to him for a time, times and half a time" (7:25). Some see this as prophesying the suffering of the Son of Man and believe Jesus had Dan 7 in mind when he spoke of the great suffering the Son of Man would endure. If Jesus had Dan 7 in mind in connection with his suffering he never explicitly says so. It is not necessary to confine the Old Testament texts about the suffering of the Son of Man to

---

[10]For discussion of the Son of Man title see the comments on 2:10.

those that use that particular phrase. Since Jesus knew that he was the referent of all the texts that speak of the Christ, regardless of the use or non-use of any pertinent title (including Son of Man), he could allude to any christological prophecies concerning himself while using any available title. In later texts in Mark Jesus alludes to or quotes at least three Old Testament passages as predicting his passion: Isa 53 (Mark 10:45), Ps 118:22-23 (Mark 12:10-11), and Zech 13:7 (Mark 14:27). Such texts may be behind the "must" of 8:31.

In Galilee Jesus had constant conflict with two overlapping groups: the scribes and the Pharisees.[11] On two occasions (3:22; 7:1) the scribes who opposed Jesus came from Jerusalem. With 8:31 the focus shifts to the religious authorities in Jerusalem. In Jerusalem the focus is on the three groups that made up the Sanhedrin: the elders, chief priests, and scribes.[12] The scribes or teachers of the law are discussed in the comments on 1:22. The chief priests were probably the leading figures in the Sanhedrin. "These were probably the former high priests and members of the priestly aristocracy from which the high priests were chosen."[13] The "elders" were powerful laymen from aristocratic families.[14] Together, these three groups made up the Sanhedrin council. The Sanhedrin, presided over by the high priest, had a significant administrative and judicial role in Jerusalem and Judea.[15] When Jesus arrived in Jerusalem, the groups that composed this council became his chief opponents.

Mark is the only Gospel writer who writes that Jesus will rise "after three days" (8:31; 9:31; 10:34).[16] In the parallel

[11]Mark also mentions the Herodians on one occasion (3:6).

[12]All three are listed together in 8:31; 11:27; 14:43, 53; 15:1. Chief priests and scribes are listed together in 10:33; 11:18; 14:1; 15:31. Chief priests or scribes are mentioned on occasion without reference to the others.

[13]G.H. Twelftree, "Sanhedrin," in *DJG*, p. 730.

[14]Sanders, *Judaism*, p. 329.

[15]Brown, p. 343.

[16]The NIV obscures the parallel in 10:34 by translating "after three days" as "three days later."

accounts Matthew (16:21; 17:23; 20:19) and Luke (9:22; 18:33; cf. 24:7, 46) have "on the third day." Mark himself portrays Jesus as crucified on Friday and raised on Sunday. His phrase cannot mean "on the fourth day." Some argue that he uses "three days" loosely to mean a short period of time.[17] Others argue that "after three days" depends on a Jewish method of reckoning by which any part of a day is counted as a day so that Jesus was raised after part of Friday, all of Saturday, and part of Sunday: that is, after three days.[18]

32. The statement that he "spoke plainly about this" indicates that Jesus was quite straightforward about his coming death and resurrection and did not speak in his usual parabolic style. He was speaking only to the disciples, not the crowd, and he wanted the disciples to understand what would happen to him. As a contrast to speaking plainly about his death, in Mark 2:20 there is an example of an obscure parabolic reference to Jesus' death, which probably was not understood as such by those who heard the parable of the bridegroom.

Peter took Jesus aside and actually rebuked him. The rebuke indicates that Peter's notion of the messiah did not involve being rejected by the religious authorities and being killed. Few if any Jews prior to Jesus had observed that certain Old Testament texts indicated a suffering messiah. There were various ideas of what the messiah might be, but all of them were glorious. The twelve, having concluded that Jesus was the messiah, must have been expecting him to assume royal authority over an earthly kingdom (cf. 10:35-37). Jesus' passion predictions involved a complete reversal of their expectations.

33. In response to Peter's rebuke, Jesus rebuked Peter. His language is extraordinarily strong. Peter's plan came from Satan's influence, not God's. Peter was focusing on the interests of men, not of God. Although this exchange of rebukes

---

[17]Lane, p. 303. See the critique of this view by Gundry, p. 447.

[18]Gundry, p. 447, with reference to Gen 42:17-18; 1 Sam 30:1, 12-13; 2 Chron 10:5, 12; Esth 4:16-5:1.

between Jesus and Peter took place in private, it is likely that Peter's rebuke, like his confession, was representative of the opinions of the twelve in general.

B. THE COSTS OF DISCIPLESHIP (8:34-9:1)

[34]Then he called the crowd to him along with his disci-
ples and said: "If anyone would come after me, he must
deny himself and take up his cross and follow me. [35]For
whoever wants to save his life[a] will lose it, but whoever loses
his life for me and for the gospel will save it. [36]What good is
it for a man to gain the whole world, yet forfeit his soul?
[37]Or what can a man give in exchange for his soul? [38]If any-
one is ashamed of me and my words in this adulterous and
sinful generation, the Son of Man will be ashamed of him
when he comes in his Father's glory with the holy angels."

[1]And he said to them, "I tell you the truth, some who are
standing here will not taste death before they see the king-
dom of God come with power."

[a]*35* The Greek word means either *life* or *soul*; also in verse 36.

As is clear in 10:35-37, the disciples' misunderstandings of the nature of Jesus' messiahship led directly to misunderstandings of the nature of discipleship. They expected to support Jesus in his rise to royal rule and then to function as dignitaries in the coming kingdom. In 8:34-9:1, immediately after apprising them of his own true role, he spells out the implications of his mission for their own. This section is central to what Mark wanted to say to his readers and what God would have modern readers learn from this Gospel. It is highlighted by the fact that 8:31-9:1 marks the central turning point in Mark's Gospel and by the fact that the pattern of 1) passion/resurrection prediction, 2) rejection or misunderstanding by the disciples, and 3) teaching on the implications of the cross for discipleship is found three times in 8:31-9:1, 9:30-35, and 10:32-45.

34. At this point Jesus turned to teach not only the disciples, but also the crowds. The disciples could more fully grasp his meaning for they alone have been told about his own future suffering and death. One of the key verses on discipleship in all of the Gospels, according to this verse would-be followers of Jesus must practice self-denial and must bear their own crosses.[19] As Luke 9:23 indicates by adding the word "daily," the cross bearing Jesus had in mind for disciples was metaphorical. It may, of course, involve martyrdom, in some cases even by way of a literal cross. But it applies widely to all sorts of suffering in the name of Christ.

35. The demands of v. 34 are continued in another famous verse. This is the first of several statements in Mark in which Jesus speaks of discipleship using the rhetoric of paradox (cf. 9:35; 10:31, 43-44). Jesus' paradoxes are statements that seem self-contradictory and opposed to common sense, yet express profound truths. As in the case of cross bearing, losing one's life is primarily a metaphorical concept (equivalent to the self-denial of v. 34), although in some circumstances it may lead to literal death as a martyr. Those who lose their lives will save them by gaining eternal life. In cases where losing one's life is metaphorical and does not involve literal death, saving one's life could also be understood in terms of experiencing spiritual life with God even before death – but the context of v. 38 suggests that Jesus was thinking primarily of life after death. V. 35 has motivated many to make great sacrifices for the sake of Jesus and his gospel.

36-37. The NIV here changes the translation of the word translated "life" (ψυχή, *psychē*) twice in v. 35. This word can be translated "soul" or "life," but in this context the translation "soul" is misleading because most modern readers probably understand it to mean a spiritual entity that dwells in the body and separates from it at death. In the New Testament

---

[19]The word translated "come" (ἀκολουθεῖν, *akolouthein*) in the NIV is more commonly and preferably translated "follow," as in the NIV translation of the same word at the end of the verse.

the term is used more holistically of the person or self.[20]

Jesus' point is a dramatic one. There is nothing, not even the totality of human wealth and power, that would compensate for the loss of eternal life with God. Nothing is more valuable than spending eternity in heaven.

38. The opposite of losing one's life for Jesus and the gospel is to be ashamed of Jesus and his words.[21] Living in an adulterous and sinful generation can easily lead a disciple to deny his Lord rather than himself. Those who are ashamed of Jesus can expect him to be ashamed of them at his second coming.

9:1. The statement in 9:1 clearly belongs in the context of 8:31-38. It underscores the truth of 8:38. Unfortunately, it is extraordinarily difficult to interpret. Keeping in mind the parallel in Matt 16:28 ("I tell you the truth, some who are standing here will not taste death before they see the Son of Man coming in his kingdom"), there are four views that need to be considered.

Two of these views are widely defended in the scholarly literature. First, in the light of Mark 8:38 and the reference to the Son of Man's coming in Matt 16:28, many believe Jesus was predicting that his second coming would occur before the death of all of those who were listening to him. Most of those who take this view believe Jesus was wrong,[22] a conclusion which is unacceptable. A few conservative commentators take this view and argue that Jesus was giving a conditional prophecy, although (as in the Jonah's prophecy of the doom of Nineveh) the conditions were left unstated. Because the prophecy was conditional, Jesus did not err when the conditions were not met and the second coming was postponed.[23]

---

[20]Robert G. Bratcher and Eugene A. Nida, *A Translator's Handbook on the Gospel of Mark* (Leiden: E.J. Brill, 1961), pp. 266-267.

[21]A few ancient witnesses have the less likely alternative "of me and mine," that is, of Jesus and his followers.

[22]E.g., Morna Hooker, *The Gospel according to Saint Mark*, Black's New Testament Commentaries (Peabody, MA: Hendrickson, 1991), p. 212.

[23]E.g., Gundry, pp. 466-469, 790. On the conditional nature of biblical prophecy, especially the phenomenon of delayed fulfillment, Gundry cites

A second view, popular among conservative commentators,[24] is that Jesus has reference to the transfiguration, in which three of those who were listening to the teaching of 8:31-9:1 were given a preview of Jesus in his coming glory and therefore an assurance that the kingdom of God had come with power. Proponents of this view cite 2 Pet 1:16-18 in which Peter relates his experience of the transfiguration as supporting his statement that "We did not follow cleverly invented stories when we told you about the power and coming of our Lord Jesus Christ, but we had been eyewitnesses of his majesty." The "coming" spoken of in this sentence is probably the second coming, to which the transfiguration event bore witness.

Two other views are found less frequently in the scholarly literature. One is that 9:1 refers to the destruction of Jerusalem.[25] The other is that 9:1 refers to the resurrection or the day of Pentecost.[26] The major weakness which causes both of these to be minority viewpoints in the scholarly literature is the contextual connection of 8:38 and 9:1. There is little doubt that 8:38 refers to the second coming, and so (especially in Matthew's version, "the Son of Man coming in his kingdom") 9:1 and its parallels apparently ought to be interpreted similarly. The destruction of Jerusalem and Pentecost views sever 9:1 from 8:38. The context of 8:38 favors the second coming view (acceptable only in the problematic "conditional prophecy" version) or the transfiguration (as a preview of the second coming) view. The transfiguration view has the least problems.

Jonah and Isa 38; Jer 18:7-10; Ezek 18:24-29; and 2 Pet 3:1-9.

[24]E.g., Lane, pp. 312-314.

[25]E.g., Norval G. Geldenhuys, *Commentary of the Gospel of Luke*, New International Commentary on the New Testament (Grand Rapids: Eerdmans, 1983), pp. 277-278; McGarvey, p. 315.

[26]I. Howard Marshall, *The Gospel of Luke*, New International Greek Testament Commentary (Grand Rapids: Eerdmans, 1978), pp. 378-379, argues for this view for the parallel in Luke 9:27. He suggests it also applies to Mark.

MARK 9

C. THE TRANSFIGURATION AND THE SUBSEQUENT DISCUSSION (9:2-13)

[2]After six days Jesus took Peter, James and John with him
and led them up a high mountain, where they were all alone.
There he was transfigured before them. [3]His clothes became
dazzling white, whiter than anyone in the world could bleach
them. [4]And there appeared before them Elijah and Moses,
who were talking with Jesus.

[5]Peter said to Jesus, "Rabbi, it is good for us to be here.
Let us put up three shelters – one for you, one for Moses
and one for Elijah." [6](He did not know what to say, they
were so frightened.)

[7]Then a cloud appeared and enveloped them, and a voice
came from the cloud: "This is my Son, whom I love. Listen
to him!"

[8]Suddenly, when they looked around, they no longer saw
anyone with them except Jesus.

[9]As they were coming down the mountain, Jesus gave
them orders not to tell anyone what they had seen until the
Son of Man had risen from the dead. [10]They kept the matter
to themselves, discussing what "rising from the dead"
meant.

[11]And they asked him, "Why do the teachers of the law
say that Elijah must come first?"

[12]Jesus replied, "To be sure, Elijah does come first, and
restores all things. Why then is it written that the Son of
Man must suffer much and be rejected? [13]But I tell you,

Elijah has come, and they have done to him everything they wished, just as it is written about him."

Whether or not the transfiguration story is the fulfilment of the statement in 9:1, it is clearly a confirmation of Peter's confession in 8:29. Peter, James, and John are singled out for a set of special events which underscore Jesus' unique status. The discussion that follows on the way down the mountain provides insight into the identity of the expected return of Elijah and further insight into the destiny of the Son of Man.

2-3. It is unusual for Mark to give a precise chronological connection such as "after six days." Some suggest the six day notation highlights the connection of the transfiguration with the prediction in 9:1,[1] but perhaps it highlights the connection with Peter's confession, or Mark may give this information simply because this is one of those rare occasions in which he had received a chronological detail. On the supposition that much of what Mark wrote came from Peter's preaching, it is easy to imagine Peter telling the story of his confession and following it with, "and after six days he . . ." to tell how the confession was confirmed on the mountain. As in 5:37 and 14:33, Peter, James, and John are singled out for this unique experience.

The transfiguring of Jesus is the first of three unusual things that happen on the mountain. The verb "transfigure" (μεταμορφόω, *metamorphoō*) has become a rare term in English. A better translation might be "transform." Jesus underwent a transformation that gave the three disciples a glimpse of his heavenly glory. As a part of this transformation, his clothing became dazzling white. Mark seeks to capture the brightness of Jesus' glorified state by saying that his clothes were brighter than any fuller (or bleacher, one who cleans woolen cloth)[2]

---

[1]Hurtado, p. 144.

[2]The NIV translates the Greek word for "fuller" (γναφεύς, *gnapheus*) as "anyone," presumably because the term "fuller" would not be readily recognized by most readers.

could whiten them. In the Old Testament and other pre-Christian Jewish literature shining white clothing is characteristic of the heavenly world – the attire of angels and the future attire of the righteous (e.g., Dan 10:5-6; 12:3).[3] In this transformation Jesus reveals his heavenly glory which will be seen by all at his second coming.[4]

4. The transfiguration of Jesus would have been a striking experience by itself, but yet another remarkable experience accompanied it. Elijah and Moses appeared and talked with Jesus. Mark does not explain why these two in particular were selected.[5] It is unlikely that they represent the law and the prophets, because Elijah was not a writing prophet and would not be representative of that part of the Old Testament canon. Some commentators suggest these two appeared because they both experienced theophanies (appearances of God) on mountains.[6] A better suggestion is that both of them were associated with eschatological (end time) expectations.[7] Moses prophesied in Deut 18:15 that God would raise up a prophet like himself. And Mal 4:5-6 predicted the return of Elijah. The experience certainly reminded the disciples of the Malachi passage, for they brought up the return of Elijah prophecy on the way down the mountain (9:11).

5-6. It is not surprising that Peter and the others were frightened by what they saw and did not know what to say. The word σκηνάς (*skēnas*) used for what Peter wanted to build could mean either "tents" (as in the well known Old Testament tent called the tabernacle) or shelters (as in the straw shelters built each year at the Feast of Booths to commemorate life during the wilderness wanderings). Peter would only have had the materials at hand to build shelters. In either case he apparently wanted to honor Jesus, Elijah, and Moses.

---

[3]See Blackburn, *Theios Aner*, pp. 117-124.

[4]Ibid., p. 120.

[5]Note that both of them are also mentioned in succession in Mal 4:4-6.

[6]Gundry, p. 459.

[7]Hurtado, pp. 144-145.

Peter addressed Jesus as "Rabbi," the first of four times this term is used to address Jesus (9:5; 10:51; 11:21; 14:45). Rabbi is a transliteration of a Hebrew form meaning "my lord." It was used as "an honorary title for outstanding teachers of the law."[8] John 1:38 says it can be translated "teacher" (cf. 4:38).

7-8. The third striking experience on the mountain was the cloud and the accompanying voice. The cloud clearly represented the presence of God who spoke in words similar to those at Jesus' baptism. The first part of the statement is identical to 1:11 except it is in third person ("this is") rather than second ("you are").[9] The second part of the divine statement in 9:5 exhorts the disciples to listen to Jesus, God's Son. The superiority of Jesus over Moses and Elijah is made clear both by identifying Jesus as God's Son and by the sudden disappearance of Moses and Elijah at the time of the heavenly voice.

9. This verse is an important part of the messianic secret theme (see 1:25; 8:31) because it provides a timetable. Jesus did not want the transfiguration experience revealed until after his resurrection. Presumably, this is also when the disciples would be free to proclaim that he was the Christ (cf. 8:30).

10. The three apostles followed Jesus' instructions and kept what had happened to themselves. They had difficulty, however, understanding what he meant by referring to his resurrection. Since they did not reckon with Jesus' coming death, the idea of being raised from the dead would be difficult to grapple with. Jesus had told them that he would be killed, but they did not accept this notion until after his death. Even then they seemed to be surprised by his resurrection.

11-13. Having just seen Elijah on the mountain, the disciples ask a related question. Mark has already alluded to the

---

[8]*BAGD*, p. 733.

[9]For comments see 1:11.

people's expectations of the return of Elijah when on two occasions (6:15; 8:28) he mentioned the speculations that Jesus might be Elijah. The disciples now refer to a similar expectation on the part of the scribes. These expectations were undoubtedly rooted in Mal 4:5-6: "See, I will send you the prophet Elijah before that great and dreadful day of the Lord comes. He will turn the hearts of the fathers to their children, and the hearts of the children to their fathers; or else I will come and strike the land with a curse." This text led many to expect Elijah's return to call for reconciliation before the judgment. For example, in the second century B.C. Sirach 48:10 says of Elijah, "At the appointed time, it is written, you are destined to calm the wrath of God before it breaks out in fury, to turn the hearts of parents to their children, and to restore the tribes of Jacob."[10]

Jesus' response to the question about Elijah alludes to Mal 4:6 and Elijah's mission of restoration. When Jesus says "Elijah has come" he has reference to John the Baptist (cf. Matt 11:13-14; 17:10-13). It is difficult to determine what Jesus had in mind when he said it was written about Elijah that they would do to him whatever they pleased. There are no predictions in Malachi of the suffering or death of the coming Elijah. However, it is commonly supposed that the trials experienced by the historical Elijah of 1 Kings, particularly his experiences with King Ahab and his wife Jezebel (1 Kgs 19), constitute a typological predecessor for the sufferings of John via Herod Antipas and Herodias.[11]

In the middle of his reply concerning Elijah Jesus treated a subject that he was more concerned to teach the disciples (as

---

[10]On the Elijah expectations see Darrell L. Bock, "Elijah and Elisha," in *DJG*, pp. 203-205. There are no pre-Christian texts that portray Jewish expectations of the chronological relationship between the coming of Elijah and the coming of the messiah. The disciples' statement that "the teachers of the law say that Elijah must come first" does not clarify the point because it is not clear whether they mean first before the messiah or first before the judgment.

[11]Gundry, p. 465.

evidenced by his repeated return to this subject). In 8:31 he had begun to teach them that he "must" be rejected and killed. Now he specifically indicates that his suffering is a matter of written prophecy (see the comments on 8:31 concerning the Old Testament texts involved). The scribes have observed correctly that Elijah must come. But they missed the predicted sufferings of both Elijah and the Son of Man.

D. JESUS CASTS A SPIRIT FROM A MAN'S SON (9:14-29)

**14When they came to the other disciples, they saw a large
crowd around them and the teachers of the law arguing with
them. 15As soon as all the people saw Jesus, they were overwhelmed with wonder and ran to greet him.**

16"What are you arguing with them about?" he asked.

**17A man in the crowd answered, "Teacher, I brought you
my son, who is possessed by a spirit that has robbed him of
speech. 18Whenever it seizes him, it throws him to the
ground. He foams at the mouth, gnashes his teeth and
becomes rigid. I asked your disciples to drive out the spirit,
but they could not."**

**19"O unbelieving generation," Jesus replied, "how long
shall I stay with you? How long shall I put up with you?
Bring the boy to me."**

**20So they brought him. When the spirit saw Jesus, it
immediately threw the boy into a convulsion. He fell to the
ground and rolled around, foaming at the mouth.**

**21Jesus asked the boy's father, "How long has he been
like this?"**

**"From childhood," he answered. 22"It has often thrown
him into fire or water to kill him. But if you can do anything, take pity on us and help us."**

**23"'If you can'?" said Jesus. "Everything is possible for
him who believes."**

**24Immediately the boy's father exclaimed, "I do believe;
help me overcome my unbelief!"**

[25]When Jesus saw that a crowd was running to the scene, he rebuked the evil[a] spirit. "You deaf and mute spirit," he said, "I command you, come out of him and never enter him again."

[26]The spirit shrieked, convulsed him violently and came out. The boy looked so much like a corpse that many said, "He's dead." [27]But Jesus took him by the hand and lifted him to his feet, and he stood up.

[28]After Jesus had gone indoors, his disciples asked him privately, "Why couldn't we drive it out?"

[29]He replied, "This kind can come out only by prayer.[b]"

[a]*25* Greek *unclean* [b]*29* Some manuscripts *prayer and fasting*

A mountaintop experience is often followed by a strong reminder of the problems of life. When Jesus and the three came to the other disciples, they found them arguing with the teachers of the law after unsuccessfully attempting an exorcism. Like several other miracle stories, this story is both a testimony to Jesus' awesome power and a summons to faith.

14-16. The antecedents of some of the pronouns in these verses are not quite clear. In v. 14, it appears that the crowd was around the disciples and that the teachers of the law were arguing with the disciples. But in v. 16, it appears as though Jesus asks the crowd (the Greek text says he asked "them," a pronoun omitted by the NIV) why they (the crowd) were arguing with the teachers of the law. Perhaps the disciples and the crowd were both arguing with the teachers of the law. The gist of the argument is never given, but apparently it was rooted in the disciples' failure to exorcise a demon from a boy brought to them by his father.

17-18. The father explained that he had brought his son hoping to see Jesus. His son was possessed by a demon that kept him from speaking and which periodically threw him into seizures. The seizures sound similar to epileptic seizures, but these are caused by a demon. Unable to see Jesus, the man asked his disciples to cast out the demons. They had been given that power by Jesus (6:7) and had had much success (6:13). But this time they were not successful.

19. Jesus' two questions in this verse indicated his discouragement with the lack of faith expressed in this incident. "O unbelieving generation" is a general phrase that might apply to the disciples, the father, the crowd, and/or the teachers of the law. The disciples revealed their weakness in faith by their inability to cast out the demon. The father asks Jesus to help him overcome his unbelief in v. 24.

20-22. The demon recognized Jesus and threw the boy into a seizure on the spot. The father explained that the boy had had the demon for some time and that it often tried to kill him by casting him into fire or water. Presumably, it did this by means of the seizures. The father's appeal for compassion and help reveals doubt ("If you can do anything") about Jesus' ability to cast out the demon.

23-24. This brief exchange about faith is an important contribution to an important theme already emphasized repetitively in Mark's Gospel (1:15; 2:5; 4:40; 5:34, 36; 6:6; cf. 7:29). Faith opens up possibilities that remain closed to unbelief. The father's request is echoed in the hearts of many of Mark's readers: "I do believe; help me overcome my unbelief!"

25-27. There was already a crowd around Jesus (cf. vv. 14-17), but it was steadily increasing. In earlier accounts the verb "rebuked" is used for Jesus rebuking the demon for identifying him (1:25; 3:12). On this occasion it applies to his command to leave the boy. The description of the demon as "You deaf and mute spirit" does not mean that the spirit itself could not speak or hear, but that it had caused the boy to be deaf and mute (cf. v.17). In the process of leaving the boy, the demon does cause the boy to cry out and convulses him violently. After the demon left, the boy looked dead and many of the bystanders thought that he was. But when Jesus lifted him by the hand, he was able to stand.

28-29. In yet another private conversation, the disciples wondered why they could not exorcise this demon. Jesus' response underscores the importance of prayer, a theme which in this case, as in Mark 11:22-24, is closely connected with the theme of faith. What the disciples needed was the kind of prayer discussed in 11:24: "whatever you ask for in prayer, believe that you have received it, and it will be yours."

After "by prayer" some ancient witnesses to v. 29 add "and fasting," a typical scribal addition.

E. THE SECOND PASSION/RESURRECTION PREDICTION (9:30-32)

30They left that place and passed through Galilee. Jesus did not want anyone to know where they were, 31because he was teaching his disciples. He said to them, "The Son of Man is going to be betrayed into the hands of men. They will kill him, and after three days he will rise." 32But they did not understand what he meant and were afraid to ask him about it.

This is the second of three passion/resurrection predictions that punctuate Mark 8-10. See the introductory comments to 8:34-9:1 concerning the threefold pattern found three times in Mark 8:31-9:1; 9:30-35; and 10:32-45.

30-31. Jesus was passing through Galilee heading toward Jerusalem. As in 7:24 he was trying to keep his whereabouts secret. This time a specific reason is given: he was teaching his disciples. In particular he was teaching them concerning his coming betrayal, death, and resurrection. The new aspect of 9:31 as compared to 8:31 is the concept of betrayal. The verb translated "betrayed" (παραδίδοται, *paradidotai*) could be translated "delivered" or "handed over," but here in 9:31 it is likely that Judas' "betrayal" is in mind. In 14:10-11, 18, 21, 42, and 44 the same verb is used to describe Judas' betrayal.

32. Peter's rebuke of Jesus in 8:32 indicates that he knew something about what Jesus meant in his passion prediction. However, what he thought he understood was diametrically opposed to what he believed the messiah's destiny to be.

Mark wrote in 9:10 that the three apostles did not understand about the rising from the dead. In 9:32 he is not specific about what aspects of Jesus' statement they do not understand. After Jesus' rebuke of Peter in 8:33, it is easy enough to see why they might be afraid to ask about this saying.

F. TEACHINGS ON SERVANTHOOD (9:33-50)

All of the teaching materials in vv. 33-49 are about servanthood and can generally be subsumed under the saying in v. 35: "If anyone wants to be first, he must be the very last, and the servant of all." Twice in this section the disciples demonstrate that they do not understand this. Jesus' teaching about servanthood for his disciples flows naturally from his teaching about his own destiny (9:31), which involves sacrificial service.

1. Who Is the Greatest? (9:33-35)

**[33]They came to Capernaum. When he was in the house,
he asked them, "What were you arguing about on the road?"
[34]But they kept quiet because on the way they had argued
about who was the greatest.**

[35]Sitting down, Jesus called the Twelve and said, "If anyone wants to be first, he must be the very last, and the servant of all."

This section completes the third part of the three part pattern identified for the passion/resurrection predictions: 1) the prediction itself, 2) rejection or misunderstanding on the part of the disciples, 3) teachings about the implications of Jesus' sacrificial service for the disciples.

33-34. Capernaum seems to be Jesus' home base during his ministry.[12] The question Jesus asked brought silence from

---

[12]See the comments on Capernaum at 1:21.

the disciples because they knew he would not like their answer. They had argued about who was the greatest among them.

35. This memorable saying is another of Jesus' paradoxes (see the comments on 8:35). It is similar to 10:43-44 where Jesus expands on the concept of servanthood.

2. An Example Based on Welcoming Children (9:36-37)

36He took a little child and had him stand among them. Taking him in his arms, he said to them, 37"Whoever welcomes one of these little children in my name welcomes me; and whoever welcomes me does not welcome me but the one who sent me."

This event flows naturally from the previous one. Jesus uses the way he receives children as an example of being last and a servant.

In a later case Jesus will use children's own attitudes as an example (10:15), but not here. By taking the child into his arms, Jesus demonstrated a welcoming, loving attitude toward the child and then summoned the disciples to have the same welcoming attitude toward little children. Those who humble themselves to welcome little children welcome Christ and ultimately the One who sent him.

3. Jesus Rebukes the Disciples' Pride (9:38-41)

38"Teacher," said John, "we saw a man driving out demons in your name and we told him to stop, because he was not one of us."

39"Do not stop him," Jesus said. "No one who does a miracle in my name can in the next moment say anything bad about me, 40for whoever is not against us is for us. 41I tell you the truth, anyone who gives you a cup of water in my

name because you belong to Christ will certainly not lose his reward.

In the context of 9:33-37, the story of the unknown exorcist portrays the disciples as acting directly counter to Jesus' instructions. They were urged to be last of all and servant of all and to welcome little ones with a spirit of humble service. Instead, they immediately demonstrate their self-serving interests by the way in which they approach the unidentified exorcist.

38. There is no question raised in the text as to whether the man casting out demons was actually able to perform exorcisms in Jesus' name. In Acts 19:14-16 the seven sons of Sceva tried unsuccessfully. This case was different and this man was apparently able to cast out demons in Jesus' name. John, who here represents the others ("we"), was not concerned about the man as a charlatan or a false teacher. He was concerned because "he was not following us." (The NIV translation "he was not one of us" masks the fact that John uses the same verb used earlier in 1:18; 2:14, 15 and 8:34 for "following" Jesus.) John's concern expressed the same attitude seen in the disciples' discussion of who was the greatest.

39-40. Jesus rebukes John and the others for their effort to stop this one who was not following them. Since he is doing miracles in Jesus' name he will presumably not say anything bad about Jesus. The proverbial wisdom, "whoever is not against us is for us," applies well in this particular circumstance.

41. The unknown exorcist that the disciples tried to stop was doing miracles in the name of Jesus. Jesus not only wants the disciples not to rebuke one who is doing such great things, but also to realize that even small acts of kindness in the name of Jesus will not go unrewarded. The disciples need to change their attitude and recognize even the value of a cup of water given to one who bears the name of Christ.

4. Getting Rid of Pride and Getting Along with Each Other (9:42-50)

42"And if anyone causes one of these little ones who believe in me to sin, it would be better for him to be thrown into the sea with a large millstone tied around his neck. 43If your hand causes you to sin, cut it off. It is better for you to enter life maimed than with two hands to go into hell, where the fire never goes out.[a] 45And if your foot causes you to sin, cut it off. It is better for you to enter life crippled than to have two feet and be thrown into hell.[b] 47And if your eye causes you to sin, pluck it out. It is better for you to enter the kingdom of God with one eye than to have two eyes and be thrown into hell, 48where

"'their worm does not die,
and the fire is not quenched.'[c]

49Everyone will be salted with fire.

50"Salt is good, but if it loses its saltiness, how can you make it salty again? Have salt in yourselves, and be at peace with each other."

[a]*43* **Some manuscripts** *out, 44where / "'their worm does not die, / and the fire is not quenched.'* [b]*45* **Some manuscripts** *hell, 46where / "'their worm does not die, / and the fire is not quenched.'* [c]*48* **Isaiah 66:24**

It is important to interpret this section in connection with the previous teachings in 9:33-41. For the most part, it continues the theme of servanthood and the rebuke of a haughty, self-serving spirit.

42. The story of the unknown exorcist provides one exemplary antecedent of "these little ones who believe in me." The disciples' efforts to stop him provide an example of putting a stumbling block before them so as to cause them to sin. Jesus makes the seriousness of this offense clear by saying it would be better to – in modern terms – be thrown in the river with a set of concrete boots.

43-48. The parables (metaphorical sayings) of the hand, foot, and eye should be understood in connection with the previous context. In the Sermon on the Mount Jesus used these metaphors in the context of a discussion of lust (Matt 5:29-30). Here in Mark the focus is on pride, the "who is the greatest" and the "you should be following us" attitude expressed in the previous sections. Jesus is saying that the disciples need to get rid of pride at all costs. Pride will cause them to be thrown into hell (γέεννα, *gehenna*), where "'their worm does not die, and the fire is not quenched.'"[13] In describing hell he alludes to Isa 66:24 ("And they will go out and look upon the dead bodies of those who rebelled against me; their worm will not die, nor will their fire be quenched, and they will be loathsome to all mankind"). The idea of eternal fire was well known in antiquity and is still widely associated with hell. The idea of undying worms was and is less common. Jesus is referring to the maggots that thrive in corpses. Hell is not only portrayed as a place of eternal fire, but as a realm whose inhabitants are inhabited by maggots that are not killed by the fire.

49-50. These are perhaps the most obscure verses in the Gospel of Mark. Some interpreters believe they have been attached to v. 48 by catchword association (v. 49 to v. 48 using the word "fire" and the two statements in v. 50 to v. 49 using the word "salt").[14] However, although catchword association may be part of the connection, it is not characteristic of Jesus or Mark to use catchword association to group together statements that have no other contextual connection. Nevertheless, in this case the contextual connections are not easily seen.

A further complication is the textual problem in v. 49. Some ancient witnesses read "For every sacrifice will be salted with salt" and others combine the two readings into "For every one will be salted with fire, and every sacrifice will be

---

[13]Vv. 44 and 46 are omitted from the NIV and other modern translations because they are absent from the best manuscripts and appear to be scribal repetitions of v. 48.

[14]E.g., Hooker, pp. 232-233.

salted with salt." These readings were apparently derived from Lev 2:13: "add salt to all your offerings." Mark probably did not write them, but they do point modern readers to something Mark and his readers knew, that sacrifices were accompanied by salt.

Hurtado provides a useful approach to understanding vv. 49-50 in the context of the previous verses:

> the fire of [v. 49] is not eternal judgment but probably the fires of trial and testing in the life of the believer, for this fire purifies. . . . The *salt* referred to in verse 50 is probably the humility and dedication that is reinforced by trial and testing. If the believer loses this *salt* he or she is not easily renewed (v. 50a), but by maintaining this *salt*, Jesus' followers can more easily be at peace with one another (v. 50b). The simple purity of dedication to Jesus that does not seek its own advantage enables one to be a servant to fellow disciples, and thus promotes peace.[15]

In this interpretation Jesus is still speaking against the disciples' "me first" attitude.

Modern readers are sometimes baffled by the idea of salt losing its saltiness. That is because we are accustomed to pure salt. The first century writer Pliny the Elder observed that the salt from the Dead Sea could lose its salty taste.[16]

---

[15]Hurtado, p. 156. Italics his.

[16]Pliny, *Natural History* 3.31.34.

MARK 10

G. JESUS QUESTIONED ABOUT DIVORCE (10:1-12)

[1]Jesus then left that place and went into the region of Judea and across the Jordan. Again crowds of people came to him, and as was his custom, he taught them.

[2]Some Pharisees came and tested him by asking, "Is it lawful for a man to divorce his wife?"

[3]"What did Moses command you?" he replied.

[4]They said, "Moses permitted a man to write a certificate of divorce and send her away."

**[5]"It was because your hearts were hard that Moses wrote
you this law," Jesus replied. [6]"But at the beginning of creation God 'made them male and female.'[a] [7]'For this reason a
man will leave his father and mother and be united to his
wife,[b] [8]and the two will become one flesh.' So they are no
longer two, but one. [9]Therefore what God has joined together, let man not separate."[c]**

**[10]When they were in the house again, the disciples asked
Jesus about this. [11]He answered, "Anyone who divorces his
wife and marries another woman commits adultery against
her. [12]And if she divorces her husband and marries another
man, she commits adultery."**

**[a]*6* Gen. 1:27 [b]*7* Some early manuscripts do not have *and be united to his wife.*
[c]*8* Gen. 2:24**

The Pharisees enter the picture again as Jesus' opponents. Mark writes that they were testing Jesus. They were not seriously seeking his counsel on marriage and divorce. But their question did provide an opportunity for Jesus to make some comments on the subject, however limited they may be due to the particular circumstances of this polemical occasion.

1. On his way to Jerusalem Jesus entered the region of Judea and the land beyond the Jordan (Perea, on the east side of the Jordan river).[1] There he was again surrounded by crowds and, as usual, he taught them.

2. In the Greco-Roman legal system it was easy to divorce a spouse. A man who wanted to divorce his wife need only give her a certificate of divorce. He did not need her consent or the consent of a judge. Women could also divorce their husbands on the same basis.[2] The Pharisees were concerned about what was lawful from the standpoint of Jewish religious law. From that standpoint, a woman divorcing her husband was generally unacceptable[3] and there was significant debate about the conditions under which a man might legitimately divorce his wife.

We know of two presumably well-known backgrounds to the Pharisees' question. One is the story of Herod Antipas and Herodias in which Antipas and Herodias each divorced their spouses and married each other. (See the comments on Mark 6:17-29 for information on this situation.) The Pharisees may have wanted Jesus to say something that would anger Antipas and Herodias, who had already killed John for his criticism of their marriage.

---

[1]There are textual variants here according to which Jesus went "into the region of Judea across the Jordan" or "into the region of Judea through the region across the Jordan." The reading adopted by the NIV is the best attested. The reading which posits a part of Judea on the east side of the Jordan does not fit the geography of Jesus' time.

[2]Everett Ferguson, *Backgrounds of Early Christianity*, 2nd ed. (Grand Rapids: Eerdmans, 1993), p. 69. Ferguson notes that one deterrent to divorce was that the husband had to return the dowry to the woman.

[3]E.g., Josephus, *Antiquities* 15.259: "Some time afterwards Salome had a quarrel with Costobarus and soon sent him a document dissolving their marriage, which is not in accordance with Jewish law. For it is (only) the man who is permitted by us to do this, and not even a divorced woman may marry again on her own initiative unless her former husband consents."

The other possible background is the dispute between the great rabbis Shammai and Hillel concerning the grounds on which a man might divorce his spouse. This dispute is reported in the Mishnah: "The School of Shammai say: A man may not divorce his wife unless he has found unchastity in her, for it is written, *Because he hath found in her* indecency *in anything*. And the School of Hillel say: [He may divorce her] even if she spoiled a dish for him, for it is written, *Because he hath found in her indecency in* anything."[4] The Mishnah was compiled about A.D. 200 and there is room for doubt about how accurately the opinions of Shammai and Hillel are represented. However, its account of their differences on the question of divorce is widely accepted. The Pharisees may have sought to test Jesus in the arena of a "hot issue" among contemporary Jewish authorities. Whichever view Jesus took would have the potential of offending some of his followers.

3-4. Jesus began by asking his opponents a question. Every informed student of the divorce question knew that the most important text was Deut 24:1-4, which was the fountainhead of the positions of both Shammai and Hillel. Deut 24:1-4 did not directly address the question of the circumstances under which a divorce was allowable. Instead, Moses' direct command in these verses was that a husband could not remarry a divorced wife who had subsequently married another. However, in the process of describing the regulated situation, Moses spoke of a man whose wife "becomes displeasing to him because he finds something indecent about her, and he writes her a certificate of divorce, gives it to her and sends her from his house." This statement was taken to mean that a divorce required a certificate of divorce. It also became the prime text for debates over the grounds for divorce. In their reply to Jesus the Pharisees do not get into the grounds debate.

5-9. Jesus apparently accepted his opponents' interpretation of Deut 24 but saw the regulations of Deut 24 as a

---

[4]*Gittin* 9.10. The italics and brackets are from Danby's translation. The Scripture cited is from Deut 24:1.

necessary expedient provided because of the hardness of the human heart. Citing first Gen 1:27 (v. 6) and then Gen 2:24 (v. 7),[5] he argued that God's intent from the beginning was that marriage would be a lifetime commitment. People should not separate what God has joined together. When divorce occurs at least one marriage partner has failed to do the will of God.

10-12. Jesus reinforced his strict view of divorce in response to the disciples' inquiry. A man who divorces his wife and marries another commits adultery against her. The main thrust of Jesus' statement is quite clear. God is opposed to divorcing one's spouse and marrying another.

But there are three aspects of this text that raise questions. First, how does Mark's unqualified statement relate to the "except for unchastity"[6] clause in the parallel in Matt 19:9 and the similar text in Matt 5:32? Some argue that Matthew contradicts Mark. Others interpret Matthew's exception clause in a way that does not permit divorce and remarriage and therefore is not contrary to Mark's statement about divorce and remarriage.[7] But the best solution is the suggestion that Mark's form of the statement is meant to be a general principle and not meant to deny the possibility of exceptions. Mark may have assumed his audience would understand that divorce and remarriage are permissible if one's spouse commits adultery.[8]

Second, how does "whoever divorces his wife and marries another" relate to "commits adultery against her"? If "commits adultery against her" is understood quite literally, then

---

[5]The two best manuscripts of Mark omit part of Gen 2:24; that is, "and be united to his wife." It is difficult to decide whether Mark originally wrote this phrase or not.

[6]The NIV translation of this exception clause, "except for marital unfaithfulness," is misleading because it may be misunderstood to include nonsexual forms of unfaithfulness. The Greek word πορνεία (*porneia*) clearly has sexual misconduct in mind.

[7]For a summary of various view see Carson, "Matthew," pp. 414-418.

[8]Ibid.

the man must in some sense still be married to the first wife.[9] In this common understanding "whoever divorces his wife and marries another" is not taken in its full literal sense, because it says that the man divorced his first wife and married a second. The literal adultery interpretation might be paraphrased as follows: "whoever divorces his wife and marries another (does this in the eyes of man; in God's eyes he is still married to the first woman and therefore) commits adultery against her." Some interpreters have advocated a different interpretation which takes "whoever divorces his wife and marries another" quite literally. If the first part of the statement is taken literally, the man is no longer actually married to the first wife and so the second part ("commits adultery against her") must be somewhat metaphorical.[10] This view might be paraphrased as follows: "whoever divorces his wife and marries another commits adultery (in the sense that what he has done is in God's eyes tantamount[11] to adultery)."[12]

Third, v. 12 has been of concern to some interpreters because of the widespread opinion that among the Jews women were not allowed to divorce their husbands. It is therefore concluded by some that Mark has created this altered version of v. 11 in the light of his non-Jewish audience outside of Palestine.[13] However, there is some debate about

---

[9]So Gundry, p. 532: "She is still his spouse."

[10]Craig Blomberg, *Matthew*, New American Commentary (Nashville: Broadman, 1992), p. 293.

[11]That is, "equivalent in value, significance, or effect." *Merriam-Webster's Collegiate Dictionary*, 10th ed. (Springfield, MA: Merriam-Webster, 1993), p. 1205. Cf. Matt 5:28 "anyone who looks at a woman lustfully has already committed adultery with her in his heart" (in the sense that what he has done is in God's eyes tantamount to adultery).

[12]Some, but by no means all, of those who take the literal adultery view believe that illegitimate remarriages involve a continuous state of adultery and therefore must be ended. The other view holds that such remarriages are sinfully conceived but are genuine marriages.

[13]So Gundry, p. 533. Lane, pp. 352 and 358, solves the problem by accepting a poorly attested variant according to which the woman in v. 12 does not divorce her husband, but deserts him.

whether women were allowed to divorce their husbands in Palestine during the days of Jesus.[14] More importantly, there was at least the famous case of Herodias divorcing Philip for Herod Antipas, a case notorious enough in its own right to account for Jesus having spoken of a woman divorcing her husband.[15]

H. RECEIVING THE KINGDOM LIKE A CHILD (10:13-16)

13People were bringing little children to Jesus to have him touch them, but the disciples rebuked them. 14When Jesus saw this, he was indignant. He said to them, "Let the little children come to me, and do not hinder them, for the kingdom of God belongs to such as these. 15I tell you the truth, anyone who will not receive the kingdom of God like a little child will never enter it." 16And he took the children in his arms, put his hands on them and blessed them.

This incident continues the emphasis on servanthood in contrast to pride and selfishness. Once again the disciples reveal that they have not learned the lesson Jesus has been teaching since 8:31.

13. According to Matt 19:13 those who brought the little children wanted Jesus to lay his hands on them and pray. The context of the disciples' behavior and Jesus' emphasis in Mark 8-10 suggests that the disciples rebuked the parents because they viewed Jesus as too important and busy to take his time with the children.

14-15. Jesus reacted with indignation to the disciples' newest demonstration that they were missing the point. Not only does he spend time with the children, but he uses them as an example to the disciples. Mark does not specify which aspect(s) of a child's attitude is the highlighted component

---

[14]See Gundry, p. 543, for references.
[15]Hurtado, p. 167.

for receiving the kingdom of God. One might speculate concerning a child's innocence, ability to trust, etc. In the light of the overall context of Mark 8-10, perhaps the best suggestion is a child's knowledge that "he is helpless and small, without claim or merit."[16] To receive the kingdom of God the disciples needed to give up their pride and recognize their humble position before God and others.

16. Jesus hugged the children and, laying his hands upon them, called down God's favor upon them.

I. THE RICH MAN AND JESUS' TEACHING CONCERNING WEALTH (10:17-31)

17As Jesus started on his way, a man ran up to him and fell on his knees before him. "Good teacher," he asked, "what must I do to inherit eternal life?"

18"Why do you call me good?" Jesus answered. "No one is good – except God alone. 19You know the commandments: 'Do not murder, do not commit adultery, do not steal, do not give false testimony, do not defraud, honor your father and mother.' "

20"Teacher," he declared, "all these I have kept since I was a boy."

21Jesus looked at him and loved him. "One thing you lack," he said. "Go, sell everything you have and give to the poor, and you will have treasure in heaven. Then come, follow me."

22At this the man's face fell. He went away sad, because he had great wealth.

23Jesus looked around and said to his disciples, "How hard it is for the rich to enter the kingdom of God!"

24The disciples were amazed at his words. But Jesus said again, "Children, how hard it is to enter the kingdom of

---

[16]Lane, pp. 360-361.

God! [25]It is easier for a camel to go through the eye of a needle than for a rich man to enter the kingdom of God."

[26]The disciples were even more amazed, and said to each other, "Who then can be saved?"

[27]Jesus looked at them and said, "With man this is impossible, but not with God; all things are possible with God."

[28]Peter said to him, "We have left everything to follow you!"

[29]"I tell you the truth," Jesus replied, "no one who has left home or brothers or sisters or mother or father or children or fields for me and the gospel [30]will fail to receive a hundred times as much in this present age (homes, brothers, sisters, mothers, children and fields – and with them, persecutions) and in the age to come, eternal life. [31]But many who are first will be last, and the last first."

[a]*19* Exodus 20:12-16; Deut. 5:16-20 [b]*24* Some manuscripts *is for those who trust in riches*

The story of the rich man (identified in Matt 19:20 as young and in Luke 18:30 as a ruler) fits well with the theme of sacrificial servanthood. This rich man well illustrates the selfish attachment of men and women to wealth and the impediment it can be to self-denying service. In the same context, Peter illustrates that though the disciples have given up riches, they have still not learned the lesson of servanthood.

17-20. The rich man sought to honor Jesus by kneeling before him and addressing him as "Good Teacher." Jesus' objection to being called "good" is surprising to many. However, as Lane suggests, "In calling in question the man's use of 'good,' Jesus' intention is not to pose the question of his own sinlessness or oneness with the Father, but to set in correct perspective the honor of God."[17] This man undoubtedly viewed himself as "good" and needed to see that "his

---

[17]Lane, pp. 365-366.

only hope is an utter reliance upon God, who alone can bestow eternal life."[18]

The question, "What must I do to inherit eternal life?" further suggests the trust that this man had in Jesus. In reply to the man's question, he recalls in summary fashion several of the ten commandments. The rich man had kept the ten commandments from childhood.

21. It is easy to think of the rich man as simply a pawn in Jesus' teaching game, as if he gave this man the challenge to give his wealth away in order to use his failure as an object lesson. But Mark says that Jesus "loved him." Jesus saw great potential in the man's trust in him, desire for salvation, and righteous lifestyle. He wanted the man to be one of his chosen followers.

22. The rich man's response reveals his sincerity. The first verb Mark uses to describe his reaction can be translated in two ways. The NIV translation, "the man's face fell" is an attempt to express one meaning of the word στυγνάσας (*stygnasas*), which is that his appearance indicated he was gloomy or sad. The NRSV "he was shocked" expresses the alternative. In either case the next phrase says that he went away grieving, because he had great wealth. His wealth was the one thing he would not give up to inherit eternal life.

23-25. Jesus used this opportunity to teach his disciples about wealth. It is hard for anyone[19] to enter the kingdom of God. It is especially hard for a rich man. In fact Jesus uses a hyperbolic illustration which characterizes a rich man's possibilities for entering the kingdom of God as nonexistent. There is no ancient evidence for the oft-cited opinion that the eye of the needle was a gate into the walls of Jerusalem that a camel could enter only with great difficulty.[20] Jesus had in mind the eye of a literal needle.

26. The shock expressed by the disciples in vv. 24 and 26

---

[18]Ibid., p. 365.

[19]Some manuscripts modify v. 24 to speak only of the rich.

[20]McGarvey, pp. 168-169, objected to this camel gate view in 1875.

may reveal an underlying theology that supposes that rich men like the one they had just seen are rich because they are blessed by God for their righteousness. Their reaction, "Who then can be saved?" seems to imply that the rich would be especially likely to be saved. If they are not saved, then who can be?

27. Fortunately, impossibilities are possible for God. Rich men can be saved and so can the rest of humanity.

28. Peter's statement sought credit for doing what Jesus told the rich man to do. The twelve had left everything they had behind and followed Jesus. Peter's language reflects the responses of Peter and Andrew in 1:18 as "they left their nets and followed him" and of James and John in 1:20 as "they left their father Zebedee in the boat with the hired men and followed him." The four fishermen had heeded the call and paid a high price.

29-30. Jesus began his reply to Peter with a commendation of his sacrifice. With his customary "I tell you the truth"[21] he emphasized the truth and significance of his promise. Those who sacrifice houses or family or fields for the sake of Jesus or the gospel will receive one hundred times what they have sacrificed in the present life and in the age to come they will receive eternal life. In a later text Jesus tells the disciples that Christians will suffer great family trials as "brother will betray brother to death and a father his child. Children will rebel against their parents and have them put to death. All men will hate you because of me . . ." (13:12-13). This statement fills out both the sense in which many may have to leave family members and the ominous reference to "and with them, persecutions" in the promise of reward. Of course, Jesus' promise does not involve literal multiplications of new family members or houses or fields. The sense in which one gains new family members may be illuminated by Mark 3:34, "Here are my mother and my brothers! Whoever does the will of God is my brother and sister and mother." For the multiple

[21]See 3:28.

returns on houses and fields one might consult Acts 2:44-45: "All the believers were together and had everything in common. Selling their possessions and goods, they gave to anyone as he had need."

31. This paradoxical saying[22] is apparently a rebuke of the down side of Peter's statement. Peter has expressed the "me-first" attitude that keeps coming through in the disciples' behavior (see 8:33-34, 38; 10:13, 35-37, 41) despite Jesus' repeated efforts to dispel it. Jesus warns Peter that those who place themselves first will be last and vice versa. This statement is more fully illuminated in Matt 19:27-20:16. There Peter's attitude is more clearly displayed by the addition of his statement, "What then will there be for us?" (19:27). The paradox of the first and last is followed by the parable of the Workers in the Vineyard and, in 20:16, a repetition of the paradox.

J. THE THIRD PASSION/RESURRECTION PREDICTION (10:32-34)

32They were on their way up to Jerusalem, with Jesus leading the way, and the disciples were astonished, while those who followed were afraid. Again he took the Twelve aside and told them what was going to happen to him. 33"We are going up to Jerusalem," he said, "and the Son of Man will be betrayed to the chief priests and teachers of the law. They will condemn him to death and will hand him over to the Gentiles, 34who will mock him and spit on him, flog him and kill him. Three days later he will rise."

This is the third and last of the passion/resurrection predictions that are the centerpieces of chapters 8-10. With the following section it repeats the pattern found in 8:31-9:1 and 9:30-35.

22On the use of paradox see the comments on 8:35.

32. The disciples are astonished and the other followers are amazed because it is clear that Jesus is leading them to Jerusalem, the center of Jewish piety and of the Jewish authorities that oppose Jesus. Again, Jesus does not make his statements about the coming events in Jerusalem in public, but takes the twelve aside. Mark's three passion/ resurrection predictions are presumably exemplary of many efforts on Jesus' part to get the disciples to understand both his destiny and theirs.

33-34. This is by far the most detailed of the predictions. Perhaps Jesus increased the detail as they drew closer to Jerusalem. Compared to the previous statements, this statement adds that the chief priests and scribes will condemn him to death and hand him over to the Gentiles, who will mock him and spit on him, and flog him before killing him. This provides a rather detailed overview from Jesus' betrayal to his death. He once again concludes with his resurrection after three days.

K. THE REQUEST OF JAMES AND JOHN (10:35-45)

35Then James and John, the sons of Zebedee, came to
him. "Teacher," they said, "we want you to do for us whatever we ask."
36"What do you want me to do for you?" he asked.
37They replied, "Let one of us sit at your right and the other at your left in your glory."
38"You don't know what you are asking," Jesus said. "Can you drink the cup I drink or be baptized with the baptism I am baptized with?"
39"We can," they answered.

Jesus said to them, "You will drink the cup I drink and be
baptized with the baptism I am baptized with, 40but to sit at
my right or left is not for me to grant. These places belong to those for whom they have been prepared."
41When the ten heard about this, they became indignant

with James and John. 42Jesus called them together and said, "You know that those who are regarded as rulers of the Gentiles lord it over them, and their high officials exercise authority over them. 43Not so with you. Instead, whoever wants to become great among you must be your servant, 44and whoever wants to be first must be slave of all. 45For even the Son of Man did not come to be served, but to serve, and to give his life as a ransom for many."

Peter has gained the reputation of being the impetuous, outspoken apostle. In Mark he does speak more often than the others and on more than one occasion he blunders (8:32; 9:5; 14:29). However, it is often not noticed that John also blunders in 9:38 and here in 10:35-37. This occasion is the most explicit demonstration of how the disciples' misunderstanding of Jesus' messiahship led them astray in understanding their own roles. It is also Jesus' most explicit teaching on the implications of his role for theirs. It is fitting that it comes on the brink of the final week of Jesus' life.

35-37. Like children, James and John asked Jesus to acquiesce to an unspecified request. Jesus, of course, did not say "yes" without hearing the request. The request is cast in the language of ancient royal customs. The king sat in his glory on the throne and those nearest in authority to him sat first on his right and second on his left. The request reveals what appears to be a earthly Davidic messianism in which Jesus is envisioned as establishing an earthly kingdom with the apostles as his chief assistants.

38-40. Jesus' counter question uses two metaphors for his coming suffering and death: drinking a cup of wine and being baptized. The use of drinking a cup as a metaphor for Jesus' death is also found in the Gethsemane account (14:36: "remove this cup from me"). A similar use of the imagery of baptism is found in Luke 12:50: "I have a baptism to undergo, and how distressed I am until it is completed!" As Jesus realized, the two brothers did not understand the question. Nevertheless, he said that they would indeed experience a cup and a baptism like his; that is, they would endure great suffering. James was one of the earliest martyrs (Acts 12:1-2). According to tradition John lived into the decade of the nineties,[23] but he too suffered, including an exile on the island of Patmos.

Jesus does not deny that he will sit on a throne or that there will be dignitaries on his right and left, but he says the choice is not his to make. He does not affirm the this-worldly implications of the brothers' request. Elsewhere, in Matt 19:28 and Luke 22:28-30, Jesus says that the twelve will sit on twelve thrones judging the twelve tribes of Israel.

41. The anger of the ten other apostles reveals their own desires to have the chief positions.

42-45. Jesus exemplifies the difference between his standards and those of the world with pagan rulers who lord it over or exercise authority over their subjects. This is not the way of Christ. His way is expressed in paradoxical parallels: "whoever wants to become great among you must be your servant" and "whoever wants to be first must be slave of all." See the parallels in 9:35 and 10:31. In connection with v. 45, these verses encapsulate the repeated theme of Mark 8-10. The "for" or "therefore" at the beginning of v. 45 indicates that the life-giving service of the Son of Man is the model and rationale for the servanthood of the disciples. If anyone deserves to be served, he did. Yet, even he did not come to be served, but to serve.

The last clause of v. 45, "to give his life as a ransom for many," probably alludes to Isa 53, especially v. 10.[24] A ransom (λύτρον, *lytron*) was a purchase price paid to free a slave, prisoner, or forfeited piece of land or other possession.[25] It is here used metaphorically for the vicarious suffering of Jesus which paid the price for the sins of others. This is one of only two statements in Mark that speak of the atoning value of

---

[23]Irenaeus, *Against Heresies* 2.22.5; 3.3.4.

[24]Lane, pp. 383-384. Gundry, p. 591, argues against an allusion to Isa 53.

[25]*BAGD*, p. 482; Lane, p. 383.

Jesus' death. The other is in the inauguration of the Lord's Supper at 14:24: "This is my blood of the covenant, which is poured out for many." Mark certainly agrees with the early Christian teaching of the atoning value of Jesus' death. But he has emphasized instead the exemplary moral value of Jesus' death as a model for sacrificial service to God and others. That is the main emphasis of vv. 43-45.

L. BARTIMAEUS RECEIVES HIS SIGHT (10:46-52)

46Then they came to Jericho. As Jesus and his disciples,
together with a large crowd, were leaving the city, a blind
man, Bartimaeus (that is, the Son of Timaeus), was sitting
by the roadside begging. 47When he heard that it was Jesus
of Nazareth, he began to shout, "Jesus, Son of David, have
mercy on me!"

48Many rebuked him and told him to be quiet, but he
shouted all the more, "Son of David, have mercy on me!"

49Jesus stopped and said, "Call him."

So they called to the blind man, "Cheer up! On your feet!
He's calling you." 50Throwing his cloak aside, he jumped to
his feet and came to Jesus.

51"What do you want me to do for you?" Jesus asked him.

The blind man said, "Rabbi, I want to see."

52"Go," said Jesus, "your faith has healed you." Imme-
diately he received his sight and followed Jesus along the
road.

The story of Bartimaeus concludes the journey to Jerusalem, leading the reader to the brink of the "triumphal entry" down the Mount of Olives. Because of the symbolism of the two-stage healing of the blind man in 8:22-26, some look for a similar symbolism in this story. They argue that the blind man miracles are symbolic bookends for the special section between them in which Jesus repeatedly teaches about his coming death as a model of sacrificial service.[26] The placement of the Bartimaeus story favors this view. However, this second healing of a blind man does not have the same sort of unique twist that needs explanation. Moreover, if a similar symbolism concerning the disciples' understanding were sought, the Bartimaeus story would seem to suggest that the disciples now understood the message that would lead them from partial to complete sight (concerning Jesus' death and their own mission of service). Subsequent events will prove that they did not.

46. Jericho is an oasis located about six miles north of the Dead Sea.[27] It is the lowest city in the world. Bartimaeus is Aramaic for "son of Timaeus." He was a blind man presumably forced by his blindness into a life of begging.

47-48. Due to his blindness Bartimaeus could not see Jesus and because of the large crowd he was not close to him to hear him or address him. When he heard who the crowd was following, he did what he could: he shouted out in hopes that Jesus would hear him and help him. The crowd tried to silence him because they were annoyed or thought Jesus might be annoyed by the cries of a street beggar. But Bartimaeus was determined to shout out above the crowd.

His cry is unique to this point in Mark in identifying Jesus as "Son of David." It leads well into the next story, the triumphal entry, in which Jesus is acclaimed with words about the "coming of the kingdom of our father David" (11:10). Despite the absence to this point in Mark of public teaching by Jesus or speculation by any other than the disciples to the effect that Jesus was the promised Davidic messiah, it is probable that Bartimaeus's cry and the shouting during the

---

[26]E.g., Hurtado, p. 173.

[27]McRay, *Archaeology*, p. 17, suggests a solution to the apparent conflict between Luke 18:35 and Mark 10:46 concerning whether Jesus healed Bartimaeus going into or out of Jericho. Over different periods of history the center of Jericho may have varied by as much as several miles. Jesus may have been leaving one area of Jericho and entering another.

triumphal entry signal the presence of messianic expectations at this point.[28] Messianic speculation presumably grew as Jesus approached Jerusalem, the city where David and his descendants ruled.

49-51. Again Jesus is more gracious than those around him (cf. 10:13-14). He is willing to take time with children and beggars. The brief exchange between Jesus and Bartimaeus establishes that it was not money that the beggar wanted from Jesus. Calling him "Rabbi" (see 9:5), he asked for sight.

52. Once again, Mark emphasizes the importance of faith. By noting that Bartimaeus followed Jesus along the road Mark leads the reader into the next story, the triumphal entry. Most of the individuals Jesus healed remain anonymous in the Gospels. Perhaps Bartimaeus followed Jesus in discipleship and thus became known by name in the early church.[29]

---

[28]Hurtado, p. 174. But see Lane, p. 388, who argues that Bartimaeus probably used "Son of David" as "a respectful form of address," but not because he recognized Jesus as the Messiah.

[29]Lane, p. 387.

MARK 11

VI. THE LAST WEEK: JERUSALEM, THE CROSS, AND THE RESURRECTION (11:1-16:8 [20])

In my opinion the traditional Christian understanding of the chronology of the major events at the end of Jesus' life is generally correct. The triumphal entry probably occurred on the Sunday before the Passover meal which was on Thursday evening. Jesus was crucified on Friday and raised on Sunday. There are a variety of questions that can be raised about this chronology, particularly from a comparative reading of the Gospel accounts. Some argue that the triumphal entry occurred several weeks prior to the crucifixion.[1] There are difficulties in reconciling John's account as to the relationship between the crucifixion and the Passover meal.[2] There are several problems of harmonization in the events leading from the entry to the cross.[3] But it is beyond my scope to deal with these issues in any detail. I will assume the parameters described above and comment primarily on Mark's apparent chronology of the intervening details.

A. THE TRIUMPHAL ENTRY (11:1-11)

[1]As they approached Jerusalem and came to Bethphage and Bethany at the Mount of Olives, Jesus sent two of his

---

[1]Lane, pp. 390-91, 401, 405, 489.

[2]See the discussion in Blomberg, *Historical Reliability*, pp. 175-178.

[3]Some of these issues are taken up in Blomberg, *Historical Reliability*, pp. 113-189.

disciples, [2]saying to them, "Go to the village ahead of you, and just as you enter it, you will find a colt tied there, which no one has ever ridden. Untie it and bring it here. [3]If anyone asks you, 'Why are you doing this?' tell him, 'The Lord needs it and will send it back here shortly.'"

[4]They went and found a colt outside in the street, tied at a doorway. As they untied it, [5]some people standing there asked, "What are you doing, untying that colt?" [6]They answered as Jesus had told them to, and the people let them go. [7]When they brought the colt to Jesus and threw their cloaks over it, he sat on it. [8]Many people spread their cloaks on the road, while others spread branches they had cut in the fields. [9]Those who went ahead and those who followed shouted,

"Hosanna![a]"
"Blessed is he who comes in the name of the Lord!"[b]
[10]"Blessed is the coming kingdom of our father David!"
"Hosanna in the highest!"

[11]Jesus entered Jerusalem and went to the temple. He looked around at everything, but since it was already late, he went out to Bethany with the Twelve.

[a]*9* A Hebrew expression meaning "Save!" which became an exclamation of praise; also in verse 10 [b]*9* Psalm 118:25,26

The triumphal entry, as it has traditionally been called, is not named for Jesus' choice of mounts, which was a colt (probably of a donkey)[4] rather than a great steed. It is named for the processional of the many who hailed Jesus as he came down the Mount of Olives toward the holy city. This event was a major turning point in that Jesus was publicly hailed with acclamations appropriate for the messiah. His decision to ride in on a colt so as to create a processional and in order to fulfill Zech 9:9 would presumably have encouraged those who wondered if he might be the messiah. Without explicitly

[4]Lane, p. 391 n. 2.

making the claim, he was stirring up messianic speculation.

1-6. The Mount of Olives is a low mountain (elevation 2500 feet) located east of Jerusalem. Bethany is less than two miles from Jerusalem on the eastern side of the mountain. Bethphage was between Bethany and the city, probably about one mile east of the temple (which was on the eastern edge of the city).[5] It is possible that Jesus had made prior arrangements with the owner of the colt. In any case he knows that whoever sees the disciples untying it will permit them to take it. The translation "The Lord needs it" may be misleading. "The Lord" translates ὁ κύριος αὐτοῦ (*ho kyrios autou*), literally "his lord (or master)." E.A. Judge argues that it is not a reference to Jesus as "the Lord," but a reference to Jesus as a "legitimate claimant ('the master') who promises to return the animal when finished with it."[6] The fact that the colt had never been ridden is meant to honor Jesus, as in 1 Sam 6:7 the ark of the covenant was placed on a new cart and pulled by oxen who had never been yoked. The disciples found the colt just as Jesus had told them.

7-10. Mark's account of the acclamation given to Jesus is brief. Many people were there and they honored Jesus in two ways. First, they spread their cloaks or fresh cut branches from the fields to make a carpet for him to ride on.[7] Second, they formed a processional in front of and behind him and shouted words of acclamation with an allusion to Ps 118:25-26. "Hosanna," found at the beginning and end of the acclamation, transliterates a Hebrew phrase found in Ps 118:25. In the context of Jesus' entry into the city it is a shout of

---

[5]On these three locations see Rousseau and Arav, *Jesus and His World*, pp. 15-16, 18-19, 210-212.

[6]E.A. Judge, "The Regional Kanon for Requisitioned Transport," in *New Documents Illustrating Early Christianity*, ed. G.H.R. Horsley (North Ryde, Australia: Macquarie University, 1976), p. 43. Of course Jesus is "the Lord." The question is how *kurios* should be translated in this particular context.

[7]Compare 2 Kgs 9:13: "They hurried and *took their cloaks and spread them under him* on the bare steps. Then they blew the trumpet and shouted, 'Jehu is king!'"

acclamation.[8] In v. 10 "Hosanna" is expanded with "in the highest," meaning "in the heavens." "Blessed is he who comes in the name of the Lord!" is from Ps 118:26. The appropriateness of the use of Ps 118 is seen in the fact that in 12:10-11 Jesus himself cites Ps 118:22-23.

In the context of the processional and praise of Jesus, the first part of v. 10 "Blessed is the coming kingdom of our father David!" is messianic. That is, those in the processional were acclaiming Jesus as the messiah, who would establish the kingdom of David.[9] His mode of entry into the city encouraged this acclamation.

11. Mark's account does not say much concerning the day of the triumphal entry. Jesus did enter the temple and look around. But since it was already late in the day, he and the twelve left the city to go to Bethany for the night. He did not spend the night in Jerusalem until the night he was betrayed. Each evening he went to Bethany (11:11-12, 19; 14:3). This may be due to a desire to avoid the authorities at night, or because of the overbooking of lodging within the city due to the Passover, or simply because Jesus desired to be with someone who lived in Bethany. In 14:3 he was in Bethany at the house of Simon the Leper. John 11:1 identifies Bethany as the home of Mary, Martha, and Lazarus.

B. CURSING THE FIG TREE AND CLEANSING THE TEMPLE (11:12-19)

12The next day as they were leaving Bethany, Jesus was hungry. 13Seeing in the distance a fig tree in leaf, he went to find out if it had any fruit. When he reached it, he found nothing but leaves, because it was not the season for figs. 14Then he said to the tree, "May no one ever eat fruit from you again." And his disciples heard him say it.

[8]Lane, p. 397.
[9]Gundry, p. 632.

[15]On reaching Jerusalem, Jesus entered the temple area and began driving out those who were buying and selling there. He overturned the tables of the money changers and the benches of those selling doves, [16]and would not allow anyone to carry merchandise through the temple courts. [17]And as he taught them, he said, "Is it not written:

"'My house will be called
a house of prayer for all nations'[a]?

But you have made it 'a den of robbers.'[b]" [18]The chief priests and the teachers of the law heard this and began looking for a way to kill him, for they feared him, because the whole crowd was amazed at his teaching.

[19]When evening came, they[c] went out of the city.

[a]*17* Isaiah 56:7 [b]*17* Jer. 7:11 [c]*19* Some early manuscripts *he*

The two stories of the cursing of the fig tree and the cleansing of the temple form another occurrence of Mark's occasional sandwiching of two stories. The cursing of the fig tree (vv. 12-14) and the next day's sighting of the withered tree frame the story of the cleansing of the temple. As usual, the two stories are thematically interrelated. In fact, the cleansing of the temple provides the clue to understanding what would otherwise be Jesus' most enigmatic miracle (since it seems so out of character).

12-14. The initial time reference sets the events of vv. 12-19 on Monday, the day after the triumphal entry. V. 13 is somewhat enigmatic. Why would Jesus look for figs when they were out of season? Gundry argues plausibly that Mark deliberately does not say Jesus looked for figs, but rather that he looked for "something" (τι, *ti*). The earliest figs do not ripen until June. Jesus was looking for the buds which form just before and as the tree leafs. These buds may appear as early as March 1st and, although they are only marginally edible, people do eat them.[10] The Mishnah refers to eating the

[10]Gundry, p. 636, based on eyewitness information from B.W. Bacon and others. The major option to Gundry's approach is that of Lane, who argues

buds when they mature, turning rosy.[11]

Regardless of the season, making a fig tree barren seems quite out of character with Jesus' use of his miraculous powers. But the next event in Mark's Gospel suggests a symbolic meaning for Jesus' unusual action. Like the two-part healing of the blind man in 8:22-26, the oddity of the fig tree miracle turns out to have a purpose. The cursing of the fig tree symbolizes God's judgment on Israel for not bearing the fruit he wanted from the temple. It foreshadows the cleansing of the temple and ultimately the prophecy of its destruction in chapter 13. Mark observes that the disciples heard Jesus' remark in order to set the stage for Peter's observations about the tree on Tuesday morning (v. 21).

15-16. The temple and its precincts were grand and imposing. The area enclosed by walls had been expanded by Herod the Great to a large irregular quadrangle containing approximately 35 acres.[12] Jesus did not, of course, enter the temple itself (only priests did that), but rather the area within these walls.

The temple tax and the payments for animals sold for sacrifice were paid in shekels.[13] Since shekels were not part of the normal Graeco-Roman coinage those who came to the temple needed to exchange their money. Those who came from a distance or who did not raise animals would need to purchase animals for sacrifice.[14] (Mark refers specifically to the sale of doves, which were required for some offerings and an option for the poor for others.)[15] These commercial activities were conducted in the Court of the Gentiles, the largest area within the temple walls.

---

that Jesus had no expectation of finding anything to eat on the fig tree. "The unexpected and incongruous character of Jesus' action in looking for figs at a season when no fruit could be found would stimulate curiosity and point beyond the incident to its deeper significance" (p. 400).

[11]*Shebiith* 4.7.

[12]Sanders, *Judaism*, p. 58.

[13]Gundry, p. 642.

[14]See Deut 14:24-26.

[15]Lev 1:14; 5:7, 11; 12:6, 8; 14:22,30; 15:14, 29; Luke 2:24.

Jesus' actions are subject to more than one interpretation.[16] He apparently did not disagree with the temple tax (cf. Matt 17:24-27) nor would he have disagreed with selling sacrificial animals to those who needed them. He probably objected to doing these things in the Court of the Gentiles. This interpretation may be supported by his citation of Isa 56:7 in which the house of God is described as "a house of prayer for all nations." He may have considered the prices to be oppressive or exploitative. This interpretation is supported by the allusion to Jer 7:11 in his statement that they had turned the temple into "a den of robbers." The fig tree incident suggests Jesus' actions represent a symbolic destruction of the temple, a prophetic action demonstrating God's judgment not only on the commercial activity, but on the temple and its authorities in general.[17] More than one of these views may be correct. They are not mutually exclusive.

V. 16 in particular is subject to two competing interpretations. The most likely view compares Jesus' concern to Mishnaic regulations against entering the temple area with a staff, sandals, or a wallet or using the forecourt of the temple area as "a short by-path."[18] According to this interpretation, Jesus was concerned with actions that desecrated the sanctity of the Court of the Gentiles. A less likely view takes the term σκεῦος (*skeuos*), which the NIV translates "merchandise," to mean "vessel" and to refer to the sacred vessels used in worship. According to this view, Jesus was virtually halting temple worship itself.[19]

17. The teachings Mark provides cast light upon the cleansing. The citation is from Isa 56:7, which in its Old Testament context refers to foreigners who serve God and offer sacrifices to him. God intended for his temple to be a place of worship not only for Jews, but also for men and

---

[16]William R. Herzog, II, "Temple Cleansing," in *DJG*, pp. 817-821.

[17]Ibid., p. 817.

[18]*Berakoth* 9.5. There is, of course, a dating problem for materials from the Mishnah, which was written about A.D. 200.

[19]Wise, "Temple Cleansing," p. 818.

women of other nations. The Court of the Gentiles, in which the commercial activities were conducted, was the place of worship for foreigners.

When Jesus makes the accusation, "You have made it 'a den of robbers,'" he alludes to Jer 7:11. There, in Jeremiah's famous temple sermon, God asked Jeremiah's contemporaries, "has this house, which bears my Name, become a den of robbers to you?" It is worthy of note that the following paragraph in Jeremiah's sermon prophesies the destruction of the temple. The destruction Jeremiah predicted took place in 587/6 B.C. In Mark Jesus will later (chapter 13) speak privately to his disciples about the destruction of the temple that would take place in A.D. 70.

18. The chief priests and teachers of the law recognized that Jesus' condemnation applied especially to them. They became fearful of Jesus' growing popularity with the crowds and therefore sought a way to kill him. This last comment by Mark echoes the plotting of the Pharisees and Herodians in 3:6.

19. Jesus and his disciples left the city to spend the night in Bethany (see 11:11-12; 14:3).

C. A LESSON FROM THE WITHERED FIG TREE (11:20-25)

[20]In the morning, as they went along, they saw the fig tree withered from the roots. [21]Peter remembered and said to Jesus, "Rabbi, look! The fig tree you cursed has withered!"

[22]"Have[a] faith in God," Jesus answered. [23]"I tell you the truth, if anyone says to this mountain, 'Go, throw yourself into the sea,' and does not doubt in his heart but believes that what he says will happen, it will be done for him. [24]Therefore I tell you, whatever you ask for in prayer, believe that you have received it, and it will be yours. [25]And when you stand praying, if you hold anything against any-

one, forgive him, so that your Father in heaven may forgive you your sins.[b]"

[a]*22* **Some early manuscripts** ***If you have*** [b]*25* **Some manuscripts** ***sins.*** [26]***But if you do not forgive, neither will your Father who is in heaven forgive your sins.***

Tuesday morning begins with the completion of the story of the fig tree. I have already commented on the symbolic meaning of the cursing in connection with the cleansing of the temple. In the conversation which follows the disciples' sighting of the withered tree, Peter makes a remark about the withering as illustrative of Jesus' power. This then becomes an opportunity for Jesus to teach a lesson about faith.

20-21. The morning marks the beginning of a third day, Tuesday. Having provided only eight verses with material from Monday, Mark dwells on Tuesday from 11:20 to 13:37. On the way back into Jerusalem the disciples saw the withered fig tree. Peter's remarks about it set the stage for Jesus' subsequent comments.

22-24. Mark repetitively emphasizes the importance of faith and this is perhaps the most striking treatment of this important aspect of the Christian life. Jesus exhorts the disciples to have faith in God.[20] Using the Mount of Olives as an example, Jesus says that one who has faith without doubt could even command the mountain to throw itself into the sea.[21] Two parallel statements urge the disciples to greater faith: "if anyone . . . does not doubt in his heart but believes that what he says will happen, it will be done for him" and "believe that you have received [whatever you ask for in prayer], and it will be yours." Both statements have a hyperbolic element. In the first case a hyperbole is found in the request of a mountain jumping into the sea. In the second a hyperbolic element is found in the tense of the verb receive:

[20]Some ancient witnesses have the less likely reading, "If you have faith in God." The meaning would be virtually the same.

[21]Cf. 1 Cor 13:2 "if I have a faith that can move mountains."

"believe that you have received it."[22] A literalistic understanding of these two statements would involve faith not only in God but also in our own ability to ask for the right things. Jesus' own example in Mark 14:36 suggests that faithful prayer is made with the qualification that God's will be done (cf. Matt 6:10). However, it is important not to blunt the force of these verses in Mark 11. Many times Christians do not receive what they ask for because they doubt God's ability or concern. These verses, along with James 1:5-8, are clarion calls to faith in God.

25. This verse is connected to the context by emphasizing another aspect of effective prayer. If we want God to forgive us, we must forgive others. Prayers are hindered both by lack of faith and by an inability to forgive, common maladies among ancient and modern people.[23]

D. ANOTHER SERIES OF CONTROVERSIES WITH THE RELIGIOUS AUTHORITIES (11:27-12:44)

Mark 2:1-3:6 contains a series of five controversies between Jesus and the religious authorities culminating in their decision to destroy him. The controversy continues in the succeeding narrative in 3:22-30; 7:1-23; 8:11-13; 9:14; and 10:1-9. It resumes with a vengeance after the cleansing of the temple which provoked the opponents of Jesus to begin looking for a way to kill him right away. The last story of chapter 11 and all seven segments of chapter 12 describe elements of the conflict during the last week.

---

[22]The tense of ἐλάβετε (*elabete*) is aorist. There are unlikely variants using the present tense ("believe that you are receiving it") and the future tense ("believe that you will receive it").

[23]V. 26 is omitted in modern translations because it is omitted in the best manuscripts and appears to be a scribal addition. The teaching of v. 26, "But if you do not forgive, neither will your Father who is in heaven forgive your sins," is implied by v. 25 and taught explicitly in Matt 6:15, the probable source of this scribal addition.

1. The Question about Authority (11:27-33)

27They arrived again in Jerusalem, and while Jesus was walking in the temple courts, the chief priests, the teachers of the law and the elders came to him. 28"By what authority are you doing these things?" they asked. "And who gave you authority to do this?"

29Jesus replied, "I will ask you one question. Answer me, and I will tell you by what authority I am doing these things.
30John's baptism – was it from heaven, or from men? Tell me!"

31They discussed it among themselves and said, "If we say, 'From heaven,' he will ask, 'Then why didn't you believe him?'
32But if we say, 'From men' . . . ." (They feared the people, for everyone held that John really was a prophet.)

33So they answered Jesus, "We don't know."

Jesus said, "Neither will I tell you by what authority I am doing these things."

The attacks made by the religious authorities typically take the form of questions. The question about the authority for Jesus' actions stems naturally from his bold act of cleansing the temple. It gets to the heart of the issue between Jesus and the religious authorities. They do not believe his teachings and actions are authorized by God.

27-28. For the third day in a row Jesus went into the temple. The questions were asked by the triumvirate first encountered in 8:31 in Jesus' prediction concerning his death: the chief priests, the scribes, and the elders. The two questions were interrelated. They wanted to know what authority Jesus had to do these things and who gave it to him. The questions arise from Jesus' presumptive act of cleansing the temple on the day before.

29-30. Jesus answered their question with one of his own, calculated both to indirectly answer their question and to simultaneously embarrass them before the people. He refuses to answer their question directly unless they answer his. The reference to John's baptism is a metonymy[24] for all of John the Baptist's work. "From heaven" is a common Jewish circumlocution for "from God," used in order to preserve the sanctity of the divine name.[25] It too is a metonymy. Jesus wanted to know if one who gave John the Baptist his authority was God. Since John testified to Jesus (1:7-8) the correct answer to Jesus' question would lead to the correct answer about Jesus' own authority.

31-33. Jesus knew the dilemma he was creating for the religious authorities. They, of course, did not believe John was authorized by God. On the other hand, John's status as a prophet sent by God was widely accepted (Mark hyperbolically says "everyone") among the people. The religious authorities were concerned about public opinion (cf. 11:18; 12:12, 38-40; 14:1-2) and refused to answer Jesus' question.

---

[24]A metonymy is "a figure of speech consisting of the use of the name of one thing for that of another of which it is an attribute or with which it is associated." *Collegiate Dictionary*, p. 732.

[25]Cf. Dan 4:26.

MARK 12

2. The Parable of the Tenants (12:1-12)

[1]He then began to speak to them in parables: "A man
planted a vineyard. He put a wall around it, dug a pit for the
winepress and built a watchtower. Then he rented the vineyard to some farmers and went away on a journey. [2]At harvest time he sent a servant to the tenants to collect from
them some of the fruit of the vineyard. [3]But they seized him,
beat him and sent him away empty-handed. [4]Then he sent
another servant to them; they struck this man on the head
and treated him shamefully. [5]He sent still another, and that
one they killed. He sent many others; some of them they
beat, others they killed.

[6]"He had one left to send, a son, whom he loved. He sent
him last of all, saying, 'They will respect my son.'

[7]"But the tenants said to one another, 'This is the heir.
Come, let's kill him, and the inheritance will be ours.' [8]So
they took him and killed him, and threw him out of the vineyard.

[9]"What then will the owner of the vineyard do? He will
come and kill those tenants and give the vineyard to others.
[10]Haven't you read this scripture:

"'The stone the builders rejected
has become the capstone;[a]
[11]the Lord has done this,
and it is marvelous in our eyes'[b]?"

[12]Then they looked for a way to arrest him because they
knew he had spoken the parable against them. But they

were afraid of the crowd; so they left him and went away.

[a] ***10*** **Or *cornerstone*** [b] ***11*** **Psalm 118:22,23**

Jesus "counterattacked" with a parable. Unlike other parables this one was directed to the religious authorities (see "them" and "they" in vv. 1 and 12). They understood the main point (v. 12). The parable is built from elements in Isa 5:1-7:

> I will sing for the one I love a song about his vineyard: My loved one had a vineyard on a fertile hillside. He dug it up and cleared it of stones and planted it with the choicest vines. He built a watchtower in it and cut out a winepress as well. Then he looked for a crop of good grapes, but it yielded only bad fruit. Now you dwellers in Jerusalem and men of Judah, judge between me and my vineyard. What more could have been done for my vineyard than I have done for it? When I looked for good grapes, why did it yield only bad? Now I will tell you what I am going to do to my vineyard: I will take away its hedge, and it will be destroyed; I will break down its wall, and it will be trampled. I will make it a wasteland, neither pruned nor cultivated, and briers and thorns will grow there. I will command the clouds not to rain on it. The vineyard of the Lord Almighty is the house of Israel, and the men of Judah are the garden of his delight. And he looked for justice, but saw bloodshed; for righteousness, but heard cries of distress.

In Isaiah's parable the owner is the Lord and the vineyard is the house of Israel, the people of Judah. The good grapes the Lord wanted were justice and righteousness. The bad fruit he got was bloodshed and cries of distress. The destruction of the vineyard referred to the coming destruction of Judah. Isaiah called upon the men of Judah to make a judgment about the fate of the vineyard (vv. 3-6) and then told them they had judged themselves (v. 7). Jesus clearly used elements of this ancient parable in constructing his own, although he altered it significantly so that it became a different story.

1. The wall, winepress, and watchtower reflect Isaiah's story. In Isaiah they represent God's loving care for his people. In Jesus' parable they perhaps just add local color to the story. Jesus' story leaves Isaiah's when the owner leaves for another country and rents the vineyard to tenants. This arrangement was common in first century Palestine. As the next verse indicates, wealthy land owners often leased their land to tenants in a share-cropping arrangement by which the owner would receive a share of the crop as payment for using the land.[1] The owner represents God and, unlike the Isaiah parable, the vineyard itself takes a back seat to the tenants, who represent the religious authorities. It is perhaps not important to decide in Jesus' parable precisely what the vineyard (God's people the Jews?) and the fruit (righteousness?) represent.

2-5. It is, however, important to observe that the servants sent by the owner represent the prophets (perhaps including John the Baptist). Jesus' parable makes the same point made by Stephen in Acts 7:51-52: "you stiff-necked people . . . You are just like your fathers: You always resist the Holy Spirit! Was there ever a prophet your fathers did not persecute? They even killed those who predicted the coming of the Righteous One."

6-8. Stephen continued in Acts 7:52-53: "And now you have betrayed and murdered him [the Righteous One]." This is the son of Jesus' parable. The son is identified as a "beloved son" as in 1:11 and 9:7. Identifying himself as the son of a vineyard owner in a parable is not as overt as saying "I am the Son of God," but it does clearly represent Jesus as uniquely related to God. He is not a servant as were the prophets, but a beloved son. The motivation Jesus portrays for the religious authorities is a selfish desire to keep control of the vineyard for themselves.

9. By using a question Jesus calls on the religious leaders to judge themselves. Then he answers his own question. Of course the owner (God) will destroy the tenants (the religious authorities) and give the vineyard (his people?) to others (the coming leaders of the church?).

---

[1]Lane, p. 417.

10-11. Jesus appealed to Scripture to underscore his main point. In Ps 118:22-23, using the imagery of a building in the place of a vineyard, God had already prophesied that the builders (= the tenants, the religious authorities) would reject the stone intended for the capstone[2] (= the son, Jesus), but that this stone would nonetheless become the capstone (= the overthrow of the tenants).

12. The religious authorities understood at least the basic point of the parable. They were afraid to arrest him in the midst of the crowd in the temple courts. They would find a less public opportunity (14:1-2, 10-11, 43-49).

3. The Question about Paying Taxes (12:13-17)

[13]Later they sent some of the Pharisees and Herodians to Jesus to catch him in his words. [14]They came to him and said, "Teacher, we know you are a man of integrity. You aren't swayed by men, because you pay no attention to who they are; but you teach the way of God in accordance with the truth. Is it right to pay taxes to Caesar or not? [15]Should we pay or shouldn't we?"

But Jesus knew their hypocrisy. "Why are you trying to trap me?" he asked. "Bring me a denarius and let me look at it." [16]They brought the coin, and he asked them, "Whose portrait is this? And whose inscription?"

"Caesar's," they replied.

[17]Then Jesus said to them, "Give to Caesar what is Caesar's and to God what is God's."

And they were amazed at him.

In 11:27-33 Jesus had embarrassed the religious authorities before the people with his question about the authority of John's baptism. They refused to answer because they would

---

[2]It is not clear whether κεφαλὴν γωνίας (*kephalēn gōnias*) should be translated "capstone" or "cornerstone." See Gundry, p. 691.

have alienated many in the crowd who viewed John as a prophet. Now they attempt to put Jesus on a similar spot. If he argues against paying the Roman taxes he would create a conflict with the Roman authorities. If he argues for paying the taxes he would alienate the many in the crowd who opposed them. The question was calculated to trap him.

13. The Pharisees and Herodians who came to Jesus were sent by the same religious authorities who had asked about Jesus' authority and who were the focus of his counterattack in the parable of the Tenants. On the Pharisees and Herodians and their collusion against Jesus see the comments on 3:6.

14-15a. It is ironic that the opponents of Jesus clearly portrayed their own lack of integrity as they addressed Jesus as "teacher" and praised his integrity which, of course, they did not believe in for a moment. In 11:32-33 Jesus' opponents declined to answer his question because of the pressure of public opinion, but now they praise Jesus for his teaching the way of God with no regard for public opinion. Once again they ask two questions that interrelate. The taxes they have in mind are those levied by Rome. They have no quarrel with the temple tax or other taxes that might be originated by Jewish authorities. In the eyes of many Jews the taxes levied by Rome were not only oppressively high, but were per se unacceptable as part and parcel of the unwanted dominion of Rome.

15b-17. Jesus' integrity contrasts with the hypocrisy of his opponents. As in other cases (2:8; 3:2-5) he knew their intent. In this case he openly declared it in his question, "Why are you trying to trap me?"

His response was so ingenious that even his opponents (the "them" and "they" of v. 17) were amazed at him. The coin he called for was a silver denarius with the head of the emperor Tiberius on its face and an inscription reading "Tiberius Caesar Augustus, Son of the Divine Augustus." Jesus reasoned that it was issued by and belonged to the emperor. The emperor could ask for it. On the other hand, one must give God what belongs to God. This qualification is vital and would certainly raise question even about the last words of the inscription on the denarius.

4. The Question about the Resurrection (12:18-27)

**18Then the Sadducees, who say there is no resurrection,
came to him with a question. 19"Teacher," they said, "Moses
wrote for us that if a man's brother dies and leaves a wife
but no children, the man must marry the widow and have
children for his brother. 20Now there were seven brothers.
The first one married and died without leaving any children. 21The second one married the widow, but he also died,
leaving no child. It was the same with the third. 22In fact,
none of the seven left any children. Last of all, the woman
died too. 23At the resurrection[a] whose wife will she be, since
the seven were married to her?"**

**24Jesus replied, "Are you not in error because you do not
know the Scriptures or the power of God? 25When the dead
rise, they will neither marry nor be given in marriage; they
will be like the angels in heaven. 26Now about the dead rising
– have you not read in the book of Moses, in the account of
the bush, how God said to him, 'I am the God of Abraham,
the God of Isaac, and the God of Jacob'[b]? 27He is not the God
of the dead, but of the living. You are badly mistaken!"**

[a]*23* Some manuscripts *resurrection, when men rise from the dead.* [b]*26* Exodus 3:6

In Mark's presentation Jesus is first approached by the religious authorities as a whole and questioned about his authority. After his rebuttal and the parable of the Tenants they no longer pursued him as a group, but the public questioning continued by sub-groups: first, the Pharisees and Herodians, and then, the Sadducees. (The final question was asked by a lone scribe.) The two sub-groups asked questions that would be typical of their concerns.

This is the only explicit reference to the Sadducees in Mark, although their presence must be assumed whenever the chief priests, scribes, and elders are referred to as a group. The Sadducees were an aristocratic party which included the high priest and presumably most of the chief priests. They accepted only the written law and denied the resurrection.[3]

18-23. Greco-Roman society in general accepted the notion of the immortality of the soul, but the resurrection of the body was another matter. The concept of a general resurrection was, however, widespread among the Jews and was supported by Jesus. The Sadducees denied it and perhaps developed certain stock questions to demonstrate its absurdity.[4] The question about the remarrying widow is based upon the levirate instructions of Deut 25:5-10. According to this law, if a man died without children, his brother should marry the widow and raise children in the first man's name. In the Sadducees' hypothetical case, the levirate rules caused a woman to sequentially marry seven brothers.[5] The purpose of the story is to set up a scenario that creates an insoluble problem for those who believe in the resurrection. The question "whose wife will she be" is supposed to be unanswerable.

24-25. But the question is answerable. If the Sadducees had known the Scriptures and the power of God, they would have known that there will be no marriage in heaven. Those who are raised will be like the angels. The angels are not portrayed as married in Scripture or in other ancient Jewish literature. It is difficult to know whether Jesus' reasoning about the resurrected ones being unmarried like the angels was common or uncommon among his contemporaries. In several relevant Jewish texts those who are raised are said to resume

---

[3]On the Sadducees see Sanders, *Judaism*, pp. 317-340.

[4]In 1 Cor 15:35 Paul addresses such a question (although I do not intend to suggest that the Sadducees were behind the Corinthians who asked it). In Corinth the question is "How are the dead raised? With what kind of body will they come?"

[5]Tobit 3:8, written in the second century B.C., tells of a woman widowed seven times without bearing children.

relationships they had on earth, although without explicit reference to marriage. 2 Baruch 51:10, a Jewish document written about A.D. 100, describes the resurrected righteous as being like angels, although again without explicit reference to marriage.[6] In any case, Jesus' contemporaries would have recognized that the angels were not married and could have followed his reasoning that being like them involved being unmarried. This would be true even of the Sadducees who did not believe in angels (Acts 23:8).

26-27. The scriptural argument Jesus gives in these verses reflects both of the items he said the Sadducees did not understand: the Scriptures and the power of God (v. 24). Jesus chose a text from the Pentateuch, Exod 3:6,[7] perhaps because the Sadducees accepted only the books of Moses. It is difficult to follow Jesus' reasoning in v. 27. Most interpreters of Exod 3:6 would think God was simply identifying himself as the God worshipped by the patriarchs during their lifetime and passed down by them to their descendants. I am inclined to follow the understanding of Dreyfuss, articulated well by Hurtado: "Jesus argues that if Abraham, Isaac, and Jacob have passed into oblivion (as the Sadducees believed happened to all the dead), then God's description of himself as the God of these patriarchs of old conveys nothing about his power to save his people, and indeed this title is a mockery of any hope that God deserves the trust of his followers. . . . God's covenant is meaningless if it is canceled by death."[8]

It should be noted that in this context Jesus is discussing the future general resurrection of the dead. He is not discussing the pre-resurrection status of Abraham, Isaac, or Jacob.

---

[6]According to 1 Enoch 62:13-16, a portion of 1 Enoch written perhaps about the same time period as 2 Baruch, "the righteous and elect ones . . . will wear the garments of glory." This metaphor may reflect an angelic status.

[7]The reference to "the account of the bush," is a sort of rough ancient counterpart to verse and chapter references.

[8]Hurtado, pp. 195-196.

5. The Question about the First Commandment (12:28-34)

[28]One of the teachers of the law came and heard them debating. Noticing that Jesus had given them a good answer, he asked him, "Of all the commandments, which is the most important?"

[29]"The most important one," answered Jesus, "is this: 'Hear, O Israel, the Lord our God, the Lord is one.[a] [30]Love the Lord your God with all your heart and with all your soul and with all your mind and with all your strength.'[b] [31]The second is this: 'Love your neighbor as yourself.'[c] There is no commandment greater than these."

[32]"Well said, teacher," the man replied. "You are right in saying that God is one and there is no other but him. [33]To love him with all your heart, with all your understanding and with all your strength, and to love your neighbor as yourself is more important than all burnt offerings and sacrifices."

[34]When Jesus saw that he had answered wisely, he said to him, "You are not far from the kingdom of God." And from then on no one dared ask him any more questions.

[a]*29* Or *the Lord our Lord is one Lord* [b]*30* Deut. 6:4,5 [c]*31* Lev. 19:18

Mark does not clarify whether the final lone questioner of Jesus was sincere or was making another attempt to ensnare him. Matt 22:34-35 clearly includes this question among those designed to test Jesus. The nature of the question makes this segment of Mark one of the most important. Here the reader finds the essence of God's will.

28. I prefer the more literal NRSV translation "Which commandment is the first of all?" because it preserves more naturally the link between v. 29 "The first is" and v. 31 "The second is." But the question does mean, "Which commandment is the most important?" According to the Babylonian Talmud, Jesus' predecessors had been asked a similar question:

> On another occasion it happened that a certain heathen came before Shammai and said to him, "Make me a proselyte, on condition that you teach me the whole Torah while I stand on one foot." Thereupon he repulsed him with the builder's cubit which was in his hand. When he went to Hillel, he said to him, "What is hateful to you, do not to your neighbor: that is the whole Torah, while the rest is commentary thereof; go and learn it."[9]

29-31. Jesus answered with a first and second commandment. In both cases he cites Scripture: Deut 6:4-5 and Lev 19:18. The first citation is of the famous Shema,[10] cited twice daily by many pious Jews from before the time of Jesus[11] to the present. The first commandment, "Love the Lord your God" is qualified by "with all your heart and with all your soul and with all your mind and with all your strength."[12] The point is to love God with all our being. The second commandment is a citation of Lev 19:18. It is parallel in structure to the first commandment: "Love your neighbor" is qualified by "as yourself."

Jesus' view of what is central in God's will was not new. Since there were hundreds of commandments it was natural from the beginning to prioritize. The ten commandments were themselves a summary and they could be further distilled into two sections. Philo, a contemporary of Jesus who lived in Alexandria, observed that the ten commandments contained five dealing with responsibilities toward God (or "piety") and five dealing with responsibilities toward other people (or "justice").[13] Seen in their contexts, the Shema and

---

[9]*Shabbath* 31a, as translated in *The Babylonian Talmud*, 35 vols., ed. Isidore Epstein (London: Soncino Press, 1935-38). There is significant question about the reliability of this account, since the Babylonian Talmud dates to the 5th-7th centuries A.D.

[10]Named by the first word in the Hebrew text, "Shema," which means "Hear."

[11]Cf. *Letter of Aristeas* 160; *Jubilees* 6:14.

[12]The Hebrew and LXX of Deut 6:5 do not contain "with all your mind."

[13]Philo, *Who Is the Heir of Divine Things* 168, 172; *Special Laws* 2.63.

Lev 19:18 appear to have served a summarizing function. In Luke 10:25-27 a (religious) lawyer asked Jesus how to inherit eternal life, and when Jesus turned the question back to him, the lawyer answered with the same answer Jesus gives in Mark: the Shema and Lev 19:18. The essence of God's will has always been plain – although many have missed it.

32-33. The scribe recognized the validity of Jesus' response. His reply indicated an appreciation for Jesus' analysis. In his reply he correctly emphasized the monotheism of the Shema ("God is one and there is no other beside him") which undergirds the absolute nature of the devotion he demands ("all" of one's being, which is not divided in the service of multiple gods). He also observed correctly, in line with the prophets, that love of God and neighbor are more important than "all burnt offerings and sacrifices" (cf. Hos 6:6; Mic 6:6-8). The focus of God's will is not ritual, but the heart.

34. As the scribe had observed that Jesus answered well, Jesus saw that the scribe's understanding of the matter was wise. "You are not far from the kingdom of God" suggests not only that this particular man was progressing in his understanding toward Jesus, but that the kingdom of God focuses on love of God and others.

Jesus' answers drove his critics out of the arena of public debate.

6. Jesus' Question about David's Son (12:35-37)

35While Jesus was teaching in the temple courts, he asked, "How is it that the teachers of the law say that the Christ[a] is the son of David? 36David himself, speaking by the Holy Spirit, declared:

"'The Lord said to my Lord:
"Sit at my right hand
until I put your enemies under your feet."'[b]

37David himself calls him 'Lord.' How then can he be his son?"

The large crowd listened to him with delight.

[a]*35* Or *Messiah* [b]*36* Psalm 110:1

Jesus now counters with a question of his own. Like the triumphal entry and the parable of the Tenants, the question about David portrays Jesus being publicly provocative concerning his messiahship, although without making clear proclamations.

35. The setting for all of the controversies in 11:27-12:44 is the temple court area. Jesus broached the subject of the messiah and at the same time criticized the religious authorities by asking about the common teaching that "the Christ is the son of David." The common idea that the messiah would be from the lineage of David is rooted solidly in 2 Sam 7:11-16. Many Jews of Jesus' time expected a ruler to arise from the lineage of David.

The question initially seems odd because it is clear that early Christians, including Mark (10:47-48; 11:10), taught that Jesus was indeed the promised messiah from the lineage of David. However, the fuller form of the question in vv. 36-37 shows that Jesus did not intend to raise doubt about the messiah being the son of David, but to raise a question about the sense in which that would be true.

36-37. Jesus cited Ps 110:1 and referred it to David and ultimately to the Holy Spirit. The point of v. 37 depends on seeing Ps 110:1 as a messianic text. Interpreted as a messianic Psalm it refers to the great future son of David. Jesus' interpretation also hinges upon seeing this Psalm as penned by David, so that he can argue that David himself calls his future son "Lord" (κύριος, *kyrios*). In the Psalm "the Lord" is Yahweh and "my lord" is the messiah. His greatness is indicated not only by David calling him "lord," but also by his positioning at

---

[14]E.g., *Psalms of Solomon* 17:21-32, written in the first century B.C. V. 21 says, "See, Lord, and raise up for them their king, the son of David, to rule over your servant Israel in the time known to you, O God."

the right hand of God's throne and his triumph over his enemies. Presumably the crowd was delighted because they understood Jesus to be saying that the messiah would be greater than David himself. They probably misunderstood the exaltation and triumph spoken of in Ps 110:1 as a reference to the messiah's coronation as king and triumph over the Roman oppressors. Such thoughts would fill them with delight.

7. Jesus Denounces the Teachers of the Law and Commends a Poor Widow (12:38-44)

38As he taught, Jesus said, "Watch out for the teachers of the law. They like to walk around in flowing robes and be greeted in the marketplaces, 39and have the most important seats in the synagogues and the places of honor at banquets. 40They devour widows' houses and for a show make lengthy prayers. Such men will be punished most severely."

41Jesus sat down opposite the place where the offerings were put and watched the crowd putting their money into the temple treasury. Many rich people threw in large amounts. 42But a poor widow came and put in two very small copper coins,[a] worth only a fraction of a penny.[b]

43Calling his disciples to him, Jesus said, "I tell you the truth, this poor widow has put more into the treasury than all the others. 44They all gave out of their wealth; but she, out of her poverty, put in everything – all she had to live on."

[a]*42* Greek *two lepta* [b]*42* Greek *kodrantes*

These two stories should be read in conjunction with each other. There is a contrast here between the religious authorities who greedily took all they could get even from widows, and the poor widow who freely gave what little she had to God. These two segments bring to an end Jesus' public teaching in the temple courts. Chapter 13 contains private teaching to the disciples. On Wednesday Mark does not indicate that Jesus entered Jerusalem (14:1-11). On Thursday he entered only in the evening for the Passover meal.

38-40. Jesus' criticisms of the scribes boil down to two basic issues. Five of the items listed indicate that they love the praise of people and use their piety for this purpose: they "like to walk around in flowing robes and be greeted in the marketplaces, and have the most important seats in the synagogues and the places of honor at banquets . . . and for a show make lengthy prayers."[15] The second basic issue is that they are greedy for money and "devour widows houses." This last phrase probably means they took advantage of widows for financial support.[16]

The observation that "such men will be punished most severely" is one of a few New Testament references to the idea of degrees of punishment (cf. James 3:1).

41-44. Many rich people put in large amounts into the temple treasury, but their gifts were small compared to the poor widow's gift. The two copper coins were leptons, the smallest coins in circulation, now commonly called "widow's mites." Mark apparently did not believe his audience would recognize the currency and so gave the value at one quadrans. The monetary value of two leptons or one quadrans was extraordinarily small. In Jesus' day a quadrans was worth 1/144 of a denarius.[17] The NIV seeks to get the point across by saying that the two copper coins were worth only a fraction of a penny.

Jesus' surprising statement in v. 43 is explained by v. 44. The poor woman put in more than all the others in terms of the amount of sacrifice she made. God measures the gift by the sacrifice involved (cf. 2 Sam 24:24). The point is parallel to the superiority of the two great love commands over all

---

[15]Cf. Luke 11:43; 14:7-11; Matt 6:5; 23:6-7.
[16]Gundry, p. 727.
[17]Gundry, p. 729.

sacrifices and burnt offerings (v. 33). Jesus' teaching about the widow's offering also implies further criticism of the scribes. They sought to squeeze the last penny from widows out of greed, but the poor widow gave the last penny to the Lord out of love and self-sacrifice.

MARK 13

E. JESUS INSTRUCTS THE DISCIPLES CONCERNING THE DESTRUCTION OF JERUSALEM AND THE SECOND COMING (13:1-37)

There is a contextual link between the cleansing of the temple, the controversies between Jesus and the religious leadership, and Jesus' statements about the destruction of the temple. As Jesus left the temple courts for the last time, he spoke to his disciples about the destruction of the entire complex. This provoked them to ask about this event and others. The difficult discourse that follows treats the A.D. 70 destruction of the temple and the city of Jerusalem, and relates that event to the second coming of the Son of Man.

This chapter is one of the most difficult sections of Mark. There are two major difficulties. The first is to determine in various segments whether Jesus is discussing a) the general events of the last days (which includes all of the period between his resurrection and his return), b) the A.D. 70 destruction of Jerusalem and the temple by the Roman army, or c) his return at the end of human history. The second is to determine how these events are related chronologically.

Before entering the details of this chapter, it would be beneficial to reread the comments on Mark 9:1, an enigmatic saying with some importance for the present chapter. I also want to make the reader aware of several of my own general perspectives on the broader issues of interpretation:

I. It seems clear to me that there are two basic points in this chapter which are of significant importance for contemporary Christianity. These are both warnings. One is the warning not to be misled by false claims that Jesus has returned or that certain signs indicate the immediate proximity of his return (vv. 5-8, 21-23, 32; cf. 2 Thess 2:1-2). The other primary warning is to be faithful and live in a state of constant preparation for his return (vv. 12-13, 33-37). It is easy to understand these warnings. It is also easy to overlook them in the effort to sort out the exegetical conundrums of this chapter. It is unfortunate that the problems of the chapter's interpretation tend to overpower these simple, basic warnings. Most of the problems concern matters that are not nearly so significant for daily Christian living as these basic admonitions.

II. There are certain perspectives on some issues in this chapter which seem to me to be so clearly erroneous that I will dismiss them here and not deal with them in the detailed comments. In the light of the major siege and destruction of Jerusalem by Roman armies in A.D. 70 it is basically ahistorical to interpret the destruction prophesied in Mark 13 as referring to a yet-to-come destruction of Jerusalem (preceded by removing the Dome of the Rock and rebuilding the Jewish temple). This dispensational premillenial view[1] of the chapter is especially contrary to the parallel in Luke 21:20 which clearly refers to the Roman armies that surrounded Jerusalem. No ancient readers would have imagined otherwise.

Another view that must be dismissed is the view that Jesus mistakenly prophesied that his return would come immediately on the heels of the destruction of Jerusalem. The dispensationalists do not have this problem because they believe the second coming will immediately follow the future destruction of Jerusalem. But for virtually everyone else the critical problem of the chapter is the apparent prophecy that the return of Christ, like the destruction of Jerusalem, will occur within Jesus' generation (vv. 24-31). Some interpreters solve the problem by assuming that Jesus made a mistake.[2] This solu-

---

[1]See the critique of the dispensational view in Carson, "Matthew," pp. 494-495.

[2]Some seek to save Jesus from error by suggesting that Mark has misrepresented him. Jesus' credibility is salvaged at the expense of Mark's.

tion creates the major problem of a fallible Jesus, an unacceptable alternative for those with an orthodox understanding of Jesus' identity. A few recent conservative interpreters have argued that Jesus did prophesy his return within his generation and was not mistaken but understood it to be a conditional prophecy.[3] He did not return within his generation because the conditions were not met. I consider this alternative possible, although not without serious problems.

A few interpreters consider all of Mark 13 to be about the destruction of Jerusalem and do not find any reference there to the return of Jesus at the end of the age.[4] This view is possible but difficult for vv. 24-27, which will be discussed in due course. It seems to me to be clearly unacceptable for vv. 32-37, especially in the light of the additional material found in the parallel to Mark 13 in Matt 24-25. Working backward section by section from the judgment of the sheep and the goats in Matt 25:31-46 it is apparent that Matthew must be discussing the return of Jesus at the end of the age in 24:36-25:46. Mark 13:32ff. is parallel to Matt 24:36ff. and also discusses the return of Jesus at the end time.

III. If the major conundrum of the chapter is the chronological relationship of the destruction of Jerusalem and the second coming, there are four possible solutions that have both strengths and weaknesses. I will attempt to set forth strengths and weaknesses of each in the course of the comments. Each of the four has major flaws, but one of them is probably correct. Each of the four can be reconciled with an orthodox and non-dispensational understanding of Christ's second coming. The four major acceptable views are:

a. That Jesus conditionally prophesied that the destruction of Jerusalem would be followed by the second coming, both

---

[3]So Gundry, p. 790.

[4]Described and rebutted by Richard T. France, *Jesus and the Old Testament*, (Downers Grove: InterVarsity, 1971), pp. 229-230. France is talking about Matt 24, but the same issues apply to Mark 13.

occurring within a generation of his prophecy (but the conditions were not met).[5]

b. That all of vv. 5-31, including everything through the statement "this generation will certainly not pass away until all these things have happened," refers to the destruction of Jerusalem (or before) and the discussion of the second coming does not begin until v. 32.[6]

c. That vv. 5-23 refer to the destruction of Jerusalem (or before), vv. 24-27 refer to the second coming, vv. 28-31 refer to the destruction of Jerusalem (or before) and vv. 32-37 refer to the second coming (an A-B-A-B pattern).[7]

d. That vv. 5-23 refer to the general characteristics of all of the last days (from Jesus' resurrection to his second coming); that within this section vv. 14-19 refer specifically to the destruction of Jerusalem; that vv. 24-27 refer to the second coming, vv. 28-31 refer to the destruction of Jerusalem and to some occurrences of all the characteristic features of the last days (described in vv. 5-13 and 20-23), and vv. 32-37 refer to the second coming.[8] This view might be represented as follows:

5-13, 20-23	Characteristic features of the last days (i.e., the period between Jesus' resurrection and his return)
14-19	The destruction of Jerusalem, a major event within the last days
24-27	The second coming
28-31	A time reference referring to vv. 5-23, the destruction of Jerusalem and some occurrences of each of the characteristic features that would occur repetitively throughout the last days

[5]Gundry, p. 790. See the critique of this view by Carson, "Matthew," p. 491.

[6]See R.T. France, *Matthew*, Tyndale New Testament Commentaries (Grand Rapids: Eerdmans, 1985), pp. 333-349.

[7]Lane, pp. 444-484; McGarvey, pp. 203-215.

[8]Carson, "Matthew," pp. 488-511.

32-37 A time reference referring to vv. 24-27, the second coming

Readers who enjoy jigsaw puzzles may be intrigued by these possibilities. Others may feel exhausted at the outset. There must be a correct view and it is presumably one of these four. All of them lead to essentially the same consequences: 1) at least vv. 14-19 refer to the destruction of Jerusalem in A.D. 70; 2) the other items prophesied in vv. 5-23 occurred by that time and many have occurred repeatedly since; 3) the second coming could occur at any time because all the preconditions mentioned in these verses have been met; and therefore, 4) all Christians living after the destruction of Jerusalem should be ready for the second coming to occur at any time. Without wishing to denigrate any of these four views, I will make a case for the fourth – despite its obvious weakness of being the most complicated view. Much of my analysis will be dependent upon Carson's comments on the parallel text in Matt 24.

1. The Setting of Jesus' Last Days Discourse (13:1-4)[9]

1As he was leaving the temple, one of his disciples said to him, "Look, Teacher! What massive stones! What magnificent buildings!"

2"Do you see all these great buildings?" replied Jesus. "Not one stone here will be left on another; every one will be thrown down."

3As Jesus was sitting on the Mount of Olives opposite the temple, Peter, James, John and Andrew asked him privately, 4"Tell us, when will these things happen? And what will be the sign that they are all about to be fulfilled?"

9The titles for the sections in chapter 13 are adapted from Carson, "Matthew," pp. 496-507.

These initial verses set the stage for the discourse that follows in vv. 5-37. The entire chapter completes Tuesday, Jesus' third and last day to enter the temple courts. This day appropriately concludes with a discourse that begins with observations about the great temple.

1. Jesus never entered the temple per se, but the temple courts, the vast area surrounding the temple and divided into the Court of the Gentiles, the Court of the Women, and The Court of the Israelites (Men). The temple complex and its buildings were truly magnificent. The walls encased approximately 35 acres. The majority of its stones weigh about two to five tons each. The largest found thus far weighs almost 400 tons! An inner wall encompassing the temple itself had ten gates, each with two doors measuring about 45 feet high and 22 feet wide! Herod wanted the complex to be impressive.[10]

2. It was surely disturbing to the disciples to hear that such great buildings would be completely destroyed. There was, of course, a well-known precedent. The great temple of Solomon had been leveled by the Babylonians in the 6th century B.C.

3-4. From the Mount of Olives on the east side of the city, visitors today still marvel at the panoramic view of the city and especially the temple mount, which is still present on the eastern side of the city, although now occupied by Moslem mosques. From this vantage point the four brothers asked Jesus to expand upon his statement concerning the temple. The question has two parts. They want to know when these things will happen and what signs will indicate they are about to happen. The use of the plural "these things" suggests the disciples have a complex of events in mind. Matthew's version of the question (Matt 24:3) indicates that this complex of events included the coming of Jesus and the end of the age. In Mark Jesus' response to their question includes not only the destruction of the temple and the city, but also general

---

[10]Sanders, *Judaism*, pp. 54-69, 306-314, provides a detailed examination and several illustrations of the entire temple complex.

characteristics of the last days and comments on his second coming.

2. General Description of the Birth Pains (13:5-13)

**[5]Jesus said to them: "Watch out that no one deceives you.
[6]Many will come in my name, claiming, 'I am he,' and will
deceive many. [7]When you hear of wars and rumors of wars,
do not be alarmed. Such things must happen, but the end is
still to come. [8]Nation will rise against nation, and kingdom
against kingdom. There will be earthquakes in various
places, and famines. These are the beginning of birth pains.**

**[9]"You must be on your guard. You will be handed over to
the local councils and flogged in the synagogues. On
account of me you will stand before governors and kings as
witnesses to them. [10]And the gospel must first be preached
to all nations. [11]Whenever you are arrested and brought to
trial, do not worry beforehand about what to say. Just say
whatever is given you at the time, for it is not you speaking,
but the Holy Spirit.**

**[12]"Brother will betray brother to death, and a father his
child. Children will rebel against their parents and have
them put to death. [13]All men will hate you because of me,
but he who stands firm to the end will be saved.**

Jesus began his response with a warning against being misled by false messiahs or by misreading the common events of the last days. Instead of being misled into erroneous speculations, what the disciples must do is be watchful and endure persecution. They will be persecuted by religious and government institutions at all levels. They will be betrayed by family members and hated by everyone. But the Holy Spirit will help them and those who endure will be saved.

5-8. The characteristic word of the chapter is the imperative verb βλέπετε (*blepete*), which the NIV translates "watch out" or "be on guard" (vv. 5, 9, 23, 33). The disciples were interested in signs. Jesus did not want them to be misled. There would be false messiahs. Outbreaks of wars, earthquakes, or famines might mislead them into believing the end of the age was imminent. But the end is still to come. Contrary to popular belief even today, these sorts of events are not signals of the immediate proximity of the end.

The wars, earthquakes, and famines experienced in the disciples' own times were the beginnings of what Jesus called the "birth pains" (ὠδίνων, *ōdinōn*). Several Old Testament texts use the image of a woman in labor to illustrate the woes of a people under siege (Isa 13:8; 26:17; Jer 4:31; 6:24; Mic 4:9-10). The birth pains Jesus speaks of are the wars, earthquakes, and famines that characterize the days from his resurrection to his return. Some non-Christian Jewish writings reflect similar ideas of end time woes. For example, 2 Baruch (a Jewish apocalyptic document written about A.D. 100) breaks the time leading up to the revelation of the messiah into twelve parts. The first will contain "the beginning of commotions"; the second through fourth, "the slaughtering of the great," "the fall of many into death," and "the drawing of the sword"; the fifth, "famine and the withholding of rain"; and the sixth, "earthquakes and terrors" (2 Baruch 27:1-7).[11]

9-13. The disciples must remain on constant guard because they will be subject to intense persecution. The book of Acts testifies to the fulfillment of these verses. The disciples have a work to do before the end can come. The gospel must be preached to all the nations. In order to help them complete their task the Holy Spirit will tell them what to say when they have opportunity to testify to various institutional leaders (from council leaders to kings). The trials seem to be described as part of the means by which the gospel will be preached to all nations – even to rulers in high places. It will be difficult to stay on task because the persecution of

---

[11]Translation of *2 Baruch* from James H. Charlesworth, ed., *The Old Testament Pseudepigrapha*, 2 vols., (New York: Doubleday, 1983, 1985). Cf. the Babylonian Talmud *Shabbath* 118a; *Sanhedrin* 98b.

Christians will be intense, even pitting family members against brother, children, or parents so that one has another put to death for faith in Christ. Everyone will hate Christians. But those who endure to the end will be saved. For some "the end" here refers to the end of their life, for others to the end of the world.[12]

3. The Sharp Pain: The Destruction of Jerusalem (13:14-19)

[14]"When you see 'the abomination that causes desolation'[a] standing where it[b] does not belong – let the reader understand – then let those who are in Judea flee to the mountains. [15]Let no one on the roof of his house go down or enter the house to take anything out. [16]Let no one in the field go back to get his cloak. [17]How dreadful it will be in those days for pregnant women and nursing mothers! [18]Pray that this will not take place in winter, [19]because those will be days of distress unequaled from the beginning, when God created the world, until now – and never to be equaled again.

[a]*14* Daniel 9:27; 11:31; 12:11 [b]*14* Or *he*; also in verse 29

With his reference to "the abomination that causes desolation," Jesus turned specifically to the issue which opened this Pandora's box in the first place. There is little doubt that vv. 14-19 focus on the events of A.D. 66-70. Most interpreters would include vv. 20-23. I will argue otherwise below.

14. The NIV translation "abomination that causes desolation" is helpful. "To desolate" means "to lay waste" or "deprive of inhabitants." The phrase refers to something detestable that causes such desolation. It has a specific background in Dan 8:13; 9:27; 11:31; and 12:11, from which it was

---

[12]See Carson, "Matthew," p. 250 (concerning the parallel statement in Matt 10:22). For a differing view see Lane, p. 460 n. 57.

used prior to Jesus also in 1 Macc 1:54. In Daniel this abomination was to be set up at the temple. 1 Maccabees correctly interprets Daniel as speaking of the actions of the Hellenistic ruler Antiochus IV when he initiated sacrifices to Zeus over the altar of burnt offering and outlawed the practice of Judaism.

Modern interpreters are not in agreement on interpreting the use of this phrase by Jesus. Mark wanted his readers to understand[13] and presumably they were in better position to do so. Matt 24:15 says that "the abomination that causes desolation" will stand "in the holy place." "Holy place" may refer to Jerusalem (which Matthew elsewhere calls the "holy city," Matt 4:5; 27:53). In that case Luke's statement, "When you see Jerusalem surrounded by armies, you will know that its desolation is near," (Luke 21:20) probably provides the key to understanding "the abomination." However, the "holy place" in Matthew might mean the temple precincts (cf. Acts 6:13; 21:28). In that case Luke's reference to the time when the Roman armies surround Jerusalem presumably is another sign and not an explanation of the abomination.[14] The abomination might refer to activities carried out by the Zealots, the leaders of Jewish opposition to the Romans, who committed sacrileges in the temple courts during the years of the Roman siege of Jerusalem. Among their own abominations were murder and the appointment of a farcical high priest.[15]

When the abomination appeared, it would be time to flee to the mountains.[16]

---

[13]Some advocate the less likely interpretation that Jesus wanted the readers of Daniel to understand. But "let the reader understand" is more naturally understood as an editorial comment by Mark.

[14]Cf. Carson, "Matthew," pp. 500-501.

[15]Lane, pp. 468-469, defends this view, basing his argument primarily on Josephus' descriptions of the Zealots' desecration of the temple.

[16]In the fourth century Eusebius wrote in his *Ecclesiastical History* 3.5.3 that "before the war, the people of the Church of Jerusalem were bidden in an oracle given by revelation to men worthy of it to depart from the city and to dwell in a city of Perea called Pella." But he does not refer to the Gospels and their warning to flee to the mountains.

15-16. These verses emphasize the necessity for immediate flight. Jesus' instructions about fleeing from a rooftop assume a flat roof and an outside staircase or ladder.[17] Those on rooftops should not take time even to enter the house. Those working in the fields should not take time to get their cloaks.

17-19. The comment about pregnant women and nursing mothers may refer to the difficulties of flight or to the living situations in the mountain caves where they would hide. The disciples should pray that the time for flight would not take place in winter, which would exacerbate the difficulties of escaping the unprecedented distress of the siege and destruction of Jerusalem.

4. Warnings against False Messiahs during the Birth Pains (13:20-23)

[20]If the Lord had not cut short those days, no one would survive. But for the sake of the elect, whom he has chosen, he has shortened them. [21]At that time if anyone says to you, 'Look, here is the Christ[a]!' or, 'Look, there he is!' do not believe it. [22]For false Christs and false prophets will appear and perform signs and miracles to deceive the elect – if that were possible. [23]So be on your guard; I have told you everything ahead of time.

[a]*21* Or *Messiah*

The most difficult element in Carson's overall interpretation of Matt 24 and in my parallel interpretation of Mark 13 is the notion that at this point (Matt 24:22-29; Mark 13:20-23) Jesus shifted focus from the destruction of Jerusalem in particular back to the characteristics of the last days in general (as in vv. 5-13). The reference to "days" (the Greek text does not include "those" before "days" as in the NIV) in v. 20 has

[17]Rousseau and Arav, *Jesus and His World*, p. 129.

seemed to most interpreters to refer to "those days" in v. 19, which in turn refer to the days of the siege and destruction of Jerusalem. However, the reference to "the elect" in v. 20 would most naturally refer to the true Christian believers who presumably escaped the tribulation of v. 19. This points to a return to the general woes (wars, earthquakes, famines, etc.) of the end times. Similarly, "all flesh" (πᾶσα σάρξ, *pasa sarx*, translated "no one" in the NIV) typically refers to everyone rather than everyone in Jerusalem. The false messiahs of vv. 21-22 are not limited to the time of the siege and destruction of Jerusalem, but have already been introduced as characteristic of the end times in v. 6. Verse 19 may be seen as a fitting end to the particular discussion of the siege and destruction of Jerusalem.[18] Although I recognize the difficulties involved and the minority status of such an interpretation, I will treat vv. 20-23 as a new paragraph which turns away from Jerusalem and back to the end times in general. From this standpoint, vv. 14-19 constitute a special subsection within the broader context of vv. 5-23. The broader context deals with the general characteristics of the end times – not just the events of A.D. 66-70.

20. The wars, famines, earthquakes, and other disasters of the end times would ultimately lead to the destruction of all humanity if they continued unabated. However, for the sake of the elect, the faithful, God has determined to shorten the period between the resurrection and the second coming.

21-22. These verses resume the theme of vv. 5-6. During the end times there will be false Christs and false prophets who will seek to deceive the people of God. They should not be misled. When the Son of Man returns, they will see him "coming in clouds with great power and glory" (v. 26).

23. Jesus repeats the chapter's watchword: "be on your guard" (see comments on v. 5). He has told them what would happen so that they would not be misled by false teachers or by misreading the signs of the end times.

---

[18]These arguments are made by Carson, "Matthew," pp. 502-503.

5. The Second Coming (13:24-27)

[24]"But in those days, following that distress,
"'the sun will be darkened,
and the moon will not give its light;
[25]the stars will fall from the sky,
and the heavenly bodies will be shaken.'[a]
[26]"At that time men will see the Son of Man coming in clouds with great power and glory. [27]And he will send his angels and gather his elect from the four winds, from the ends of the earth to the ends of the heavens.

[a]*25* Isaiah 13:10; 34:4

R.T. France is probably the best representative of those interpreters who believe that vv. 24-27 refer to the destruction of Jerusalem.[19] This point of view deserves careful consideration. Numerous Old Testament texts (e.g., Isa 13:10; 34:4) use cosmic imagery similar to that in vv. 24-25 to describe the overthrow of nations within human history. In Mark 13 the coming of the Son of Man might be a heavenly coming to God for vindication (cf. Dan 7:13-27) and the sending of the angels might be the sending of missionaries (the word translated "angels" [ἀγγέλους, *angelous*] also means "messengers") to gather the elect into the church.

Nevertheless, France's view is difficult to maintain, especially in vv. 26-27. The descriptions of the Son of Man "coming in clouds with great power and glory" and "sending out the angels to gather his elect" are most naturally seen in the context of numerous New Testament references to the second coming, several of which refer to Jesus coming with clouds and to the role of the angels (see especially Matt 13:37-43; 25:31; 2 Thess 1:7; Rev 1:7).[20]

24-25. According to the interpretation presented above for vv. 20-23, the distress referred to in v. 24 is not limited to the

[19]France, *Matthew*, pp. 333-350.
[20]Carson, "Matthew," p. 493.

destruction of Jerusalem, but presumably refers to the general characteristics (wars, earthquakes, famines, etc.) of all of the period between Jesus' resurrection and his return. God has cut short the days of such tribulations (v. 20). They will be brought to an end by the second coming (vv. 24-27).

The NIV puts the celestial upheavals of vv. 24-25 in quotation marks because they reflect such Old Testament texts as Joel 2:10; 3:15; Ezek 32:7-8; Amos 8:9; and especially Isa 13:10 and 34:4. In general, the Old Testament texts use this language in a metaphorical sense for events that occur within human history. It is difficult to decide whether to take Jesus literally or metaphorically. Since he is speaking of the second coming and the end of the world, it may be appropriate to take his language literally.[21]

26-27. The description of "the Son of Man coming in clouds with great power and glory" alludes to Dan 7:13-14 (cf. Mark 14:62). The angels come with him and are sent out to gather the elect. This description of the second coming of Christ resonates with many other New Testament texts, especially Matt 13:37-43; 25:31; 2 Thess 1:7; and Rev 1:7.[22]

6. The Significance of the Birth Pains for the Second Coming (13:28-31)

28"Now learn this lesson from the fig tree: As soon as its twigs get tender and its leaves come out, you know that summer is near. 29Even so, when you see these things happening, you know that it is near, right at the door. 30I tell you the truth, this generation[a] will certainly not pass away until all these things have happened. 31Heaven and earth will pass away, but my words will never pass away.

[a]*30* Or *race*

---

[21]Cf. 2 Pet 3:10-12.

[22]Matthew's parallel, 24:31, adds the trumpet call, further underscoring the reference to the second coming (cf. 1 Cor 15:52; 1 Thess 4:16).

28-29. With a brief parable (the word translated "lesson" is παραβολή [*parabolē*]) about a fig tree, Jesus reflects on both parts of the disciples' question: when will these things be and what will be the sign that they are about to be fulfilled? When the fig tree begins sprouting leaves, everyone knows the summer is near. Similarly, when the disciples see these things happening, they will know that his return is near. Interpreters have argued over the meaning of "these things" and over what Jesus says is near.

It is illogical to consider "these things" to include the second coming itself.[23] There would then be nothing left to describe as near. It would not make sense to say that when the second coming happened the disciples would know it was near. Since the celestial events of vv. 24-25 seem to be a part of the second coming, they are not likely to be included either. In v. 29 "these things" presumably refers to everything in vv. 5-23, the destruction of Jerusalem and the general characteristics of the period between Jesus' resurrection and return.[24]

If this is correct, then that which is near is the second coming. There is a slight ambiguity in the Greek text in that the pronoun subject of "is near" is simply implied in the verb (ἐστιν, *estin*) and could be translated "it" (as in the NIV) or "he" (as in the NRSV). In either case, the reference is probably to the second coming ("it") of the Son of Man ("he").[25] After the occurrence of the general characteristics of the end times and of the destruction of Jerusalem, the second coming would be near. That does not mean it must happen immediately after the destruction of Jerusalem, for Jesus goes on to say that "about that day or hour no one knows" (v. 32) and "you do not know when the master of the house will come" (v. 35). It does mean that it could happen at any time after the signs had occurred.

---

[23]Carson, "Matthew," p. 507.

[24]Ibid.

[25]Contra Lane, who argues that "it is near" refers to the abomination of desolation and the destruction of Jerusalem (p. 478 n. 99).

30-31. "All these things" should be understood in the light of "these things" in v. 29. The second coming itself is not included. According to this understanding there is no need to resort to some unusual interpretation of the phrase "this generation." Within roughly forty years of Jesus' discourse, the disciples had witnessed examples of all the general characteristics of the end times (which continue today) and the destruction of Jerusalem. It would be especially problematic to assert that Jesus erred in his prediction regarding what would happen in his generation since he begins his statement with "I tell you the truth" (cf. 3:28) and follows it with "my words will never pass away."

7. No One Knows the Day or Hour of the Second Coming (13:32-37)

[32]"No one knows about that day or hour, not even the angels in heaven, nor the Son, but only the Father. [33]Be on guard! Be alert[a]! You do not know when that time will come. [34]It's like a man going away: He leaves his house and puts his servants in charge, each with his assigned task, and tells the one at the door to keep watch.

[35]"Therefore keep watch because you do not know when the owner of the house will come back – whether in the evening, or at midnight, or when the rooster crows, or at dawn. [36]If he comes suddenly, do not let him find you sleeping. [37]What I say to you, I say to everyone: 'Watch!'"

[a]*33* **Some manuscripts** ***alert and pray***

32. Although the events of vv. 5-23 would all take place within a generation and from that time forward the second coming would be near, no one knows the day or hour of the second coming. It is remarkable that those who do not know the day or hour include not only the angels but also the Son.

33. After the occurrence of characteristic end time events and the destruction of Jerusalem, the disciples would know that the second coming was near – but they would not know the time. Therefore, they (and we) must live in a constant state of readiness. Jesus again repeats his watchword, "Beware" (βλέπετε, *blepete*, cf. comments on v. 5).

34-36. Jesus emphasizes the point with another parable, which might be called the parable of the Doorkeeper. The disciples will be like a slave whose master went away for an unspecified period and left him to keep watch at the door. The doorkeeper must stay alert at all times so that whenever the master returns he will not catch the doorkeeper sleeping. Like the second coming, the master's return is described as "sudden" (ἐξαίφνης, *exaiphnēs*) and as occurring at any time of the day or night.

37. The chapter ends with a virtual synonym for the characteristic watchword *blepete* (vv. 5, 9, 23, 33). The word translated "watch" is γρηγορέω (*grēgoreō*), chosen over *blepete* because of its use in the parable where it describes the doorkeeper's responsibility. Jesus' discourse begins and ends with an exhortation to "watch" (*blepete*, v. 5; *grēgoreite*, v. 37). Its major thrusts are to warn the disciples to watch out in order not to be deceived and in order to be constantly ready for the Son of Man's return.

MARK 14

F. JESUS HONORED AND BETRAYED (14:1-11)

[1]Now the Passover and the Feast of Unleavened Bread
were only two days away, and the chief priests and the
teachers of the law were looking for some sly way to arrest
Jesus and kill him. [2]"But not during the Feast," they said,
"or the people may riot."

[3]While he was in Bethany, reclining at the table in the
home of a man known as Simon the Leper, a woman came
with an alabaster jar of very expensive perfume, made of
pure nard. She broke the jar and poured the perfume on his
head.

[4]Some of those present were saying indignantly to one
another, "Why this waste of perfume? [5]It could have been
sold for more than a year's wages[a] and the money given to
the poor." And they rebuked her harshly.

[6]"Leave her alone," said Jesus. "Why are you bothering
her? She has done a beautiful thing to me. [7]The poor you
will always have with you, and you can help them any time
you want. But you will not always have me. [8]She did what
she could. She poured perfume on my body beforehand to
prepare for my burial. [9]I tell you the truth, wherever the
gospel is preached throughout the world, what she has done
will also be told, in memory of her."

[10]Then Judas Iscariot, one of the Twelve, went to the
chief priests to betray Jesus to them. [11]They were delighted
to hear this and promised to give him money. So he watched
for an opportunity to hand him over.

[a]5 Greek *than three hundred denarii*

Throughout chapters 14 and 15 every segment of the narrative relates directly to Jesus' death. The death and resurrection (chapter 16) of Jesus are the climactic events of Mark's Gospel and indeed of any telling of the gospel story.

The first two stories in Mark 14 are another instance of a "sandwich" in which one story frames another. In this case the story of the arrangements for Judas' betrayal brackets the story of the woman anointing Jesus for burial. The contrast is remarkable.

1-2. After the lengthy account of events set on Tuesday of Jesus' last week (11:20-13:37), the account of events on Wednesday is brief (14:1-11). Jesus does not enter the city of Jerusalem again until Thursday evening when he enters for the Passover meal. Mark, of course, does not say "Wednesday" but relates Wednesday and Thursday to the Passover celebration and the week-long Feast of Unleavened Bread. On the Passover see the introductory comments below on vv. 12-31. The Feast of Unleavened Bread was a week-long celebration of the Exodus connected with the Passover meal (Exod 12:15-20; 23:15; 34:18; Deut 16:1-8).[1]

The religious leaders' fear of arresting Jesus in a public setting while Jerusalem was swelled with pilgrims to the Feast resonates with their earlier refusal to answer Jesus' question about John the Baptist "because they feared the people" (11:32). Both Jesus and John had significant followings among the people.

3. In the midst of the story of the arrangements for Jesus' betrayal Mark breaks to Bethany and a moving counter-story. The Greek text identifies the owner of the house Jesus was dining at as Simon the leper. The NIV translation "a man known as" presumably reflects the translators' opinion that if

---

[1]In popular usage the Passover and the Feast of Unleavened Bread were sometimes distinguished, but at other times one term or the other was used to include both. For discussions with references see Robert H. Gundry, *Matthew* (Grand Rapids: Eerdmans, 1982), p. 524; Sanders, *Judaism*, pp. 132-133.

Simon were still a leper the Mosaic laws concerning cleanliness would prevent him from entertaining guests.[2]

The expensive perfume is identified as nard, an oil extracted from a plant native to India.[3] It was sealed in a small alabaster flask.[4] The woman presumably broke the neck of the bottle to release the perfume.

4-5. The nard was worth more than three hundred denarii, each of which represented a day's wage for a common laborer – more than a year's wages altogether. Some of those present[5] rebuked her for her extravagance. Would it not be better to sell the perfume and give the money to the poor?

6-9. Jesus, however, commended the woman's action. In the light of his impending death he interpreted it as preparing his body for burial. The Jewish burial custom was to lay the body in a niche within a natural or man-made cave until it decayed and could be removed to an ossuary (a wooden or stone box for the bones of the deceased). The body was prepared with perfume before or as it was placed in the niche. It is not likely that the woman knew the full import of her action, because she presumably did not understand that Jesus was about to die.

Jesus' statement about always having the poor is misunderstood if it is seen as in any way callous to the plight of the poor and the need to give to them. In fact, his wording alludes to Deut 15:11 in which "There will always be poor people in the land" leads to "Therefore I command you to be openhanded toward your brothers and toward the poor and needy in your land." What justified the woman's extravagant act was Jesus' impending death.

Through the Gospels what this woman did has in fact been told throughout the world wherever the gospel has been preached. Here Jesus apparently uses the term "gospel" with

---

[2]So Lane, p. 492.

[3]In his *Natural History* 12.25.42 the first century writer Pliny the Elder describes nard as holding "the foremost possible rank among perfumes."

[4]Ibid., 13.3.19: "The best ointment is preserved in alabaster."

[5]The disciples according to Matt 26:8.

reference to the message of his death and resurrection, a message to be proclaimed after his death.

10-11. Mark now returns to the story of betrayal begun in vv. 1-2. Judas Iscariot, one of the Twelve, provided a means for the chief priests to accomplish the goal of vv. 1-2, to arrest Jesus away from the crowd. It would not be long before Judas found the opportunity he was looking for.

G. THE PASSOVER MEAL (14:12-31)

Jesus' last meal before his death was the most important meal in the Jewish calendar (Exod 12:1-13, 21-27, 43-49; Num 9:1-14; Deut 16:1-8). During the afternoon hours of the 14th day of the month of Nisan the lambs were slaughtered for the Passover meal, which was eaten on the evening of the 15th day (which began, according to the Jewish calendar, at sundown). According to our system the preparation took place on Thursday afternoon and the meal was eaten Thursday evening. The day would have been in our month of March or April.[6]

The Passover meal was an annual memorial to the Exodus, when the Lord "passed over" the Israelite homes and took the firstborn of each Egyptian family, provoking Pharaoh to let the Israelites escape into the desert. The Exodus was the benchmark event of Old Testament history just as the death of Jesus would become the benchmark event of New Testament history. It was no accident that Jesus' last meal and the meal during which he established the Lord's Supper memorial was the Passover meal.

---

[6]Most first century Jews used a lunar calendar. The average lunar month is roughly 29½ days. By alternating between 29 and 30 day months a lunar calendar produces a year of 354 days. The Jews inserted a thirteenth month every three years or so to keep the calendar related to the seasons created by the sun. The date of Easter in Western nations moves in a way similar to the old lunar calendar because it is observed on the first Sunday after the first full moon after the vernal equinox. (Unlike Easter, Passover was not tied to a particular day of the week.) See the discussion in Sanders, *Judaism*, pp. 131-132.

1. Preparation for the Passover (14:12-16)

**[12]On the first day of the Feast of Unleavened Bread,
when it was customary to sacrifice the Passover lamb, Jesus'
disciples asked him,"Where do you want us to go and make
preparations for you to eat the Passover?"**

**[13]So he sent two of his disciples, telling them,"Go into
the city, and a man carrying a jar of water will meet you.
Follow him. [14]Say to the owner of the house he enters, 'The
Teacher asks: Where is my guest room, where I may eat the
Passover with my disciples?' [15]He will show you a large
upper room, furnished and ready. Make preparations for us
there."**

**[16]The disciples left, went into the city and found things
just as Jesus had told them. So they prepared the Passover.**

12. The first day of the Feast of Unleavened Bread is another chronological marker, which brings us to Thursday. That afternoon the lambs would be sacrificed and all the other preparations for the Passover meal would be made. The meal involved the Passover lamb, unleavened bread, and bitter herbs (Exod 12:8).

13-16. These verses follow the same pattern as 11:1-6, when Jesus sent two disciples to bring the colt for his entry into Jerusalem. In both cases he sent two disciples, told them exactly what they would encounter, and gave them a message for the responsible party. In both cases, the disciples' mission went just as Jesus had said.

The Passover was eaten within the walls of Jerusalem. The house Jesus used had an upper room large enough for thirteen and furnished for dining.

2. Jesus Predicts His Betrayal (14:17-21)

**[17]When evening came, Jesus arrived with the Twelve.
[18]While they were reclining at the table eating, he said,"I tell**

you the truth, one of you will betray me – one who is eating with me."

[19]They were saddened, and one by one they said to him,"Surely not I?"

[20]"It is one of the Twelve," he replied,"one who dips bread into the bowl with me. [21]The Son of Man will go just as it is written about him. But woe to that man who betrays the Son of Man! It would be better for him if he had not been born."

17-20. Thursday evening Jesus and the Twelve came to the upper room for the Passover. All but one of the Twelve must have been shocked at Jesus' statement that one of them would betray him. With the rhetorical question "Surely not I?" each one denied any such intent. But Jesus reaffirmed that it would be someone at that very table, dipping bread into the bowl. One who was sharing the meal would commit the offense. Jesus probably alluded to Ps 41:9: "Even my close friend, whom I trusted, he who shared my bread, has lifted up his heel against me."[7]

21. Ps 41:9 may be part of what Jesus had in mind in speaking of the Son of Man going as it is written about him, although he may have been thinking of other Old Testament texts about his suffering (see comments at 8:31). In any event, even though the death of the Son of Man was prophesied, his betrayer would be culpable and would be punished severely.

3. The Institution of the Lord's Supper (14:22-25)

[22]While they were eating, Jesus took bread, gave thanks and broke it, and gave it to his disciples, saying,"Take it; this is my body."

[23]Then he took the cup, gave thanks and offered it to them, and they all drank from it.

---

[7]Cf. John 13:18.

**24"This is my blood of the[a] covenant, which is poured out
for many," he said to them. 25"I tell you the truth, I will not
drink again of the fruit of the vine until that day when I
drink it anew in the kingdom of God."**

[a]*24* Some manuscripts *the new*

22. Jesus used two of the items found in the memorial Passover meal and gave them a new meaning in relationship to his coming death. By so doing he established a new memorial meal.

The NIV translation that having taken the bread Jesus "gave thanks" is slightly misleading. For the bread Mark uses the term εὐλογέω (*eulogeō*), "to bless." For the cup he uses the term εὐχαριστέω (*eucharisteō*), "to give thanks." There is, however, little difference.[8] The bread which he used is not specified as unleavened, but must have been to be part of the Passover meal.

It seems extraordinarily unlikely that Jesus would expect the Twelve to understand "this is my body" literally when he (and his body) was personally with them at the table.[9] The Passover meal itself involved a heavy use of symbolism and the apostles would surely have understood Jesus to be using the bread symbolically.[10]

23-24. Wine would have been part of virtually every meal, including the Passover. Jesus' actions with respect to the cup of wine parallel those with respect to the bread, except he cannot break the wine into pieces for distribution and so he passes the cup for all to drink of it. His words reflect not only his coming death but its atoning value. The phrase "blood of the covenant" echoes Exod 24:8 in which, during the process of confirming the covenant at the foot of Mount Sinai, Moses sprinkled sacrificial blood on the Israelites and described it as "the blood of the covenant that the LORD has made with you."

---

[8]Luke 22:19 uses *eucharisteō* for the bread.
[9]Gundry, p. 831.
[10]Hurtado, p. 235.

The shedding of Jesus' blood would inaugurate a new[11] covenant with God. The statement that Jesus' blood is "poured out for many" alludes to Isa 53:12 ("he poured out his life unto death . . .For he bore the sin of many") and parallels Jesus' statement in Mark 10:45 that he would die "as a ransom for many." These two verses describe Jesus' death as a vicarious sacrifice which atones for the sins of the many.

25. Jesus implicitly speaks of his death in saying he will not drink the vine again until he drinks it in the kingdom of God. This statement parallels his statement in Luke 22:15-16 that he will not eat the Passover until it is fulfilled in the kingdom of God. He presumably speaks of the messianic banquet, when "many will come from the east and the west and will take their places at the feast with Abraham, Isaac and Jacob in the kingdom of heaven" (Matt 8:11; cf. Isa 25:6; Rev 19:9). At that time he will again eat and drink the Passover – in a transformed sense.

H. JESUS PREDICTS THE FLIGHT OF THE DISCIPLES AND PETER'S DENIAL (14:26-31)

26When they had sung a hymn, they went out to the Mount of Olives.

27"You will all fall away," Jesus told them, "for it is written:

"'I will strike the shepherd,
and the sheep will be scattered.'[a]

28But after I have risen, I will go ahead of you into Galilee."

29Peter declared, "Even if all fall away, I will not."

30"I tell you the truth," Jesus answered, "today – yes, tonight – before the rooster crows twice[b] you yourself will disown me three times."

---

[11]The better manuscripts do not contain the word "new," but of course the covenant inaugurated by Jesus' death was new (cf. Luke 22:20; 1 Cor 11:25).

[31]But Peter insisted emphatically,"Even if I have to die with you, I will never disown you." And all the others said the same.

[a]*27* Zech. 13:7 [b]*30* Some early manuscripts do not have *twice*.

Chapter 14 repeatedly underscores the failures of the Twelve. Judas arranges to betray Jesus (vv. 10-11), Jesus predicts the betrayal (vv. 18-21), Jesus predicts the flight of the others and in particular Peter's denial (vv. 27-31), the three cannot remain awake (vv. 37-38, 40-41), Judas betrays Jesus (vv. 43-45), the others flee (vv. 50-52), and Peter fulfills the prophecy of his denials (vv. 66-72). On the last two days before his death, Jesus' teachings on discipleship in Mark 8-10 seem to have fallen on deaf ears.

26. According to later rabbinic materials the singing at the conclusion of the Passover would have been from the Hallel Psalms (Pss 114-118).[12] Leaving the city of Jerusalem, they went back to the Mount of Olives. Jesus had left the city, presumably for Bethany, each night since his entry on Sunday.

27. Jesus' prediction that the Twelve would all fall away was rooted in Zech 13:7. The latter chapters of Zechariah, 9-14, appear repeatedly in quotations or allusions in connection with Jesus' last days.[13]

28. Jesus' references to his death are customarily accompanied by references to his resurrection (cf. 8:31; 9:9, 12, 31; 10:33-34). Although the shepherd will be struck down he will rise. There is also a note of hope here for the Twelve. Although the sheep will be scattered, they will reunite with the shepherd in Galilee. This verse forms the background to the message for the disciples from the angel at the empty tomb: "He is going ahead of you into Galilee. There you will see him, just as he told you" (16:7).

---

[12]Mishnah *Pesahim* 10:5-7. Brown, pp. 122-123, rightly questions the validity of these Mishnaic traditions for the time of Jesus.

[13]E.g., Zech 9:9 (Mark 14:24); 12:10 (John 19:37).

29-31. Peter was certain he would not be like the others. His declaration provoked a particularly foreboding prediction for Peter himself. That very night Peter would deny his connection with Jesus three times. This would happen before the cock crowed twice.[14] (Several Graeco-Roman sources indicate that the second cock crow was associated with dawn.[15]) But Peter – and the others – assured Jesus they would die with him if necessary. Their actions would demonstrate otherwise.

Mark presumably wants his audience to learn from the mistakes of the Twelve. Those who believe Mark was written in connection with the Neronian persecution see direct relevance to that setting throughout chapter 14. Although I date the setting of Mark too early for the Neronian persecution, it seems apparent that throughout the first several decades of early Christianity there would be Christians in various locations who could directly appropriate the lessons learned from Judas' betrayal (cf. 13:12), the flight of the Twelve, and Peter's denial.

I. PRAYER IN GETHSEMANE (14:32-42)

[32]They went to a place called Gethsemane, and Jesus said to his disciples,"Sit here while I pray." [33]He took Peter, James and John along with him, and he began to be deeply distressed and troubled. [34]"My soul is overwhelmed with sorrow to the point of death," he said to them. "Stay here and keep watch."

---

[14]There are textual variants at each of Mark's references to two cock crows: 14:30, 68, 72a, and 72b. The references to two cock crowings in vv. 30, 72a, and 72b were probably part of Mark's original text, removed by some scribes who thought they conflicted with the other Gospels. The reference to the first cock crowing in v. 68 is more weakly attested. It is not a necessary accompaniment to Mark's references to two cock crows and it may have been added by scribes who believed there needed to be a specific reference to the first cock crow. See Metzger, *Textual Commentary*, pp. 96-98.

[15]Brown, p. 137, citing Aristophanes, *Ecclesiazusae* 30-31, 390-391; Juvenal, *Satire* 9.107-108; and Ammianus Marcellinus, *Res Gestae* 22.14.4.

[35]Going a little farther, he fell to the ground and prayed that if possible the hour might pass from him. [36]"Abba,[a] Father," he said,"everything is possible for you. Take this cup from me. Yet not what I will, but what you will."

[37]Then he returned to his disciples and found them sleeping. "Simon," he said to Peter,"are you asleep? Could you not keep watch for one hour? [38]Watch and pray so that you will not fall into temptation. The spirit is willing, but the body is weak."

[39]Once more he went away and prayed the same thing. [40]When he came back, he again found them sleeping, because their eyes were heavy. They did not know what to say to him.

[41]Returning the third time, he said to them,"Are you still sleeping and resting? Enough! The hour has come. Look, the Son of Man is betrayed into the hands of sinners. [42]Rise! Let us go! Here comes my betrayer!"

[a]*36* Aramaic for *Father*

This third instance in which Mark speaks of Jesus praying (cf. 1:35; 6:46) is the most important of the three. It is well known to modern Christians as portraying the humanity of Jesus and as a model for prayer. In Mark's account the focus seems to fall on the contrast between how Jesus faced the impending crisis of his life in submissive prayer vs. the disciples' failure to prepare. In terms of Mark's focus on christology, the Gethsemane scene portrays Jesus as "overwhelmed with sorrow" at the prospects of the cross and yet unflinchingly submissive to the Father's will. In terms of the focus on discipleship, it calls on the reader to watch and pray as did Jesus and not to follow the example of the disciples.

32. The name Gethsemane comes from a Hebrew phrase meaning "oil presses."[16] It was probably an olive grove with an oil press. This grove was located on the Mount of Olives.

---

[16]*BAGD*, p. 153. See also Brown, pp. 606-607.

Jesus went there to pray in preparation for the events that he knew were imminent.

33-34. Once again he selected the three to go along with him. Mark's statement that he was distressed and troubled and Jesus' self-description as "overwhelmed with sorrow to the point of death" graphically portray the distress he felt concerning his impending fate. Jesus' own comment probably means something like, "I am so very sorrowful that it is killing me."[17] The exhortation to the three to "keep watch" should be viewed in the light of the use of the same word (γρηγορέω, *grēgoreō*) in the parable of the Doorkeeper (13:34-37) and in 14:37-38. It has religious overtones of watching out for temptation and keeping alert against Satan. A similar idea is found in 1 Pet 5:8: "Be sober and watch (*grēgoreō*), for your adversary, the devil, as a roaring lion walks about seeking whom he will devour" (NRSV).[18]

35-36. Jesus alone went on "a little farther" – Luke 22:41 says about "a stone's throw." There he "fell to the ground," a humble posture for prayer and another indication of his distraught condition. The metaphors of the hour passing from him and the cup being taken away from him are parallel descriptions of the same request. Both refer to his impending suffering and death. The metaphor of drinking a cup of suffering has already appeared in Mark 10:38-39. The metaphor of the hour is clarified in the immediate context when Jesus says, "The hour has come. Look, the Son of Man is betrayed into the hands of sinners" (14:41).

The Aramaic word *abba* is transliterated into Greek three times in the New Testament: Mark 14:36; Gal 4:6; and Rom 8:15. In each case it is immediately translated by the Greek πατήρ (*patēr*), which means "Father." These texts indicate that the Aramaic word became known and remembered even in the Greek speaking church. Its precise meaning on the lips of Jesus continues to be a matter of debate. In an influential

---

[17]Brown, pp. 155-156, discusses this possibility and others.
[18]See Brown, pp. 156-157.

study J. Jeremias argued that it was the term used by children for their fathers, that it therefore expressed an intimate family relationship, and that Jesus' use of the term was without precedent among the Jewish people.[19] However, the form used by children for their parents was not *abba*, but *abi* (אבי).[20] The form used by Jesus was an unusual form of address and was, so far as existing evidence demonstrates, unprecedented as a personal address to God. It was not, however, the intimate term used by children for their fathers.[21]

Jesus expressed his intense desire not to have to endure the suffering he knew awaited him in the immediate future. At the same time he expressed his acknowledgment of God's control of all things and his willingness to submit to the will of God, however different his own desires might be. Mark's summation of Jesus' prayer provides both insight into Jesus himself and a model for Christian prayer.

37-38. Despite the fact that Jesus had revealed to them the state of his heart (v. 34) the disciples fell asleep. Jesus perhaps chose to speak to Peter because he was the one who so boldly insisted that he would not leave Jesus and he was the one who would soon deny him three times. He, and the others, desperately needed to pray not to fail. The NIV should provide at least a footnote alternative to "fall into temptation." The verb ἔλθητε (*elthēte*) is literally "come" not "fall" and the noun πειρασμόν (*peirasmon*) may be translated "trial."[22] The NRSV translates "come into the time of trial." That very evening Peter would encounter one of the great trials of his life. He was eager and willing to remain faithful to Jesus ("Even if all fall away, I will not" v. 29), but he would be too weak to live up to his intentions. He needed to pray. So did they all, because all the disciples would flee at the time of Jesus' arrest.

---

[19]Joachim Jeremias, *The Central Message of the New Testament* (New York: Charles Scribner's Sons, 1965), pp. 9-30.

[20]This form of the word is found in a Dead Sea Scroll prayer-psalm (4Q372) in reference to God. See Brown, p. 172.

[21]Brown, p. 173.

[22]*BAGD*, p. 640.

39-40. The threefold repetition of Jesus' prayer and the disciples' sleeping underscores both behaviors. The statement, "They did not know what to say to him," does not necessarily imply that he asked them anything. They knew what he expected.

41-42. The question "Are you still sleeping and resting?" is not an inquiry, but a criticism. They knew they were supposed to be praying. The word translated "Enough!" (ἀπέχει, *apechei*) is extraordinarily difficult to translate in this context. I am inclined to agree with Raymond Brown. After a survey of suggested alternatives, he chooses the translation "It is paid," which "preserves the most frequently attested meaning of *apechei* in ordinary life."[23] Jesus is saying that Judas has received his money. The betrayal is at hand.

"The hour" is the hour Jesus prayed to avoid. When the Son of Man is betrayed into the hands of sinners he will suffer and die upon a cross. Jesus must know at this point that the hour will not pass from him (cf. v. 35).

J. BETRAYAL, ARREST, AND FLIGHT (14:43-52)

43Just as he was speaking, Judas, one of the Twelve, appeared. With him was a crowd armed with swords and clubs, sent from the chief priests, the teachers of the law, and the elders.

44Now the betrayer had arranged a signal with them:"The one I kiss is the man; arrest him and lead him away under guard." 45Going at once to Jesus, Judas said,"Rabbi!" and kissed him. 46The men seized Jesus and arrested him. 47Then one of those standing near drew his sword and struck the servant of the high priest, cutting off his ear.

48"Am I leading a rebellion," said Jesus,"that you have come out with swords and clubs to capture me? 49Every day I was with you, teaching in the temple courts, and you did not

---

[23]Brown, pp. 208-209, 1379-1383.

arrest me. But the Scriptures must be fulfilled." [50]**Then everyone deserted him and fled.**

[51]**A young man, wearing nothing but a linen garment, was following Jesus. When they seized him,** [52]**he fled naked, leaving his garment behind.**

The arrest apparently took place in the olive grove. Christologically, this scene portrays Jesus willingly submitting to the will of God and fulfilling the Scriptures. It begins Jesus' ordeal with the indignity of being arrested as though he were a criminal. In terms of discipleship, this is a low point in which the disciples serve as a strong counter example to the behavior Mark wants to commend. One of them betrays Jesus and the others flee, leaving him to face his ordeal alone.

43. The crowd with Judas is armed with swords and clubs. The reference to swords suggests the idea of military or paramilitary arms. This is not a lynch mob, but a delegation sent by the Sanhedrin.[24] One member of the crowd is described in v. 47 as the servant of the high priest.

44-45. The crowd Judas was leading was not a group of men who knew Jesus well. The prearranged signal was a kiss. It is probable that a kiss was a common method of greeting at the time.[25] With a kiss and the greeting "Rabbi,"[26] Judas perhaps sought to appear "disarmingly normal."[27]

46-47. As the men seize and arrest Jesus as though he were a common criminal, someone present strikes out momentarily in defense and cuts off the ear of the servant of the high priest. John 18:10 identifies the sword wielder as Peter. His courage was short-lived, for in v. 50 he fled with the rest.

48-49. Jesus' complaint has two parts. "Am I leading a rebellion?" is a dubious translation of "Am I a criminal (ληστής, *lēstēs*)?" The word *lēstēs* is used in the Gospels and

---

[24]Cf. Matt 26:47; John 18:3.

[25]Brown, pp. 254-255.

[26]On the term Rabbi see the comments on 9:5.

[27]Brown, p. 254.

elsewhere of violent criminals of various types. It was *lēstai* (the plural form) who beat and robbed the man going down to Jericho who was later aided by the Good Samaritan (Luke 10:30, 36). Such men could be involved in a rebellion (Mark 15:7; cf. John 18:40; Josephus, *War* 2.57), but they might be merely common thugs.[28] Jesus' point is that coming after him with swords and clubs suggest he is a violent man who needs to be subdued with weapons.

The second part of Jesus' complaint is that he could easily have been arrested during one of his visits to the temple courts, visits characterized by public teaching. He had not hidden like some criminal who needed to be sought out in the hills.

Jesus viewed what had just happened and what it was leading to as the fulfilment of Scripture (cf. 8:31; 9:12; 10:45; 12:10-11; 14:21, 27).

50-52. One such fulfilment is immediately mentioned. In 14:27 Jesus had referred to Zech 13:7 in predicting the disciples' coming desertion. Now it is fulfilled. The English translation hides an unfortunate contrast between 1:18, 20 and 14:50. In the former verses the four fishermen "left" (ἀφίημι, *aphiēmi*) their nets and their families and followed Jesus. Now, along with all the others, they "left" (*aphiēmi*) Jesus. Mark does not identify the young man who even left his clothes behind when the arresting party got a hand on them. The point he apparently had in mind with this little extra is to illustrate the intensity of the desire to flee. This young man ran out of his clothes and fled naked rather than be caught along with Jesus.

K. JESUS AND PETER PUT ON TRIAL (14:53-72)

In another "sandwich" of two stories, Mark clearly juxtaposes the trial[29] of Jesus and his brave confession before the

[28]Brown, p. 283.

[29]Brown, p. 329, suggests that "hearing" or "legal proceeding" might be

high priest with the testing of Peter and his cowardly denials before a servant girl who worked for the high priest.

Some scholars have raised historical questions about the trial before the Sanhedrin based upon traditions found in the Mishnah. According to these traditions the trial contains various illegalities. For example, capital cases were not tried at night, such cases required two consecutive days of trial, and Jesus should have been offered a defense attorney. However, the Mishnah was compiled about A.D. 200 and there are serious dating problems with the legal traditions and their applicability to the days of Jesus. Furthermore, the Sanhedrin may very well have engaged in illegal proceedings in their efforts to destroy Jesus. Part of the impetus behind many historical critics with respect to the trial scene is the accusation that the portrayals of the trial are anti-Semitic. It is certainly true that racists have used the trials and various aspects of the sentencing and death of Jesus to promote anti-Semitic sentiments and to stir up hatred against all Jews. Such twisting of Scripture has been used to promote many grievous offenses including the Jewish holocaust of the mid-twentieth century. However, it is another matter to accuse the Gospels themselves (three of which were written by Jews) of anti-Semitism because they report the participation of some Jews, even of the leading council, in the death of Jesus. On the matter of anti-Semitism and on the historical debates consult Carson's commentary on Matthew.[30]

1. Jesus' Trial before the Sanhedrin (14:53-65)

53They took Jesus to the high priest, and all the chief priests, elders and teachers of the law came together. 54Peter followed him at a distance, right into the courtyard

---

more technically correct in their modern senses. I follow him and others in using the traditional term "trial," without intending technical precision.

[30]Carson, "Matthew," pp. 549-552.

of the high priest. There he sat with the guards and warmed himself at the fire.

[55]The chief priests and the whole Sanhedrin were looking for evidence against Jesus so that they could put him to death, but they did not find any. [56]Many testified falsely against him, but their statements did not agree.

[57]Then some stood up and gave this false testimony against him: [58]"We heard him say, 'I will destroy this man-made temple and in three days will build another, not made by man.'" [59]Yet even then their testimony did not agree.

[60]Then the high priest stood up before them and asked Jesus, "Are you not going to answer? What is this testimony that these men are bringing against you?" [61]But Jesus remained silent and gave no answer.

Again the high priest asked him, "Are you the Christ,[a] the Son of the Blessed One?"

[62]"I am," said Jesus. "And you will see the Son of Man sitting at the right hand of the Mighty One and coming on the clouds of heaven."

[63]The high priest tore his clothes. "Why do we need any more witnesses?" he asked. [64]"You have heard the blasphemy. What do you think?"

They all condemned him as worthy of death. [65]Then some began to spit at him; they blindfolded him, struck him with their fists, and said, "Prophesy!" And the guards took him and beat him.

[a]*61* Or *Messiah*

53. The meeting of the high priest, the chief priests, the elders, and the scribes is clearly defined in v. 55 as an assembly of the Sanhedrin, the governing body of the Jews.[31] On this occasion they met at the home of the high priest Caiaphas, whose term of office lasted nineteen years, from A.D. 18 to 37.

---

[31]See the comments at 8:31.

54. The next sentence begins the story of Peter's denials, which is completed in vv. 66-72. Peter kept his distance in following Jesus, but went on into the courtyard of the high priest. The guards he was sitting with are identified by the term ὑπηρέτης (*hypēretēs*), a term which in this context probably refers to police attendants as in Matt 5:25 ("the judge may hand you over to the *officer*") or Acts 5:26 ("the captain went with his *officers* and brought the apostles"). John 18:3 identifies such *hypēretas* from the Sanhedrin as being among the arresting party. They now sat around the fire in the chilly spring night.

55-56. According to Mark the Jewish leadership had known since 3:6 what they wanted to do with Jesus. However, they had difficulty at first finding sufficient evidence to warrant the death penalty. Their witnesses could not agree. They needed the agreement of at least two witnesses (cf. Deut 17:6; 19:15; Num 35:30).

57-59. Mark provides a climactic example of the conflicting testimony. The accusation sounds like a genuine saying of Jesus recorded in John 2:19, "Destroy this temple and I will raise it again in three days." The alterations in the testimony against Jesus are significant. They say Jesus himself planned to destroy the "made-with-hands" temple. Jesus did not say that he himself would destroy the temple and he was not speaking of the temple made by hands. He had spoken metaphorically of his own body (cf. John 2:21). Mark does not say what aspects of the testimony there was disagreement upon, but in any case the witnesses were not completely consistent with one another.

60-62. Since the testimony against Jesus was getting nowhere, Caiaphas addressed him directly, initially asking for a response concerning the testimony against him. Receiving no answer, the high priest pursued the question of Jesus' messiahship. (In his question "Son of the Blessed One" stands in apposition to "Christ" and means essentially the same thing.)[32]

[32]On the titles Christ and Son of God see the notes on 1:1, where Christ and Son of God are also juxtaposed.

Jesus answered this question directly and forcefully. He not only frankly admitted being the Christ, the Son of God, but he went on to add to the offense, bringing together allusions to Ps 110:1 ("The Lord says to my Lord: 'Sit at my right hand until I make your enemies a footstool for your feet'") and Dan 7:13 ("Before me was one like a son of man, coming with the clouds of heaven. He approached the Ancient of Days and was led into his presence") to assert that the Sanhedrin members themselves would one day see him enthroned at the right hand of God. Mark has already portrayed Jesus as citing Ps 110:1 in connection with the Messiah (12:36). In both cases what is being asserted is that he will reign at the right hand of God. The allusion to Dan 7:13 alters somewhat the imagery of Daniel. There the son of man figure comes *to* God on the clouds. In Mark it appears that he comes *from* his position at the right hand of God and to humanity (cf. 13:26).[33] At this "coming on the clouds" his position as second in command will be seen by all, including his enemies in the Sanhedrin.

In these two verses the three major titles of Jesus in Mark are brought together. For treatments of "Christ" and "Son of God" see the comments on 1:1. For a treatment of "Son of Man" see the comments at 2:10. All three are messianic titles in the Gospels. Clearly, the title "Christ" would be recognized as such by virtually all first century Jews. The high priest's use of "Son of the Blessed One" in apposition to "Christ" suggests that he and others viewed that title as messianic as well. It is difficult to know to what extent the phrase "Son of Man" was recognized before Jesus as a messianic title.

63-64. Tearing one's clothes was a way of expressing great grief.[34] In this case the high priest expressed his grief over

---

[33]Brown, p. 497.

[34]Brown, p. 517, cites Old Testament (Gen 37:34; 2 Sam 1:11-12) and Greco-Roman (Cassius Dio, *History* 54.14.1-2; 56.23.1) examples of tearing one's clothes upon hearing of a death or a political or military defeat. He also cites the example of those who tore their clothes upon hearing that the commander of the Assyrian armies blasphemed by saying God could not deliver Israel from the Assyrians (2 Kgs 18:30, 37; 19:1).

hearing something he believed was offensive to God. I have already noted in the comments on 2:5 that the term blasphemy was understood loosely. Since the high priest viewed Jesus as a heretic, his claim to be the messiah was considered a major affront to God. As a blasphemer Jesus was condemned to death.

65. In ancient (e.g., Num 12:14; Deut 25:9) and in modern times, spitting in someone's face is a way of showing disdain for them. Matt 26:67-68 and Luke 22:64 make explicit what Mark's context suggests concerning the challenge to Jesus to prophesy. The opponents of Jesus blindfolded him; then, various ones would strike him and ask him to identify (by prophecy) who did the striking.[35] This "game" seemed appropriate mockery for one who claimed to be sent from God. Mark's readers know the irony that the only one who saw clearly was the one blindfolded.

The mocking of Jesus after the Sanhedrin trial contains three basic elements: spitting in his face, the blindfolding "game," and a beating by the guards.[36] The term translated "beat" is found in various ancient contexts, some of which involve beating someone with a club or rod and others of which involve striking someone with an open hand (slapping).[37] The LXX of Isaiah 50:6-7 uses the noun form of the same word and was probably in Mark's mind as he wrote of Jesus being spit upon and slapped: "I gave . . . my cheeks to slaps; I did not turn my face from the shame of spitting. And the Lord God became my helper, and so I was not ashamed."

---

[35]Brown, pp. 574-575, surmises that the background of this adult mockery may be in widely known children's games. He cites three blindfolding games from a second century B.C. work (Pollux, *Onomasticon* 9.113, 123, and 129).

[36]On the guards see the comments on 14:54.

[37]*BAGD*, p. 734.

2. Peter's Denials (14:66-72)

**66While Peter was below in the courtyard, one of the ser-
vant girls of the high priest came by. 67When she saw Peter
warming himself, she looked closely at him.**

"You also were with that Nazarene, Jesus," she said.

**68But he denied it. "I don't know or understand what
you're talking about," he said, and went out into the entryway.[a]**

**69When the servant girl saw him there, she said again to
those standing around, "This fellow is one of them." 70Again
he denied it.**

After a little while, those standing near said to Peter, "Surely you are one of them, for you are a Galilean."

**71He began to call down curses on himself, and he swore
to them, "I don't know this man you're talking about."**

**72Immediately the rooster crowed the second time.[b] Then
Peter remembered the word Jesus had spoken to him:
"Before the rooster crows twice[c] you will disown me three
times." And he broke down and wept.**

[a]*68* Some early manuscripts *entryway and the rooster crowed* [b]*72* Some early manuscripts do not have *the second time.* [c]*72* Some early manuscripts do not have *twice.*

V. 54 left Peter sitting in the courtyard with the guards warming himself around the fire. Having portrayed what happened indoors as Jesus appeared before the Sanhedrin, Mark now turns to what was happening at the same period of time to Peter.

66-68. The remark that Peter was "below" in the courtyard indicates that Jesus' hearing took place in an upper room. While Jesus was being interrogated by the high priest, outside Peter was interrogated by one of the high priest's servant girls. At some point she had seen him with the "Nazarene" (the man from Nazareth, cf. 1:24; 10:47; 16:6).

69-70a. The servant girl found Peter again and repeated

her accusation, this time asserting he was one of them, that is, of Jesus' entourage. Peter made his second denial.

70b-71. Only a short time elapsed before another bystander joined the servant girl's accusation. He inferred she must be right because Peter was a Galilean.[38] This time Peter's denial was vehement. He swore an oath that he did not even know Jesus. The NIV translation "began to call down curses on himself" provides an object for "began to curse," although there is not one in the Greek text. The NIV may be correct. The idea would be that Peter supported his oath by calling down curses upon himself if what he was saying was not true. Brown and others, however, believe the implied object of the cursing is Jesus.[39] That is, Peter cursed Jesus and denied he had anything to do with him.

72. On the variant concerning the second rooster crowing and on the meaning of the references to the rooster crowing see the comments on v. 30. Peter recognized that he had just fulfilled Jesus' prophecy. His emphatic assertion that he would stay with Jesus even until death was broken. His spirit had been willing, but his flesh was weak. He broke down and wept.[40]

---

[38]Matt 26:73 indicates that Peter's accent gave away his Galilean heritage ("Surely you are one of them for your accent gives you away").

[39]Brown, pp. 604-605.

[40]The verb ἐπιβαλών (*epibalōn*) which the NIV and NRSV translate "broke down" is difficult to translate in this context. See Brown, pp. 609-610.

MARK 15

L. JESUS' TRIAL BEFORE PILATE (15:1-15)

[1]Very early in the morning, the chief priests, with the
elders, the teachers of the law and the whole Sanhedrin,
reached a decision. They bound Jesus, led him away and
handed him over to Pilate.
[2]"Are you the king of the Jews?" asked Pilate.
"Yes, it is as you say," Jesus replied.
[3]The chief priests accused him of many things. [4]So again
Pilate asked him,"Aren't you going to answer? See how
many things they are accusing you of."
[5]But Jesus still made no reply, and Pilate was amazed.
[6]Now it was the custom at the Feast to release a prisoner
whom the people requested. [7]A man called Barabbas was in
prison with the insurrectionists who had committed murder
in the uprising. [8]The crowd came up and asked Pilate to do
for them what he usually did.
[9]"Do you want me to release to you the king of the Jews?"
asked Pilate, [10]knowing it was out of envy that the chief
priests had handed Jesus over to him. [11]But the chief priests
stirred up the crowd to have Pilate release Barabbas instead.
[12]"What shall I do, then, with the one you call the king of
the Jews?" Pilate asked them.
[13]"Crucify him!" they shouted.
[14]"Why? What crime has he committed?" asked Pilate.
But they shouted all the louder,"Crucify him!"
[15]Wanting to satisfy the crowd, Pilate released Barabbas
to them. He had Jesus flogged, and handed him over to be
crucified.

According to John 18:31 the Sanhedrin turned to Pilate because they could not legally carry out the death sentence. This subject has been discussed extensively in the twentieth century. Brown provides a useful summary of the debate and evidence. He concludes that there were some types of criminal cases in which the Roman authorities would have permitted the Sanhedrin to execute a criminal, but that these were clearly restricted and did not include a case like that of Jesus.[1] In most cases, including that of Jesus, they needed the judgment of the Roman governor.

The local Roman governor for the province of Judea was Pontius Pilate. His official title was "prefect," an office he held from A.D. 26-36.[2] He administered the province from Caesarea, but frequently went to Jerusalem, especially during Jewish festivals. In both Caesarea and Jerusalem his residence was called the "praetorium," the name for the residence of any such governor. There is continuing debate over whether his praetorium in Jerusalem was the Fortress Antonia near the temple (the traditional location that begins the Via Delorosa, the "path of sorrow" Jesus took to Golgotha) or the Herodian Palace at the western edge of the city.[3]

The trial before Pilate has several parallels to the Sanhedrin trial. The high priest and Pilate both ask Jesus two questions, which are parallel to each other, although the order is reversed. Both ask a direct question about his identity ("Are you the Christ/king of the Jews?") and a question about why he refused to respond to the accusations made against him. Both trials lead to a death sentence followed by mockery that includes spitting and beating.

1. It is a debatable point whether this verse describes the conclusion of the night meeting of the Sanhedrin or a

---

[1]Brown, pp. 363-372.

[2]A first century inscription discovered in 1961 at Caesarea Philippi refers to "Pontius Pilate Prefect of Judea." See Brown, p. 695.

[3]See the discussion by Brown, pp. 706-710, who favors the Herodian Palace.

reassembling for final considerations.[4] In either case, they bound Jesus and led him to the praetorium to appear before Pilate. The proceedings took place in a public area outside Pilate's residence. The statement that they "handed over" Jesus to Pilate is part of a string of occurrences of the Greek word παραδίδωμι (*paradidōmi*), some of which are translated "betrayed" and some "handed over." Judas handed over or betrayed Jesus to the Jewish authorities (14:11, 18, 21, 41). The Sanhedrin handed him over to Pilate (15:1). Pilate handed him over to be crucified (15:15). The first two parts of this string fulfill the words of 10:33: "the Son of Man will be betrayed (*paradidōmi*) to the chief priests and teachers of the law. They will . . . hand him over (*paradidōmi*) to the Gentiles."

2. Apparently, the Sanhedrin approached Pilate with the accusation that Jesus was a threat to Roman rule, a man who wanted to be king of the Jews. Pilate would not have been interested in the religious charge of blasphemy. But he was interested in the charge of insurrection, and asked Jesus directly if he was the king of the Jews. The NIV translation of Jesus' reply, "Yes, it is as you say," is an interpretive translation of a two word statement (σὺ λέγεις, *su legeis*) which the NRSV more literally translates, "You say so." It is difficult to decide the connotations of this reply. The context would seem to suggest that it is a qualified affirmative (contrary to the NIV translation).[5] Jesus affirmed that he was the king of the Jews, but not in the sense Pilate presumably had in mind.

3-5. The various accusations made by the chief priests probably supported the fundamental accusation of insurrection, as in Luke 23:2 where Jesus is accused of telling the Jews not to pay taxes to Caesar. Mark's comments about Jesus' silence in the face of these accusations (cf. 14:60-61a) and Pilate's amazement at his lack of response may be intended to recall Isa 53:7: "He was oppressed and afflicted, yet he did

[4]Ibid., pp. 630-631.
[5]Ibid., p. 733.

not open his mouth; he was led like a lamb to the slaughter, and as a sheep before her shearers is silent, so he did not open his mouth."

6-8. It was Pilate's custom to release one prisoner of the people's choosing in connection with the Passover Feast. One possible candidate for this release was Barabbas. He was one of several men imprisoned for committing murder in a riot. The nouns which the NIV translates "insurrectionists" and "uprising" are cognate nouns (στασιαστής, *stasiastēs* and στάσις, *stasis*) which could refer to a range of activities from general rioting to a major insurrection.[6] Whatever level of disturbance Barabbas was involved in, there is a certain irony to keeping Jesus and releasing a man who was a genuine violent threat to the Roman authorities.

7-11. Pilate's use of the phrase "the king of the Jews" in addressing the people might suggest that he was taunting them with sarcasm. But Mark's statement that he was motivated by his understanding of the envy of the chief priests suggests that he did actually hope to release Jesus. However, the chief priests incited the crowd to ask for Barabbas. The popular assumption that this crowd represents the same people who had hailed Jesus during his triumphal entry is an assumption with no basis in the text. Thousands of people lived in Jerusalem and even more were there for the Festivals. There is no basis for the claim that the same people who loved Jesus on Sunday were clamoring for his crucifixion on Friday.

12-15. By saying "the one you call[7] the king of the Jews," Pilate may be taunting the crowd, or simply identifying Jesus by their accusation against him. The question "What crime has he committed?" suggests he genuinely hoped to exonerate Jesus, although it would be hard to determine the level of his concern. It was not enough to keep him from releasing Barabbas and crucifying Jesus in order to satisfy the crowd.

---

[6]Brown, pp. 796-797.

[7]The phrase translated "the one you call" is missing in some significant ancient witnesses and may be a scribal addition.

"Flogging" (φραγελλώσας, *phragellōsas*) often preceded crucifixions. The prisoner was stripped and bound to a post or thrown to the ground. The scourge was generally made of leather thongs, often fitted with pieces of bone or lead or with spikes.[8] The beatings varied in severity. Josephus describes incidents in which men were flogged until their bones lay visible.[9] Two features of Jesus' story suggest a severe beating. He seems to have had difficulty carrying his cross (15:21) and he died in less time than usual (15:44).

M. PILATE'S SOLDIERS MOCK JESUS (15:16-20)

16The soldiers led Jesus away into the palace (that is, the Praetorium) and called together the whole company of soldiers. 17They put a purple robe on him, then twisted together a crown of thorns and set it on him. 18And they began to call out to him,"Hail, king of the Jews!" 19Again and again they struck him on the head with a staff and spit on him. Falling on their knees, they paid homage to him. 20And when they had mocked him, they took off the purple robe and put his own clothes on him. Then they led him out to crucify him.

This second mocking is roughly parallel to the first (14:65), but it is based on the more political concept of Jesus as a king rather than the more religious concept of Jesus as a messiah.

16. Mark probably envisions a large courtyard inside the praetorium as the scene of the mockery by the soldiers. When he says they called together the "whole company" he uses the term σπεῖρα (*speira*), which the NRSV translates "cohort." A cohort consisted of about 600 soldiers, so there may have been hundreds involved in this scene.

17. The purple robe and the crown are symbols of royalty.

---

[8]Brown, p. 851.

[9]Josephus, *War* 2.612; 6.304.

The type of crown the Gospel writers had in mind was a wreath. The word used to describe the plant used to make the wreath could refer to any of several thorn plants. In addition to mocking the wreaths worn by rulers, the thorns may have brought to mind the royal image of a diadem with the sun's rays radiating on all sides. This radiate image was used on depictions of the emperors to represent their divine nature.[10]

18-20. Having robed and crowned Jesus as a king, the soldiers mockingly bowed before him as king of the Jews. "Hail, king of the Jews!" corresponds to the standard acclamation "Ave Caesar!" Falling on one's knees was an appropriate way to pay homage to a king. Striking Jesus on the head and spitting on him add physical abuse to the whole sorry scene. When the soldiers grew tired of their charade they removed the purple cloak.[11] It is somewhat surprising that they put Jesus' clothes back on him. Normally the criminal would carry his cross beam naked to the place of crucifixion.[12]

N. THE CRUCIFIXION (15:21-41)

[21]A certain man from Cyrene, Simon, the father of Alexander and Rufus, was passing by on his way in from the country, and they forced him to carry the cross. [22]They brought Jesus to the place called Golgotha (which means The Place of the Skull). [23]Then they offered him wine mixed with myrrh, but he did not take it. [24]And they crucified him. Dividing up his clothes, they cast lots to see what each would get.

[25]It was the third hour when they crucified him. [26]The written notice of the charge against him read: THE KING OF THE JEWS. [27]They crucified two robbers with him, one

[10]Brown, pp. 866-867.

[11]The Gospel writers do not say whether they removed the crown of thorns.

[12]Brown, p. 870.

**on his right and one on his left.[a] 29Those who passed by
hurled insults at him, shaking their heads and saying,"So!
You who are going to destroy the temple and build it in
three days, 30come down from the cross and save yourself!"**

**31In the same way the chief priests and the teachers of
the law mocked him among themselves."He saved others,"
they said,"but he can't save himself! 32Let this Christ,[b] this
King of Israel, come down now from the cross, that we may
see and believe." Those crucified with him also heaped
insults on him.**

**33At the sixth hour darkness came over the whole land
until the ninth hour. 34And at the ninth hour Jesus cried out
in a loud voice,"Eloi, Eloi, lama sabachthani?" – which
means,"My God, my God, why have you forsaken me?"[c]**

**35When some of those standing near heard this, they
said,"Listen, he's calling Elijah."**

**36One man ran, filled a sponge with wine vinegar, put it
on a stick, and offered it to Jesus to drink."Now leave him
alone. Let's see if Elijah comes to take him down," he said.**

37With a loud cry, Jesus breathed his last.

**38The curtain of the temple was torn in two from top to
bottom. 39And when the centurion, who stood there in front
of Jesus, heard his cry and[d] saw how he died, he said,
"Surely this man was the Son[e] of God!"**

**40Some women were watching from a distance. Among
them were Mary Magdalene, Mary the mother of James the
younger and of Joses, and Salome. 41In Galilee these women
had followed him and cared for his needs. Many other
women who had come up with him to Jerusalem were also
there.**

[a]*27* Some manuscripts *left, [28]and the scripture was fulfilled which says, "He was counted with the lawless ones"* (Isaiah 53:12) [b]*32* Or *Messiah* [c]*34* Psalm 22:1 [d]*39* Some manuscripts do not have *heard his cry and.* [e]*39* Or *a son*

The event portrayed in these verses is both the supreme tragedy and the supreme victory of human history. For all who were there, friend and foe, it appeared to be the end of the story of Jesus. And there could be no more tragic end. Crucifixion was bitterly painful and scandalously shameful.[13] The tragic aspect most strongly underlined in Mark's account is the horrible shame of dying on a cross. Jesus was publicly paraded from the praetorium to Golgotha. His clothes were divided by lots by his torturers. He was mocked by the inscription "King of the Jews." He was placed between two bandits. He was insulted by those who passed by, by the religious authorities, and even by the criminals hanging beside him.

Yet throughout Mark's portrait the reader is also reminded that this event was a part of God's plan. Although these verses are devoid of explicit references to the fulfilment of Scripture and contain only one direct citation of Scripture (v. 34), they are laced with allusions to Scripture for those with ears to hear them. The alert reader is continuously reminded that this event was the fulfilment of prophecy.

21. It is highly unusual that someone else was made to carry Jesus' cross.[14] It is often surmised that the flogging was so severe that he could not carry it. According to the usual custom what Simon carried was probably not the entire cross, but the horizontal beam. The vertical beams would be left implanted at the place of crucifixion. (When the victim had been affixed to the crossbeam, forked poles could be used to raise it with the body into place on the vertical pole.)[15]

Simon was from Cyrene, the capital city of ancient Cyrenaica in northern Africa (in the area of Libya). He may

---

[13]See the excellent survey of ancient information on crucifixions by Martin Hengel, *Crucifixion in the Ancient World and the Folly of the Message of the Cross* (London: SCM, 1977).

[14]Plutarch (late first, early second century A.D.) *De sera numinis vindicta* 9; #554AB says "Every wrongdoer who goes to execution carries out his own cross." Artemidorus Daldianus (late second century A.D.) *Oneirokritika* 2.56 says, "The person who is nailed to the cross first carries it out." Cited by Brown, p. 914.

[15]Brown, pp. 913, 949.

have been a Jew (cf. Acts 2:10; 6:9 for Cyrenian Jews in Jerusalem). Simon happened by on his way into the city from the countryside and was pressed into an unpleasant task. Mark's identification of Simon through his sons Alexander and Rufus suggests that his audience knew about the sons. A plausible explanation for this is that they became Christians and thus were known to the Christian community Mark envisions in his audience.[16]

22. The place of the crucifixion was Golgotha. It was important to both the Jews and the Romans that such places of execution be outside the city. Golgotha was probably located at the traditionally revered site of the Church of the Holy Sepulchre. There crucifixions were conducted atop a small hill.[17] Mark provides the Semitic name Golgotha and then translates it with a Greek phrase meaning "place of the skull."

23. The Babylonian Talmud makes reference to Jewish women in Jerusalem who gave the condemned wine mixed with frankincense as a narcotic to relieve their pain.[18] On this basis many have proposed that Mark here refers to these women and their narcotic drink. But the Babylonian Talmud was written several centuries after Jesus' death, Mark refers to myrrh rather than frankincense, and Mark does not mention any Jewish women – the natural antecedent of "they" in v. 23 is the Roman soldiers. It is possible that the myrrh was mixed in for a narcotic effect. Lane references a first century A.D. army physician Dioscorides Pedanius as commenting on the narcotic properties of myrrh.[19] The myrrh may have been mixed in for taste (or both taste and narcotic value). The first century writer Pliny says, "The finest wine in early days was

---

[16]Although both suggestions are speculative, it is possible that one of Simon's sons was the Rufus of Rom 16:13 and that the other should be identified with an inscription "Alexander, son of Simon" found on an ossuary in a burial cave near Jerusalem that belonged to a family of Cyrenian Jews. See Lane, p. 563; and Brown, p. 916.

[17]Brown, p. 937.

[18]*Sanhedrin* 43a.

[19]Dioscorides Pedanius, *Materia Medica* 1.44.3. Lane, p. 564.

that spiced with the scent of myrrh," and "I also find that aromatic wine is constantly made from almost the same ingredient as perfumes, from myrrh, as we have said."[20] The suggestion that wine mixed with myrrh was meant to be a fine wine seems to conflict with Matt 27:34 in which "they offered Jesus wine . . . mixed with gall; but after tasting it, he refused to drink it." Matthew suggests a bitter taste. A possible solution is the analogy of modern vermouth, which includes wormwood (*absinthium*), which (I am told) like myrrh has a certain bitterness.[21] It is possible that one or more of the soldiers offered the wine sincerely. On the other hand, the soldiers may have expected Jesus not to like it.

24. "And they crucified him" is extraordinarily brief, but Mark's readers would presumably have firsthand knowledge of what was involved. Although there was a wide variety of crucifixion practices, the Gospels make it clear that Jesus was nailed to the cross at both his hands and his feet (Luke 24:39; John 20:25, 27). Many assume that the evangelists use the term χεῖρας (*cheiras*, hands) loosely and that the nails went into Jesus' wrists – arguing that nails in one's palms would not hold the weight of the body. One recent discovery provides a possible understanding of how Jesus' feet were nailed. In 1968 Jerusalem archaeologists discovered the bones of a man crucified several decades before A.D. 70. In his case it appears that his feet were placed one on each side (not on the front) of the vertical post. A nail for each foot was driven first through an olive wood plaque (to prevent him from pulling his feet free from the nail), then through the heel bone, and then into the cross.[22] Christian art and imagination are not to be counted on for an accurate picture. In the early centuries several Christian writings refer to four nails being used.

---

[20]Pliny, *Natural History* 14.15 (#92), 19 (#107); cited by Brown, p. 941.

[21]The analogy is suggested by Brown, p. 943, although he disagrees with using it to harmonize Matthew and Mark.

[22]Ibid., p. 950. Many sources of information concerning this find are based on the first 1970 report, which contained major flaws. See Brown's references to more recent articles which provide correctives.

Helena, Constantine's mother, investigated various traditions in Palestine and supposedly found only three nails, which from her time (4th century) became the standard concept.[23]

The soldiers had put Jesus' own clothes back on him after the mocking scene (v. 20). At Golgotha they took them off. The late second century A.D. writer Artemidorus Daldianus indicates that the normal Roman practice was to crucify criminals naked.[24] However, the Romans might have made a concession to the Jews and allowed a loincloth.[25] Although most Christian art portrays Jesus in a loincloth, the earliest representations both written and artistic are divided on the issue. In the late second century Melito of Sardis wrote concerning "his body naked and not even deemed worthy of a clothing that it might not be seen. Therefore the heavenly lights turned away and the day darkened in order that he might be hidden who was denuded upon the cross."[26] The purpose of such exposure would be to expose the criminal to public shame.

Mark's reference to the soldiers casting lots over Jesus' clothes serves both to underscore the experience of humiliation and to allude to Ps 22:18: "They divide my garments among them and cast lots for my clothing."

25. This is the second of a series of time references in Mark's account of Jesus' crucifixion: v. 1 "very early in the morning," v. 25 "the third hour," v. 33 "at the sixth hour . . . until the ninth hour," v. 34 "at the ninth hour," and v. 42 "as evening approached." According to the common way of reckoning the hours of the day, each hour was reckoned from dawn. The third hour would therefore correspond with our 9:00 AM. Unfortunately, there is an apparent conflict with John 19:14 which portrays Jesus still on trial at the praetorium "about the sixth hour." This is the most difficult time

---

[23]Brown, p. 951, who notes also that in Christian art the single nail pierces first the right foot and then the left, except in Spanish art.

[24]*Oneirokritika* 2.53.

[25]Brown, p. 953.

[26]Melito, *On the Pasch* 97. See Brown, p. 953.

problem in the Gospel accounts. All of the proposed answers have significant flaws,[27] provoking Lane to argue that this verse was not part of the original text of Mark[28] – despite the fact that no manuscript omits it. In the absence of a clearly preferable solution to this problem, one can only say that Jesus' crucifixion began between nine o'clock and the early afternoon.

26. It was not uncommon to use an inscription describing the crime of a condemned man.[29] Mark does not describe the location of the inscription, but Matt 27:37 says they put it above his head. The purpose of such an inscription was to bring further shame on the condemned man and to warn passersby not to follow in his footsteps.

27. Two other men were crucified at the same time as Jesus. The term used to describe them is the Greek word ληστής (*lēstēs*) commented on at 14:48. These men were violent men of some sort. They may have been common thugs. Possibly they were involved in the same incident as Barabbas, who is described in John 18:40 as a *lēstēs*. Mark 15:7 mentioned that Barabbas was one of several men imprisoned for the same incident. Mark's reference to the two criminals further underscores the indignity to which Jesus was subjected. V. 28, "and the scripture was fulfilled which says, 'He was counted with the lawless ones" is not attested in the best manuscripts and is therefore omitted from most modern translations.

29-30. Mark has recounted a mocking incident at the end of each of the two trial scenes. Now in vv. 29-32 he portrays three groups mocking Jesus during the crucifixion. Again, the emphasis is on humiliation and shame. The first group is sim-

[27]Brown, p. 959, lists the major alternatives and provides an objection to each one. I do not agree with his conclusion that there is an unavoidable contradiction between the accounts, but I do see significant weaknesses in the available solutions.

[28]Lane, p. 567.

[29]References in Brown, p. 963.

ply the passersby. The NIV's "hurled insults" translates the Greek word βλασφημέω (*blasphēmeō*), the word used for Jesus' own supposed blasphemy in 2:7 and 14:64. In describing the passersby shaking their heads and verbally deriding Jesus Mark alludes to another verse from Ps 22: "All who see me mock me; they hurl insults, shaking their heads" (v. 8; he had previous alluded in 14:24 to Ps 22:18).[30] The passersby know about Jesus and his supposed statement that he would destroy the temple and build it in three days (cf. 14:58). They use it to insult him, for one who could do such things should be able to save himself and come down from the cross.

31-32a. The second group mocking Jesus is the chief priests and scribes, those who had condemned Jesus for blasphemy and turned him over to Pilate. Recalling his healing ministry, they observe that he saved others, but now he cannot save himself. They, too, taunt him to come down from the cross. If he could do that, they mockingly say they would believe he was the Christ, the King of Israel.

32b. The third group is the two crucified with Jesus. Being taunted even by these criminals adds to the total scene of humiliation.

33. From roughly noon until three in the afternoon darkness overshadowed the land.[31] The word translated "land" (γῆν, *gēn*) could also be translated "earth." It is not clear whether Mark meant the land of Judea alone or had a broader reference in mind. In any case darkness is clearly a symbol of divine displeasure. Many Old Testament texts use this motif, including Jer 15:9 ("Her [Jerusalem's] sun will set while it is still day; she will be disgraced and humiliated") and Amos

---

[30]Cf. also the similarities to Jer 48:27. There God speaks to Moab concerning her treatment of Israel, saying, "Was not Israel the object of your ridicule? Was she caught among thieves, that you shake your head in scorn whenever you speak of her?" See Brown, p. 989 n. 12.

[31]This could not be a natural eclipse, which does not last for three hours and would never occur in the middle of one of the Jews' lunar months. On the eclipse notion see Brown, pp. 1041-1042, who wrongly suggests confusion and exaggeration on the part of the Gospels.

8:9-10 ("'In that day,' declares the Sovereign LORD, 'I will make the sun go down at noon and darken the earth in broad daylight'"). Since this darkness comes close to the Passover feast, perhaps one should be reminded of the plague of darkness preceding the Exodus which showed God's displeasure with the Egyptians.[32]

34-37. In Mark the only statement Jesus makes while on the cross is his well-known citation of Ps 22:1. Mark provides a Greek transliteration of Jesus' original Semitic[33] language and then a Greek translation. In this case the reason for preserving the original language seems apparent from the subsequent storyline. It explains to the reader why some of the bystanders thought he was calling Elijah. That would not be understood from the Greek θεός (*theos*), but it is understandable from the Semitic word *eloi*. The meaning of Jesus' cry has been extensively discussed. Some have argued that Jesus actually cited the entire Psalm, which ends on a strongly positive note. However, the Gospel writers only cite the first verse, and the context of the crucifixion suggests that the words should be taken literally. Most modern interpreters understand the cry as an expression of Jesus' sense of being abandoned by God.[34]

It is difficult to assess whether the man who offered Jesus a drink and commented about Elijah taking him down was or was not being hostile toward Jesus. The drink (ὄξος, *oxos*) he offered Jesus is known from Greek and Roman literature as a common drink and need not have an unpleasant connotation.[35] On the other hand, the LXX of Ps 69:21 (LXX=Ps 68:22) uses the same word in a context that clearly suggests a negative connotation: "They put gall in my food and gave me

---

[32]So Lane, p. 572; Brown, p. 1035.

[33]On the problems of deciding between Hebrew and Aramaic see Brown, pp. 1051-1053.

[34]E.g., Brown, pp. 1044-1051; Lane, p. 573. This is not to suggest that Jesus, even in the depths of anguish, did not also have the faith expressed in the latter parts of Ps 22.

[35]Brown, p. 1063.

vinegar (*oxos*) for my thirst." If Mark intended an allusion to this Psalm, then the bystander's gesture was hostile and his words ("Let's see if Elijah comes to take him down") were presumably sarcastic. A negative intent would fit the context of Mark's references to the insults from three differing groups in vv. 29-32.

After this final insult, Jesus made a loud cry and breathed his last.

38. The rending of the curtain of the temple[36] is quite evidently a miraculous sign from God. It calls attention to the momentous nature of Jesus' death. In the light of the prediction of the destruction of the temple in 13:2 it seems likely that it is a warning of that coming event and that it connects that event with the rejection and killing of Jesus.[37] In order to be more precise in determining the connotations of this rending, interpreters ancient and modern have sought to determine which of two possible curtains is the one the Gospel writers had in mind: the "outer veil" at the entrance to the holy place or the "inner veil" between the holy place and the holy of holies. One difference would be that the inner veil would only be visible to priests inside the holy place. It seems unlikely that one can determine which veil was meant and many of the differences suggested between rending one or the other are problematic.[38]

39. A centurion was a commanding officer over one hundred soldiers. The centurion, whom Pilate will summon in 15:44 to see if Jesus is dead, was presumably in charge of the execution. Unlike Matthew (27:54) Mark is not very specific about what the centurion saw that led to his confession. The NIV notes that the word translated "heard his cry and" is absent in some ancient manuscripts. The NRSV is probably

[36]The word Mark uses for the temple in this instance is ναός (*naos*). Most of his references to the temple (9 occurrences in chapters 11-14) use ἱερόν (*hieron*). The previous occurrences of *naos* are when Jesus' opponents accuse him of having said he would destroy the temple (14:58; 15:29).

[37]Cf. Lane, p. 575; Brown, pp. 1113-1116.

[38]Brown, pp. 1109-1113.

correct to leave it out of the text. One feature of how Jesus died that presumably made a deep impression on the centurion was the three hours of darkness. But whatever factors contributed to his impression, the centurion saw that Jesus was the Son of God. As the NIV footnote indicates, some interpreters would emphasize the absence of a Greek article (the word "the") before Son of God and translate "a son of God." This argument overlooks other occasions in the Gospels in which "son of God" is anarthrous (without the article) but clearly means "the Son of God" (Matt 4:3, 6; 27:40, 43; Luke 1:32, 35) and "Colwell's Rule" that a definite predicate noun which precedes the verb usually lacks the article.[39] As Peter did not understand the full import of his confession that Jesus was the Christ, the centurion represents the correct identification of Jesus, but in all likelihood he did not understand the full meaning of his remark.

The centurion's confession is a climactic moment in Mark's Gospel. It is one of four standout instances of Jesus being identified as God's Son: the opening verse (1:1), the voice from heaven at his baptism (1:11) and at his transfiguration (9: 7), and this declaration immediately following his crucifixion. In Mark it is only after the crucifixion that a human being declares Jesus to be God's Son. This underscores Mark's emphasis on the suffering and death of Jesus and on Jesus' frequent efforts to correct the mistaken messianic understandings of his followers and teach them about his coming death. It suggests a motive for the "messianic secret" motif by which Jesus' messianic status is kept secret during his ministry.[40] Only in the light of the cross could his identity be fully understood. The centurion's confession is in this respect more true than was Peter's.

40-41. Mark has left the women followers of Jesus unmentioned until this point. He brings them in at this point in order to set the scene for their discovery of the empty tomb.

---

[39]Brown, p. 1147.

[40]See the comments on the messianic secret at 1:25 and 8:31.

Since they were watching the crucifixion at a distance they were able to see where Jesus was buried so that after the sabbath they could return to anoint Jesus' body. The three women Mark introduces by name are the ones who will go to the tomb on Sunday (16:1). Mary Magadalene means Mary from Magdala, a village on the northwest shore of the Sea of Galilee. The second Mary is identified by her sons, James the younger and Joses. Apparently, like Rufus and Alexander in 15:21, these were men known to the Christians Mark addressed. The parallel in Matt 27:56 might suggest that Salome was the mother of the apostles James and John. Having introduced the women by name Mark goes on to identify them as followers of Jesus who had ministered to him in Galilee.[41] These three and others had come with Jesus to the Passover/Feast of Unleavened Bread in Jerusalem.[42]

O. THE BURIAL OF JESUS (15:42-47)

42It was Preparation Day (that is, the day before the Sabbath). So as evening approached, 43Joseph of Arimathea, a prominent member of the Council, who was himself waiting for the kingdom of God, went boldly to Pilate and asked for Jesus' body. 44Pilate was surprised to hear that he was already dead. Summoning the centurion, he asked him if Jesus had already died. 45When he learned from the centurion that it was so, he gave the body to Joseph. 46So Joseph bought some linen cloth, took down the body, wrapped it in the linen, and placed it in a tomb cut out of rock. Then he rolled a stone against the entrance of the tomb. 47Mary Magdalene and Mary the mother of Joses saw where he was laid.

---

[41]Concerning their ministry to Jesus see Luke 8:1-3.

[42]It seems odd to the modern reader to say that they came "up" from Galilee (in the north) to Jerusalem (in the south). But Jerusalem was in the hills of Judea. "Up" refers to altitude.

The death of Jesus is only half of the climax of the Gospel. It would be a pointless tragedy without the rest of the climax, the resurrection. The story of the burial sets the stage for the resurrection.

42-43. The Jews often placed the dead in niches carved in the sides of natural or manmade caves. According to Josephus, "The Jews are so careful about funeral rites that even those who are crucified because they were found guilty are taken down and buried before sunset."[43] This practice was rooted in Deut 21:22-23: "If a man guilty of a capital offense is put to death and his body is hung on a tree, you must not leave his body on the tree overnight. Be sure to bury him that same day, because anyone who is hung on a tree is under God's curse." In Jesus' case, the coming day was a sabbath and so the burial had to take place before the sabbath began at sunset or it could not be done until Sunday.[44]

"Of Arimathea" designates Joseph's birthplace, a city of unknown location. He was a member of the Council, another name for the Sanhedrin. In fact he was a "prominent" member. Mark here uses a term often found in ancient inscriptions honoring some individual.[45] The observation that he was "waiting for the kingdom of God" along with his willingness to go "boldly" before Pilate to ask for the body indicates that he had a serious level of interest in Jesus. The NIV leaves out the word "also" in "who was also himself waiting for the kingdom of God." Like the women of vv. 40-41, Joseph was "also" waiting for the kingdom. (The other Gospels indicate Joseph was a secret disciple: Matt 27:57; Luke 23:50-51; John 19:38). His need for "boldness" may refer both to possible recrimination from his fellows in the Sanhedrin and from

---

[43]*War* 4.317.

[44]The NIV translation "as evening approached" is technically incorrect. Mark says it was already evening (καὶ ἤδη ὀψίας γενομένης, *kai ēdē opsias genomenēs*). The term Mark uses for evening (*opsia*) may refer to late afternoon (cf. Matt 14:15 vs 23). Brown, p. 1211.

[45]Cf. Acts 13:50; 17:12.

Pilate. The Sanhedrin members would consider his sentiments heresy. Pilate might consider them seditious.[46]

44-45. Jesus died more quickly than most victims of crucifixion.[47] Pilate's investigation of Jesus' death undercuts the possible suggestion that Jesus did not actually die and later only appeared to be raised from the dead. The centurion confirmed his death.

46. Joseph wrapped Jesus' body in a linen cloth and placed it in a manmade cave. The stone rolled against the entrance could be a large boulder or possibly a disc-shaped stone which rolled in a track across the entrance to the tomb.[48]

47. The two Marys saw where the body was laid. The Gospels do not describe them as participating with Joseph. They perhaps kept their distance, but located the body so that they could return on Sunday to anoint it.

---

[46]Tacitus, *Annals* 6.8 observes that the emperor Tiberius was suspicious of the friends of Sejanus, who had been guilty of treason.

[47]Brown, p. 1222.

[48]Ibid., p. 1248.

MARK 16

P. THE RESURRECTION (16:1-8)

1When the Sabbath was over, Mary Magdalene, Mary the
mother of James, and Salome bought spices so that they
might go to anoint Jesus' body. 2Very early on the first day
of the week, just after sunrise, they were on their way to the
tomb 3and they asked each other, "Who will roll the stone
away from the entrance of the tomb?"
4But when they looked up, they saw that the stone, which
was very large, had been rolled away. 5As they entered the
tomb, they saw a young man dressed in a white robe sitting
on the right side, and they were alarmed.
6"Don't be alarmed," he said. "You are looking for Jesus
the Nazarene, who was crucified. He has risen! He is not
here. See the place where they laid him. 7But go, tell his dis-
ciples and Peter, 'He is going ahead of you into Galilee.
There you will see him, just as he told you.'"
8Trembling and bewildered, the women went out and fled
from the tomb. They said nothing to anyone, because they
were afraid.

However one assesses the problem of the ending of Mark (16:9-20), the story of the resurrection completes the climax of the book. Jesus' death is followed by his triumph over death.

1-3. The visit of the three women was quite early on the first day of the week, not long after sunrise. Because of the sabbath and then the darkness after the sunset which began the first day of the week, this was the first opportunity they had to anoint Jesus' body for burial. Typically the body would be anointed with oil (by rubbing or pouring) and/or treated with spices. Oil and spices could be combined in a fragrant oil. That seems to be the case here since the verb "anoint" (ἀλείφω, *aleiphō*) is used with reference to the spices.[1]

The boulder or disc-shaped carved stone at the entrance to the tomb was large enough that the three women anticipated needing help to move it. Obviously, they did not anticipate it being moved already. In all of the Gospel accounts the disciples seem quite surprised by the resurrection, even though Jesus had repeatedly predicted it. They did not understand (cf. Mark 9:10, 31-32).

4-5. The large stone had been rolled back. So they entered the tomb to find a young man sitting on the right side. The young man's white robe suggests what Matt 27:2-3 specifies: he was an angel. The women apparently recognized him as such and they were alarmed.

6-7. The women's alarmed reaction and the initial reassurance of the angel are standard parts of angelic appearances (cf. Luke 1:12-13, 28-30; 2:9-10). The angel's message has two parts. First, he declares that Jesus has risen. They had seen not only the tomb, but "where he was laid" (15:47). Now the angel uses that awareness to show them that "the place where they laid him" is vacant.

The second part of the young man's message is a message to the disciples and to Peter. Peter is perhaps singled out because of his denials of Jesus. It was in the very context of Jesus' prediction concerning all of them deserting him and Peter denying him that he had said "after I am raised up, I will go before you to Galilee" (14:28). The message the women are to take to Peter and the others recalls that resurrection promise and assures them that they will see him in Galilee.

8. Although the ending of Mark's Gospel is uncertain (see

---

[1]Brown, p. 1261.

the appendix on 16:9-20), there is some probability that he intended to end with this verse. If so, then the Gospel ends on the note of the women's overwhelming awe in response to their experience at the tomb. Every item in v. 8 underscores this point. The more literal translation of the NRSV accurately portrays the two sections of Mark's sentence and how each begins with an action that is then grounded in the women's sense of awe:

a) "So they went out and fled from the tomb, *for* terror and amazement had seized them; and

b) they said nothing to anyone, *for* they were afraid."

Three words described their emotional state: "terror," "amazement," and "afraid." Two actions demonstrate the same: they "fled from the tomb" and "they said nothing to anyone." Of course their silence was temporary. Of course they and others saw the risen Lord. The other Gospels enter into what happened next. But if Mark stopped here these events are all left to the implied future of the story. The point of vv. 1-8 might be paraphrased as follows: "He has risen! You will see him! How awesome!"[2]

Q. POST-RESURRECTION APPEARANCES (16:9-20)

The text critical problem concerning these verses is discussed in the appendix. Although I am inclined to think that Mark ended his book at 16:8, the problem is difficult and divergent opinions ought to be respected.[3] Furthermore, the

---

[2]Lane, pp. 590-592, points out that "Fear is the constant reaction to the disclosure of Jesus' transcendent dignity in the Gospel of Mark (cf. 4:41; 5:15, 33, 36; 6:50; 9:6, 32). . . . With his closing comment he wished to say that 'the gospel of Jesus the Messiah' (Ch. 1:1) is an event beyond human comprehension and therefore awesome and frightening."

[3]In 1896 J.W. McGarvey wrote: "The question of the genuineness of these verses is one of the most intricate with which textual critics of the New Testament have to deal. . . . I think that, after a candid study of the evidence as a whole, it must be conceded that the question is as yet unsettled." ("Biblical Criticism," *Christian Standard* 32 [1896]: 1367).

material in vv. 9-20 is in harmony with the other Gospels and may be studied with profit.[4] Therefore I have chosen to comment on these verses.

These verses emphasize two themes: faith and mission.[5] The emphasis on faith can be seen in the following phrases: "they did not believe it" (v. 11), "they did not believe them either" (v. 13), "he rebuked them for their lack of faith and their stubborn refusal to believe" (v. 14), "whoever believes and is baptized will be saved, but whoever does not believe will be condemned" (v. 16), and "these signs will accompany those who believe" (v. 17). The theme of faith is also undergirded by the appearances of Jesus, the testimony of those who saw him, and the emphasis (in vv. 17-18 and 20) on confirmatory signs.

The emphasis on mission can be seen in the following phrases: "she went and told those who had been with him" (v. 10), "they returned and reported it to the rest" (v. 13), "go into all the world and preach the good news to all creation" (v. 15), and "then the disciples went out and preached everywhere" (v. 20).

These verses do form another fitting ending to the Gospel. They call the reader to believe the message and to proclaim it to others.

1. The Appearance to Mary Magdalene (16:9-11)

9When Jesus rose early on the first day of the week, he appeared first to Mary Magdalene, out of whom he had driven seven demons. 10She went and told those who had been

---

4McGarvey, p. 1367: "I think it safe to say, as I did before, that the statements contained in them [Mark 16:9-20] are authentic, whether written by Mark or appended by another hand." On McGarvey's opinions see Stanley N. Helton, "Churches of Christ and Mark 16:9-20," *Restoration Quarterly* 36 (1994): 32-52.

5Lamar Williamson, Jr., *Mark*, Interpretation Commentary (Atlanta: John Knox, 1983), p. 287.

with him and who were mourning and weeping. [11]When they heard that Jesus was alive and that she had seen him, they did not believe it.

Verse 9 reemphasizes that Jesus rose on the first day of the week. Mary Magdalene was first introduced in 15:40. This verse adds the observation that Jesus had exorcised seven demons from her. Luke 8:2 also refers to this exorcism, but none of the Gospels provide an account of the story. The main point in this paragraph is that Mary told the disciples she had seen Jesus alive, but they did not believe her. Appearances to Mary Magdalene are also found in Matt 28:9 (with others) and John 20:11-18.

2. The Appearance to Two Disciples (16:12-13)

[12]Afterward Jesus appeared in a different form to two of them while they were walking in the country. [13]These returned and reported it to the rest; but they did not believe them either.

This brief report is apparently the same story as Luke 24:13-35 tells in some detail about two disciples on the road to Emmaus. The point emphasized in these two brief verses is that the two disciples saw and reported that Jesus was alive, but the others did not believe.

3. The Appearance to and Commission of the Eleven (16:14-18)

[14]Later Jesus appeared to the Eleven as they were eating; he rebuked them for their lack of faith and their stubborn refusal to believe those who had seen him after he had risen.

[15]He said to them,"Go into all the world and preach the

good news to all creation. [16]Whoever believes and is baptized will be saved, but whoever does not believe will be condemned. [17]And these signs will accompany those who believe: In my name they will drive out demons; they will speak in new tongues; [18]they will pick up snakes with their hands; and when they drink deadly poison, it will not hurt them at all; they will place their hands on sick people, and they will get well."

14. The reason the number is now eleven is of course due to Judas' betrayal. This verse resonates with the two previous stories in which the disciples refused to believe the testimony of Mary Magdalene and then of the two unnamed disciples. It implicitly warns the reader not to follow "their lack of faith and their stubborn refusal to believe."

15-16. Jesus commissions the eleven to go into all the world and preach the gospel. At this point in the story the gospel must be the good news about Jesus Christ, especially the good news that he rose from the dead. This good news calls for a response. Those who hear it should believe it and be baptized. Those who do so will be saved. Those who do not believe (it goes without saying that unbelievers will not be baptized) will be condemned. Salvation and condemnation here presumably refer to eternity in heaven or hell.

17-18. The miracles Jesus speaks of in these verses are viewed as "signs" (σημεῖα, *sēmeia*) acts which point beyond themselves to the truth of the message. The book of Acts provides examples of most of the signs that Jesus says would be performed by those who accepted the gospel. Healings, exorcisms, and tongue-speaking are frequent occurrences in Acts. On one occasion Paul was accidentally bitten by a poisonous snake, but the poison had no effect on him (Acts 28:3-6). The reference to drinking deadly poison presumably refers to occasions in which a disciple might be forced to drink poison as a form of execution for his or her faith, but would be protected by the Lord. Of course this is not a blanket promise of protection. The New Testament records examples both of miraculous protection (e.g., Acts 12:3-10) and of martyrdom (e.g., Acts 12:2).

4. The Ascension and the Disciples' Mission (16:19-20)

[19]After the Lord Jesus had spoken to them, he was taken up into heaven and he sat at the right hand of God. [20]Then the disciples went out and preached everywhere, and the Lord worked with them and confirmed his word by the signs that accompanied it.

19. The phrase "Lord Jesus" is common in Acts and in Paul's writings. Otherwise, it occurs here, once in Luke (24:3), and twice in Revelation (22:20-21). Jesus ascended from the disciples to the right hand of God. The reference to "the right hand of God" echoes Ps 110:1 as in Mark 14:62 where Jesus told the Sanhedrin they would "see the Son of Man sitting at the right hand of the Mighty One."

20. The disciples did what Jesus told them to do. They "went out" ("Go into all the world") and "preached everywhere" ("and preach the good news to all creation"). And the Lord fulfilled his promise concerning the confirmatory signs (cf. vv. 17-18).

APPENDIX
THE TEXT CRITICAL PROBLEM OF MARK 16:9-20

It is unfortunate that the ending of Mark is uncertain, but it is important not to overrate the significance of the problem.[1] There is no doctrine or practice discussed in vv. 9-20 that is not taught elsewhere in the New Testament.[2] The only religious practices which need 16:9-20 as their basis are snake handling and poison drinking. And these practices are, of course, erroneously based on v. 18, which is not recommending that Jesus' disciples deliberately pick up snakes or drink poison as religious ceremonies.

There are actually five different endings represented in the ancient manuscripts, versions, and church fathers:[3]

1) After v. 8 one Old Latin manuscript provides what is called the "shorter ending" of Mark: "And all that had been commanded them they told briefly to those around Peter. And afterward Jesus himself sent out through them, from east to west, the sacred and imperishable proclamation of eternal salvation" (NRSV).

2) After v. 8 several manuscripts and versions add this "shorter ending" plus the "longer ending," vv. 9-20.

3) One manuscript (Washingtonianus) contains the "longer ending," vv. 9-20, in an expanded version with a long addition between vv. 14 and 15: "And they excused themselves saying, 'This age of lawlessness and unbelief is under Satan, who does not allow the truth and power of God to prevail over the unclean things of the spirits. Therefore reveal your righteousness now' – thus they spoke to Christ. And

---

[1]See the comments from McGarvey in chapter 16, footnotes 3 and 4.

[2]In fact this is generally true of the text critical problems throughout the New Testament, which has many fewer textual problems than other ancient writings. Our God has not seen fit to exempt the New Testament from the copying problems that existed in all books prior to the invention of the printing press. But by his grace those problems do not create significant variations in Christian beliefs and practices.

[3]*UBS*[4], pp. 189, 191; Metzger, *Textual Commentary*, pp. 102-106.

Christ replied to them, 'The term of years of Satan's power has been fulfilled, but other terrible things draw near. And for those who have sinned I was handed over to death, that they may return to the truth and sin no more, that they may inherit the spiritual and imperishable glory of righteousness that is in heaven.'"

4) The majority of witnesses conclude the book with vv. 9-20, although some of them provide a critical note or sign indicating an awareness that there was a problem with the ending after v. 8.

5) The two oldest and best manuscripts (Sinaiticus and Vaticanus), one late manuscript (304), several ancient versions, and some of the church fathers end the book after v. 8. In the time of Eusebius (early fourth century) and Jerome (late fourth, early fifth) "almost all" of the Greek manuscripts known to these church leaders ended at v. 8.[4]

The first three alternatives can be immediately dismissed as poorly attested. The last two are the viable alternatives. The issue is whether vv. 9-20 were written by Mark or added to the text by a scribe who either composed them for this purpose or found them already existing and joined them to Mark.

In the twentieth century most New Testament text critics (those who study the ancient texts), commentators, and translators have concluded that Mark did not write vv. 9-20.[5] The primary reasons for doubting that Mark penned vv. 9-20 are:

1) The best ancient manuscripts (Sinaiticus and Vaticanus) both omit vv. 9-20. Furthermore, Eusebius and Jerome indicate that most Greek manuscripts of the fourth and early fifth centuries did not have them.

2) Some of the words and grammatical features of vv. 9-20 differ from Mark's usual style. For example, although Mark uses the word καί (*kai*, "and") to begin nearly sixty percent of his

---

[4]Lane, p. 601, citing Eusebius, *Quaestiones ad Marinum* 1 and Jerome, *Epistle* 120.3, *ad Hedibiam*. Both churchmen used the phrase "almost all."

[5]For a detailed defense of Mark's authorship of vv. 9-20 see William R. Farmer, *The Last Twelve Verses of Mark*, Society for New Testament Studies Monograph Series 25 (Cambridge: Cambridge University Press, 1974).

sentences, in vv. 9-20 only one sentence begins with *kai* (v. 15). (But such stylistic judgments are often highly subjective.)

Those who argue that Mark did write vv. 9-20 point out that all or at least some of these verses were known to Irenaeus[6] and probably to Tatian[7] in the late second century. Justin Martyr may have known the long ending at the middle of the second century.[8] This information is important but in the opinion of most scholars it does not overthrow the evidence against the longer ending. As is also true for a number of textual problems in other New Testament books, both the shorter and longer readings existed by the late second century. We are still faced with the problem of deciding between them.

Another reason advanced in favor of Mark having written vv. 9-20 is the opinion that without them Mark does not have a proper ending. Even if that were true, it would not necessarily mean that vv. 9-20 are Mark's original ending. Gundry and others believe the original ending was lost.[9] But most interpreters believe that vv. 1-8 are a proper ending. It was not necessary to end a Gospel by telling several stories of Jesus' post-resurrection appearances. It is clear that Mark believed he did appear. But perhaps he chose to end with the sense of awe created by the empty tomb.

---

[6]Irenaeus, *Against Heresies* 3.10.6.

[7]They are found in the Arabic version of his harmony of the Gospels called the *Diatesseron*. Lane, p. 605.

[8]Justin Martyr, *Apology* 1.45, has a sentence which includes five words that appear in v. 20, although in Justin they are in a different sequence. See Metzger, *Textual Commentary*, p. 104.

[9]Gundry, p. 1009-1012.